Verification
Monitoring Disarmament

A Pugwash Monograph

Verification

Monitoring Disarmament

EDITED BY

Francesco Calogero, Marvin L. Goldberger, and Sergei P. Kapitza

Westview Press
BOULDER • SAN FRANCISCO • OXFORD

Copyright © 1991 by Pugwash Conferences on Science and World Affairs

Published in 1991 in the United States of America by Westview Press, Inc., 5500 Central Avenue, Boulder, Colorado 80301, and in the United Kingdom by Westview Press, 36 Lonsdale Road, Summertown, Oxford OX2 7EW

Library of Congress Cataloging-in-Publication Data
Verification : monitoring disarmament / edited by Francesco Calogero,
    Marvin L. Goldberger & Sergei P. Kapitza.
        p. cm.
At head of title: Pugwash Conferences on Science and World
    Affairs.
    Includes bibliographical references and index.
    ISBN 0-8133-0965-4
    1. Nuclear disarmament.   2. Nuclear arms control—Verification.
I. Calogero, F.   II. Goldberger, Marvin L.   III. Kapitsa, Sergei
Petrovich.   IV. Pugwash Conferences on Science & World Affairs.
JX1974.7.V39   1990
327.1′74′028—dc20   90-47954
                                                               CIP

Printed and bound in the United States of America

The paper used in this publication meets the requirements
of the American National Standard for Permanence of Paper
for Printed Library Materials Z39.48-1984.

10   9   8   7   6   5   4   3   2   1

Contents

Preface

The idea of a project aimed at producing a book with chapters co-authored by individuals from East and West was conceived at the end of the 1987 Annual Pugwash Conference (Gmunden, Austria, 1-6 September 1987). Martin Kaplan, then Secretary General of Pugwash, immediately supported the idea and suggested "verification" as the most appropriate topic. A plan of the book, a list of prospective authors, and a request for financial support were then put quickly together, with the help of John Holdren and Catherine Kelleher, who have played a key role as advisors throughout this project. Most of the authors then met in May 1988 in New York, in September 1988 in Moscow and in December 1988 in London; the task to produce final agreed texts was then turned over to the co-authors of each chapter. Although all authors profited from the interactions provided by the meetings of the entire group, it is understood that each author is responsible solely for the chapter he/she signs; this applies as well to the editors. And of course all authors and editors contribute in their personal capacity; any mention of the institutions with which they have been or are associated is reported merely for the purpose of identification.

Since this project was conceived, the global political situation has greatly changed. In particular East-West contacts have become much easier. But to produce agreed texts remains a nontrivial achievement; indeed in some cases it has been made quite difficult by the avalanche of commitments that have crowded the schedules of some of the authors of this book, precisely due to the latest political developments and their role in them. Moreover the time of completion of the whole book has, of course, been set by the chapter handed in last. Nevertheless, as the reader may verify, most of the material of this book remains up to date; largely because of its lasting character; but also, in part, due to the unfortunate fact that progress in arms control and disarmament so far has not been as rapid and dramatic as the political developments might have warranted. A case that stands out in this respect is the chapter on conventional forces--there indeed the pace of political change in Europe, as well as arms control developments (including unilateral arms reductions and breakthroughs on verification issues), have challenged the authors to deal with a fast moving target--but they have managed to cope.

Only a summary is printed below of Chapter 3 on verification of a test ban treaty. The reason for this is that the version of this chapter that was drafted turned out to be much more technical, more detailed and more extended than any of the other chapters; moreover some details had still to be ironed out among the co-authors well after all other chapters had been completed. For these reasons we regrettably had to omit the complete version of this chapter from the English version of the book. We expect that the complete agreed text will appear soon in English as a journal article; and it might perhaps be included in the Russian version of this book. Comments on this chapter, as well as on all other chapters, are in any case included in the last chapter of this book.

All chapters were prepared specifically for this book, except Chapter 5 on the verified elimination of nuclear warheads, which constitutes a joint elaboration of an article published earlier by one of the two co-authors. Chapter 10 on the verification of conventional reductions has been distributed as an occasional paper by the American Pugwash Committee through the American Academy of Arts and Sciences.

The book is published in English by Westview Press and in Russian by Mir. The camera-ready copy of this English version has been produced by Andrea Belloni and by Stefano Leonardi, both of them working in the Rome Pugwash Office as "conscientious objectors". They deserve our thanks; as does Marco De Andreis, for his help in proofing the camera-ready copy and especially in preparing the index. The Russian version has been translated in Moscow by Mir, under the supervision of Ms. Valentina Samsonova, whom we also wish to thank for her cooperation in the whole project.

Last but not least, we wish to thank the John D. and Catherine T. MacArthur Foundation and the Carnegie Corporation of New York for providing the financial support to the English version of this book which has made this project possible, the Peace Fund of the Soviet Union for support of the Russian version, as well as the Istituto Nazionale di Fisica Nucleare (INFN) and the Consiglio Nazionale delle Ricerche (CNR) of Italy for the financial support provided to the Pugwash Office in Rome, where the final editing of the book has been done and the camera-ready copy produced.

F. Calogero, M. L. Goldberger, S.P. Kapitza

Acronyms

ABM	Anti-Ballistic Missile
ABMT	ABM Treaty
ACDA	Arms Control and Disarmament Agency
ALCM	Air Launched Cruise Missile
ASAT	Anti-Satellite
ATC	Armored Troop Carrier
ATTU	Atlantic To The Urals
BSTS	Boost-phase Surveillance and Tracking Satellite
BW	Biological Weapons
BWC	Biological Weapons Convention
CBM	Confidence Building Measure
CBW	Chemical and Bacteriological Warfare
CD	Conference on Disarmament
CDE	Conference on Disarmament in Europe
CEES/PU	Center for Energy and Environmental Studies/Princeton University
CFE	Conventional Forces in Europe
CIA	Central Intelligence Agency
CISSM	Center for International Security Studies at Maryland
CSBM	Confidence and Security Building Measure
CSCE	Conference on Security and Cooperation in Europe
CTB	Comprehensive Test Ban
CTBT	CTB Treaty
CW	Chemical Warfare
CWC	Chemical Weapons Convention
DIA	Defense Intelligence Agency
DOE	Department Of Energy
EEP	Exit/Entry Point
EURATOM	European Atomic Energy Agency
FEL	Free Electron Laser
FY	Fiscal Year
GEO	Geosynchronous Earth Orbit

HEU	High Enrichment Uranium
HLVA	Hessisches LandesVermessungs Amt
IAEA	International Atomic Energy Agency
ICBM	Intercontinental Ballistic Missile
IEEE	Institute of Electrical and Electronic Engineering
IISS	International Institute for Strategic Studies (London)
IMEMO	Institute of World Economy and International Relations (Moscow)
INF	Intermediate-range Nuclear Forces
IR	Infrared
IRBM	Intermediate Range Ballistic Missile
JSTARS	Joint Surveillance and Target Attack Radar System
KKV	Kinetic-Kill Vehicle
LEU	Low Enrichment Uranium
LPAR	Large Phased-Array Radar
MBFR	Mutual and Balanced Force Reduction Negotiations
MIRV	Multiple Independently-targetable Re-entry Vehicle
MIT	Massachusetts Institute of Technology
MUF	Material Unaccounted For
NASA	National Aeronautics and Space Administration
NATO	North Atlantic Treaty Organization
NCND	Neither Confirm Nor Deny
NPB	Neutral Particle Beam
NPT	Non-Proliferation Treaty
NTM	National Technical Means
OPANAL	Organization for the Prohibition of Nuclear Arms in Latin America
ORAE	Operational Research and Analysis Establishment (Ottawa)
OSI	On Site Inspection
PIV	Physical Inventory Verification
RV	Re-entry Vehicle
SALT	Strategic Arms Limitation Talks
SBI	Space Based Interceptor
SBL	Space Based Laser
SCC	Standing Consultative Commission
SDI	Strategic Defense Initiative
SDIO	Strategic Defense Initiative Office
SICBM	Small ICBM
SIPRI	Stockholm International Peace Research Institute
SLBM	Submarine Launched Ballistic Missile
SLCM	Sea Launched Cruise Missile
SNDV	Strategic Nuclear Delivery Vehicle

SP	State Party
SRAM	Short Range Attack Missile
SSBN	Nuclear Ballistic Missile Submarine
SSSF	Single Small Scale Facility
START	Strategic Arms Reduction Talks
SVC	Special Verification Committee
TASM	Tomahawk Anti Ship Missile
TEL	Transporter Erector Launcher
TLAM	Tomahawk Land Attack Missile
TLE	Treaty Limited Equipment
TTBT	Threshold Test Ban Treaty
UCLA	University of California - Los Angeles
UN	United Nations
UNGA	United Nations General Assembly
URENCO	Uranium Enrichment Company
USAF	United States Air Force
VERTIC	Verification Technology Information Center
WEU	Western European Union
WTO	Warsaw Treaty Organization

About the Contributors

JÜRGEN ALTMANN (FRG). Scientific Staff Member, Institute of Experimental Physics, Ruhr-Universität Bochum. Formerly, Researcher, Peace Research Institute Frankfurt. Professional background: applied physics. Current research project: new technical means for cooperative verification in Europe.

CHARLES B. ARCHAMBEAU (USA). Adjunct Professor of Geophysics and a member of the scientific research staff at the Cooperative Institute for Research in the Environmental Sciences (CIRES), which is jointly sponsored by the U.S. Department of Commerce (NOAA) and the University of Colorado. He was formerly a Professor of Geophysics at the California Institute of Technology, from 1966 through 1974. In May of 1986 he was a member of a U.S. citizens' delegation to the Soviet Union that negotiated a seismic monitoring agreement between the Soviet Academy of Sciences and the Natural Resources Defense Council of the U.S., which was designed to monitor both U.S. and Soviet nuclear tests.

FRANCESCO CALOGERO (Italy). Professor of Theoretical Physics (on leave), University of Rome "La Sapienza"; Secretary-General, Pugwash Conferences on Science and World Affairs; Member, Governing Board, Stockholm International Peace Research Institute (SIPRI). Professional activity: theoretical and mathematical physics (in recent years, mainly nonlinear evolution equations and dynamical systems).

PETER DEAK (Hungary). Retired Colonel, Professor of International Military Affairs, and an expert on conventional forces and military doctrines. Currently, Special Advisor to the Director of the Hungarian Institute of International Affairs, and Head of the international research program on "Armies in a Democracy". Born in Budapest in 1931, educated in the military college until 1953, in the military academy of the General Staff until 1961, and in the History Faculty of the Eötvös Lóránd University until 1966. Professor of Logistics and Military Economy at the Technical Military University for 12 years. Last position in the Army: Head of the Scientific Department of the General Staff. He has been involved with Pugwash Conferences since 1984.

GLORIA DUFFY (USA). Founder and President of Global Outlook, Dr. Duffy has been the Executive Director of the Ploughshares Fund, a consultant to the MacArthur Foundation, a resident consultant at the Rand Corporation,

Assistant Director of the Arms Control Association and Editor of *Arms Control Today*. She is the author of two books: *Compliance and the Future of Arms Control* and the textbook *International Arms Control Issues and Agreements* (with Coit Blacker). Dr. Duffy obtained her doctorate from Columbia University.

LEV P. FEOKTISTOV (USSR). Doctor of Physics/Mathematics. Head of Department, Lebedev Physical Institute, USSR Academy of Sciences. Professional field of activity: applied nuclear physics.

STEVE FETTER (USA). Assistant Professor, School of Public Affairs, University of Maryland, College Park. Formerly, Research Fellow, Center for Science and International Affairs at Harvard University and Lawrence Livermore National Laboratory. Professional interests: arms control, space policy, energy policy and radioactive waste disposal.

RICHARD L. GARWIN (USA). IBM Fellow and Science Advisor to the Director of Research, IBM Research Division, Yorktown Heights, NY. Adjunct Professor of Physics, Columbia University. Formerly Professor of Public Policy, Harvard University. Member, President's Science Advisory Committee 1962-1965, 1969-1972. Consultant to the U.S. government on military technology and arms control since 1950. Member, USA National Academy of Sciences' Committee on International Security and Arms Control.

MIKHAIL B. GOKHBERG (USSR). Doctor of Physics/Mathematics. Deputy Director, Institute of Earth Physics, USSR Academy of Sciences. Co-director, US-Soviet Seismic Data Exchange Project. Professional field of interest: seismoelectromagnetic phenomena.

VITALI I. GOLDANSKII (USSR). Member, Academy of Sciences of the USSR. Member of Soviet Parliament. Director, Institute of Chemical Physics. Vice-chairman, Committee of Soviet Scientists for Global Security. Chairman, Soviet Pugwash Group; Member, Pugwash Council. Lenin Prize. Numerous publications on chemical physics, nuclear physics, problems of science and society.

MARVIN L. GOLDBERGER (USA). Director, Institute for Advanced Study, Princeton, New Jersey. Formerly, President, California Institute of Technology. Member, President's Science Advisory Committee (1965-1969). Involved in consulting for the U.S. government on national security issues since 1959. First chairman and now member of the USA National Academy of Sciences' Committee on International Security and Arms Control. Professional background: elementary particle physics.

IRAKLI G. GVERDZITELI (USSR). Member, Academy of Sciences of the Georgian Soviet Socialist Republic. Professor, Tbilisi University. Chairman, Georgian Scientific and Educational Center, World Laboratory. Member, Committee of Soviet Scientists for Global Security. Research in atomic and solid state physics.

JOHN P. HOLDREN (USA). Professor of Energy and Resources at the University of California, Berkeley, Chairman of the Pugwash Executive Committee and of the U.S. Pugwash Group and a former Chairman of the Federation of American Scientists. His research interests include fusion energy technology, global environmental problems, energy and environmental policy and arms control.

SERGEI P. KAPITZA (USSR). Doctor of Physics/Mathematics. Head of Laboratory at the Institute for Physical Problems. President, Physical Society of the Soviet Union. Vice-chairman, Committee of Soviet Scientists for Global Security. Member of Pugwash Council and Club of Rome. Research on: design and use of electron accelerators. Publications on public matters and the history of science, moderator of major TV science programs.

MARTIN M. KAPLAN (Switzerland/USA). Microbiologist and Epidemiologist. He was a staff member (1949-1976) of the World Health Organization in the Division of Communicable Diseases and Director of Research Promotion and Development in the Office of the Director General. He served as Secretary-General of the Pugwash Conferences from 1976 to 1988 and continues to be active in Pugwash while serving as a consultant to WHO.

OLEG K. KEDROV (USSR). Doctor of Physics/Mathematics. Head, Laboratory of Explosion Seismology, Institute of Earth Physics, Academy of Sciences of the USSR. Member of Ad-hoc group of Scientific Experts to Conference on Disarmament. Research on: seismic monitoring methods.

CATHERINE MCARDLE KELLEHER (USA). Director of the Center for International Security Studies at Maryland (CISSM) and Professor in the School of Public Affairs at the University of Maryland. She served on the National Security Council staff during the Carter Administration and has had a wide range of academic involvements in international security studies. She has published extensively on issues of arms control, alliance relations, East-West relations and European security. Her recent publications include contributions in S. Sloan (ed.), *NATO in the 1990s* (1989), in S. Szabo (ed.), *The Bundeswehr* (1990), and in S. Biddle and P. Feaver (eds.), *Battlefield Nuclear Weapons: Issues and Options* (1989).

ANDREI A. KOKOSHIN (USSR). Corresponding Member, Academy of Sciences of the USSR. Vice director, Institute of USA and Canada, USSR Academy of Sciences. Vice-chairman, Committee of Soviet Scientists for Global Security. Professional fields of interest: theory of international relations and US foreign policy.

ITSHAK LEDERMAN (Israel), a lieutenant colonel in the Israeli Defence Forces, is currently on sabbatical at the University of Maryland at College Park, where he is finishing his Ph.D. in the government and politics department. As a senior MacArthur scholar at the Center for International Security Studies in Maryland, he is focusing on verification regimes of arms control agreements, which is also the subject of his doctorate.

JEREMY LEGGETT (UK). Geologist, Director of Science at Greenpeace UK. Before joining Greenpeace in May 1989 he spent eleven years lecturing in earth sciences at Imperial College of Science, Technology and Medicine, and was Director of the Verification Technology Information Centre from 1985 to 1989. He has written over fifty scientific papers and has won two major awards for his research, including in 1980 the President's Prize of the Geological Society, the UK's premier award for geologists aged 30 or under. He has sat for several years on one of the three main advisory panels to the Ocean Drilling Program, a multi-million-dollar international research project which investigates the past history of the oceans. He has published numerous articles on arms control, environmental issues and science policy.

KARLHEINZ LOHS (GDR). Education: in chemistry at the University of Leipzig; Dr. rer. nat. (1955); Dr. rer. nat. habil (1962); Professor 1965; Member of the Academy of Sciences since 1970; Director of the Research Department on Chemical Toxicology, Leipzig, of the Academy of Sciences of the GDR; Dr. h.c. at Martin-Luther University (Halle-Wittenberg), 1987. Main research work in chemistry and toxicology of organo-phosphorus compounds, pesticides and environmental protection, risk assessment of industrial compounds and of waste disposals. Since 1955 connected with disarmament problems (especially destruction of CW stocks, CW compounds). Part-time member of the Disarmament Delegation of the GDR in Geneva. Member of the Pugwash Council. Member of the SIPRI Governing Board (since 1980). Author of 15 books and approximately 200 scientific publications, more than 200 articles in the daily press (including interviews, reports and the like).

VITALI A. LOUKIANTZEV (USSR). Senior Advisor, Soviet Foreign Ministry. Negotiator in talks within the Conference on Security and Cooperation in Europe and in the Soviet-American space nuclear weapons talks. Publications on the history of international relations, problems of arms limitation and disarmament.

VADIM I. MAKAREVSKY (USSR). Major-General, retired. Candidate of Military Science. Senior Researcher, Institute of World Economy and International Relations (IMEMO), USSR Academy of Sciences. Member of Presidium, Soviet Association of Assistance for UN. Member of Commission on Security and Cooperation, Soviet Generals and Admirals for Peace and Disarmament, Soviet Peace Committee. Military expert of the Soviet Pugwash Committee. Professional interests: general issues in disarmament and security of conventional forces.

MATTHEW MESELSON (USA). Thomas Dudley Cabot Professor of the Natural Sciences at Harvard University. Member, US National Academy of Sciences, the Royal Society, and the Academie des Sciences. Professional interests: molecular genetics, chemical and biological weapons and arms control.

MIKHAIL A. MILSTEIN (USSR). Lt. General (rt.), professor, doctor of history. Consultant, Institute of USA and Canada Studies, Academy of Sciences of the USSR. Author of many books and articles on military and arms control problems. Graduated from two military academies. Held a chair at the Academy of the General Staff. Member, Soviet Pugwash committee, Soviet committee on European Security. Was scientific advisor to the Palme Commission.

MARK A. MOKULSKY (USSR). Doctor of Physics/Mathematics. Head of Department, Institute of Molecular Genetics, Academy of Sciences of USSR. Member, Committee of Soviet Scientists for Global Security. Research on: radiation-matter interaction, space structure of biological macromolecules, space research, plasma physics, ecology.

JULIAN P. PERRY-ROBINSON (UK), a chemist and lawyer by training, is a Senior Fellow of the Science Policy Research Unit, University of Sussex, England, where he heads the Military Technology & Arms Limitation research group. He had previously held research appointments at the Stockholm International Peace Research Institute (SIPRI), the Free University of Berlin and the Center for International Affairs at Harvard University. At SIPRI during 1968-71 he wrote much of the 6-volume study *The Problem of Chemical and Biological Warfare*, and during 1982-86 was the founding editor of the series *SIPRI Chemical & Biological Warfare Studies*. He has served as an advisor or consultant to a variety of national and international organizations, governmental and nongovernmental, including the World Health Organization, other agencies of the United Nations and the International Committee of the Red Cross. With Matthew Meselson of Harvard University, he now edits *Chemical Weapons Convention Bulletin*, published in Washington.

STANISLAV N. RODIONOV (USSR). Doctor of Physics/Mathematics. Head of Section, Institute of Space Research, USSR Academy of Sciences. Member, Committee of Soviet Scientists for Global Security. Professional background: high energy physics.

JOSEPH ROTBLAT (UK). Emeritus Professor of Physics at the University of London. Work on the atom bomb during World War II, in Liverpool and Los Alamos. Signatory of the Russell-Einstein Manifesto. Formerly (1957-1973) Secretary-General, and, since 1988, President of the Pugwash Conferences. Professional background: nuclear and medical physics, radiation biology, disarmament and social responsibility of scientists.

ROALD Z. SAGDEEV (USSR). Member, Academy of Sciences of the USSR. Member of Soviet Parliament. Head of Center for Analytical Research, Space Research Institute, USSR Academy of Sciences. Chairman, Committee of Soviet Scientists for Global Security. Numerous publications on space, plasma physics, non-linear mechanics.

LAWRENCE SCHEINMAN (USA). Professor of Government and Acting Director of the Peace Studies Program at Cornell University. He has been actively involved in nuclear nonproliferation and arms control as an academic, U.S. State Department official and member of the staff of the International Atomic Energy Agency. His most recent book in this field is *The International Atomic Energy Agency and World Nuclear Order*, published in 1987.

NIKITA P. SMIDOVICH (USSR). Head of Division at the Department of Arms Limitation and Disarmament Problems, Ministry of Foreign Affairs of the USSR. Professional interests: chemical weapons.

THEODORE B. TAYLOR (USA). Independent consulting physicist, West Clarksville, New York. Staff member, Los Alamos National Laboratory, working on nuclear weapon design, 1949-1956. Senior Research Advisor at General Atomic Company, 1956-1964. Deputy Director, Defense Nuclear Agency, 1964-1966. Chairman, International Research and Technology Corporation, 1967-1976. Visiting Lecturer, Princeton University, 1976-1980.

1

Introduction

*Francesco Calogero (Italy), Marvin L. Goldberger (USA),
Sergei P. Kapitza (USSR) & Mikhail A. Milstein (USSR)*

There is something very paradoxical about arms control and arms control treaties: The process is one where adversary nations agree to manage their military competition by signing binding covenants, almost like agreeing to fight by Marquis of Queensbury rules. This is done in the belief that their individual security is thus better served than the alternative of an unrestrained arms race; although they are in a sense enemies, they share an overriding interest in lowering the probability of conflict, in decreasing the level of such conflict should it occur, and in lightening the burden of the cost of maintaining military establishments. There is a tacit assumption that some degree of an adversarial relationship is inevitable for the foreseeable future, since many treaties specify their being of unlimited duration.

Because arms control treaties are agreements between adversaries, a central feature of them are provisions for verification of compliance. Each side may believe that the other has some incentive to cheat and all modern arms control agreements contain detailed descriptions of what is or is not permitted along with procedures of various kinds that attempt to make evasion difficult and unattractive. It is unfortunate that so much attention is focused on discussing verification as an abstract concept whereas in fact it has meaning only in connection with specific situations. What might constitute "adequate" verification in one case could be unacceptable in another. Generally speaking, however, minimum requirements for a verifiable treaty would include the following:

1. No significant risk to the national security of either party that might be caused by a treaty violation shall go undetected and unidentified.
2. No violation that would undermine in a basic way the purpose of the treaty should go undetected and unidentified.

The true purpose of verification provisions in a treaty is to deter violations by making the costs and risks of evasion unacceptably high as compared to the conceivable gain. Eventually the very existence of verifiable treaties will allow nations to move away from the concept of deterrence, as practiced up to now.

In any discussion of arms control treaties and verification it is important to put the treaty, rigorous adherence to it, and violation by an adversary into the proper perspective. One must contrast the dangers of a no-treaty situation with the gain achieved when both sides abide by the treaty provisions as compared to the risks incurred if the other side cheats. A treaty can be judged as advantageous if the gain in security from its presence in force is large compared to the loss in security if it is violated by one side. For such a treaty verification procedures can be minimal. If on the other hand the risks associated with violation are large compared to the gain in the security of a treaty regime, very rigorous verification would be required and the value of the treaty is dubious. In the present world of vast nuclear arsenals almost any treaty that has been or is being discussed between East and West is advantageous in the above sense since a violation by one side scarcely perturbs the capability of either to destroy the other. When the numbers of nuclear weapons get truly small, verification will play a much more important role and what will constitute a good or bad treaty will become much more complicated.

Links Between Technical and Political Dimensions

There is a close link between the technical and political dimensions of arms control treaty verification provisions. They must be perceived by the public as being sufficient to preserve national self-interest: indeed, public opinion has always played an important role in this respect in the United States, and it now appears likely that it will play an analogous role in the Soviet Union as well. There is great difficulty, however, in convincing a largely technically illiterate public that in spite of the fact that absolute adherence to a treaty is impossible to insure, verification can be quite satisfactory even if it leaves some margin of uncertainty. It is unfortunate that proponents of absolute standards are often those who oppose any kind of arms control agreements while posturing for political purposes as supporters of arms control "provided that it is verifiable."

Arms Control Treaties and Verification Measures

There are two general approaches to arms control treaties each with advantages and disadvantages. One can imagine formulating broad principles to deal comprehensively with a particular agreement. In this approach the object is to emphasize intent in a general fashion with the advantage of avoiding the specification of a laundry list that may turn out at a later time to be incomplete.

The very lack of specificity can, however, lead to "gray areas" of eventual disagreement. The Biological Weapons Convention is an example of this approach to a treaty.

The SALT II Treaty is illustrative of the other approach where the language is highly specific and technical. It is the belief that in this way gray areas can be more readily avoided and disputes over definitions over what is or is not included or what is or is not allowed in research and development, etc., will be less frequent. But an attempt to be exhaustive can also be dangerous: It is hard to think of everything and hard to come up with language that will cover unanticipated technical development that can open up a legal slalom course through treaty restrictions.

As technology advances and the capabilities of military systems expand, the boundaries between permitted and forbidden activities become fuzzy. For example, space-based defensive systems can acquire pronounced offensive capabilities, and tactical systems under certain circumstances can be quickly adapted to have strategic uses. If the provisions of a treaty are too narrowly drawn, compliance in a broad sense can become irrelevant. Those negotiating treaties on each side have differing views and interests to say nothing of the differences between the two sides. These are often best breached by some level of ambiguity rather than engaging in Talmudic arguments about every detail. Drafting provisions for arms control seems to require what is known in the US legal profession as "creative ambiguity."

There is, of course, a strong correlation between what is required in the way of verification of treaties and whether they are structured in the general or very specific form. The structure of verification provisions is also a function of the degree of trust that obtains at a given time. The better the political climate the quicker the parties concerned might agree on mutual concessions and the easier they might arrive at an agreement on control and verification measures.

Verification, Intelligence, and Conflict Resolution

The whole process of verification is one of intelligence gathering specifically directed to arms control provisions. By and large what can or cannot be verified puts the limits on what can legitimately be controlled by treaty. What cannot be "inspected" cannot be expected is an old business adage and it has truth in agreements between groups with somewhat conflicting self-interests.

In the subsequent chapters of this book verification requirements and technical means are discussed in detail in connection with specific arms control areas. Here we content ourselves with some general remarks. Verification measures fall into the following general groups:

1. Cooperative measures: Openness of features of military systems, exchange

of information on military doctrine, non-interference with verification means, funneling weapons and delivery systems through monitored check points, etc.

2. National Technical Means (NTM) such as non-intrusive surveillance from satellites, radar and optical surveillance from locations outside the monitored country, seismic stations, etc.
3. Technical monitoring devices placed at or near sites.
4. On-site inspections.
5. "Normal intelligence channels" such as agents, emigree interviews, communication intercepts, information leaks, etc.

There is clearly a price to be paid by allowing foreign intrusion for arms control monitoring since there is inevitable ancillary intelligence potential.

Of all the verification measures none has stirred up more controversy than on-site inspections. The utility of such inspections is vastly overrated and problems arising over how inspections are to be initiated and how they are to be conducted have occupied much time and effort of arms control negotiators. The mechanisms that would trigger them have to be very carefully specified by the treaty language to prevent abuse. Examples of possible arrangements are the following: A seismic disturbance of a certain magnitude at a nuclear test site; on-site inspection of sensitive locations to check production levels of weapons or materials. In general, the treaty will be structured so that detection of a clear violation will be unlikely. The purpose of the measure is to discourage cheating or to make the cost of evasion in money or complexity unattractive.

The recently concluded INF Treaty between the US and the USSR has very specific provisions governing on-site inspections, including notification of an inspection intent, limitations on travel by inspectors, restrictions on the types of measurements and instruments that may be used, etc. This treaty marks the first time such arrangements have been agreed to by these countries. In general, the verification provisions of that treaty have set a new standard of rigor. And it should also be noted that on-site inspections have yet another dimension, as rather conspicuous performances done in public. This certainly helps to defuse mutual secretiveness and leads to greater public understanding and trust.

Treaty Violations

The manner by which real or perceived treaty violations are dealt with has a bearing on verification.

Arms control agreements are concluded because they are perceived to be in the security self-interest of the parties involved. Treaties are drafted in such a way that violations unless flagrant have little value. Yet real or perceived violations have historically been the rule. For the most part they have been technical in nature and have usually arisen from the zeal of the military bureaucracy operating behind the cloak of highly compartmentalized classification without high-level approval rather than signifying a deliberate national policy of deception. It is likely that the Soviet radar at Krasnoyarsk and the US modifications of the radars at Thule and Fylingdales fall into this category. But once initiated such violations are hard for political leaders to control both from the standpoint of internal affairs and a natural unwillingness to publicly acknowledge a mistake that violates an international agreement and gives evidence of lack of control.

Another set of activities that can be troublesome involves taking advantage of legal loopholes or pushing too aggressively into the gray areas. These can be interpreted as violations of intent by the other side and tend to poison the atmosphere.

There appears to be an unavoidable class of alleged "violations" arising from unclear or ambiguous conduct or disputes over the interpretation of data. The SALT Treaty of 1972 recognized this and created the Standing Consultative Committee (SCC) to deal with such disputes; the Special Verification Committee (SVC) of the INF Treaty is to play the same role. These and analogous future committees must have a broad problem-solving approach and should operate entirely privately, dealing with disputes in such a way that public national honor doesn't come into play. There is a time when an overall assessment of treaty compliance must be made public, but this should be done in a non-confrontational way. Clearly as verification techniques improve and as trust between the parties grows there will be increasingly less work for these committees.

Verification and Trust

On the other hand, the procedure for verification, the very operation of the inspection groups, invites the parties involved into a growing degree of cooperation. This cooperative effort, manifest already in the lengthy process of negotiation, is an important part in establishing greater understanding, even a team spirit. This new degree of cooperation may be important in dealing with unexpected and unforeseen circumstances. Just as a conflict imposes a confrontational logic in the behavior of opposing sides, so the collaborative effort of negotiation and verification will lead to a new sense of mutual comprehension and hopefully of trust.

In the long run this common understanding may help in moving towards a world in which we will not only renounce and hopefully get rid of nuclear weapons, but we will revoke the old doctrine that war is a natural phenomenon among nations, a mere continuation of politics by other means. And verification is the first step towards killing one of the sacred cows of the military--that of secrecy and concealment.

In this time of dramatic change in Eastern Europe and the Soviet Union, an atmosphere is prevailing which is conducive to arms reductions, secured by treaties and by verification provisions. This constitutes significant progress towards a higher level of truly international security. Moreover, the growing inter-dependence of nations based on economics and information exchange provides a basis for a new spirit of world-wide allegiance and a sense of shared values.

The necessity of involving international organizations in the verification process takes on added importance as the arsenals of the superpowers are drawn down. Although it will be a long time before the nuclear forces of even Great Britain, France and China will be comparable in size to those of the Soviet Union and the United States, that time will eventually come.

The verification process was pioneered first by the mutual acceptance of national means of verification. Next came bilateral agreements entailing a more extensive collaborative effort in verification. Multilateral agreements, such as the Non Proliferation Treaty with its associated safeguards by the International Atomic Energy Agency, have also played an important role in promoting the notion that international verification is acceptable and useful. Eventually we may expect the international effort in verification to be placed under the auspices of the United Nations. Hence it is important to involve in a major way the United Nations in the global verification process. A system of international reconnaissance satellites related to a Global Military Information Centre attached to the U.N. Security Council would be an important positive step in such direction.

Verification has many dimensions and with its development we are moving more and more into an open world. Greater information and mutual understanding will certainly help in defusing the arms race, which was so often spurred by lack of information, secrecy and worst case analysis. Science and technology have provided the arms in the past and provide the instruments of verification today. We hope that in the future their contribution towards common security and cooperation will safeguard our world against any outbreak of violence that would be a menace to the very survival of our civilisation, in this world where the powers of destruction have reached a global scale.

2

Arms Limitation and Control: Improving the Institutional Mechanisms for Resolving Compliance Issues

Gloria Duffy (USA) & Vitali A. Loukiantzev (USSR)

Introduction

In the period 1981-87, the arms control environment was characterized more by controversies over compliance with past agreements than by progress toward new limitations. The United States and the Soviet Union, especially, accused one another of numerous treaty violations. In 1983-87, the Reagan Administration issued annual reports elaborating charges of Soviet cheating. In 1986, the United States unilaterally ended its voluntary adherence to the SALT II limits on strategic nuclear weapons, citing concerns about Soviet non-compliance.

The Standing Consultative Commission (SCC) is the vehicle for resolution of compliance problems arising from the SALT and ABM Treaties and the main institutional model for dealing with compliance issues. It worked to the satisfaction of the United States and the Soviet Union during the 1970s. During the 1980s, however, this body ceased to function effectively.

A general sense emerged from this difficult period that "something" needs to be done to improve the ability and willingness of the Soviet Union and the United States to resolve constructively their differences about treaty interpretation without resort to public condemnations or withdrawal from agreements.

To a lesser extent, the 1980s were also a time of controversy about other countries' compliance with multilateral arms control agreements. Among other issues, questions were raised at the UN about the use of chemical weapons by Iraq (a party to the 1925 Geneva Convention) in the Iran-Iraq war, and about the suspected use of toxin weapons in the late 1970s and early 1980s by the governments of Vietnam and Laos (both parties to the 1972 Biological and Toxin

Weapons Convention).

Other concerns about states' behavior--such as alarm about Pakistan's move toward acquiring nuclear weapons--were not strictly compliance issues. Some nations defied international norms without technically violating any agreement. Pakistan, for example, is not a signatory of the Non-Proliferation Treaty.

Nonetheless, in the case of multilateral accords as well as superpower arms control agreements, the ability to resolve disputes over treaty compliance to the satisfaction of concerned parties seemed low. This added to the sense that "something" should be done to improve the mechanisms for settling disagreements.

Causes of Compliance Problems in the 1980s

In the 1990s, the challenge will be to remember and to draw lessons from the compliance problems of the 1980s, notwithstanding the flush of optimism in U.S.-Soviet relations and the rush to new agreements. The period of better East-West relations that began in 1988 should be exploited to reform the dispute-resolution process in ways that would be impossible when relations were more difficult.

Many suggestions have been made for improving the process for resolving compliance disputes. In determining the complexion of the necessary reforms, it is crucial to assess correctly the nature of the compliance problems in the 1980s. Was cheating on the terms of arms control agreements actually as rampant as the 40-or-so charges levelled against one another by the United States and the Soviet Union would suggest? If violations did occur, why? Because treaty provisions were inadequate? Because verification methods were ineffective in deterring the nations accused of cheating from producing and deploying weapons in defiance of treaty limits? And why did attempts to resolve questions of compliance end in stalemate? Due to inadequate dispute-resolution mechanisms, or because the parties involved lacked the will to settle their differences?

A very telling point in seeking the causes of the compliance controversies of the 1980s is that, while cheating concerns dominated the arms control dialogue for the six years prior to 1988, suddenly in 1988 these concerns vanished from the public U.S.-Soviet discourse. And they barely surfaced through the end of the 1980s.

A variety of factors help to explain this curious phenomenon. In 1985, the Soviet Union began to take steps to improve its performance on treaty commitments where it had been poor or questionable. Such steps included halting construction of, and ultimately, in 1989, announcing the dismantling of the Krasnoyarsk radar. In addition, expert studies in the United States began to analyze Soviet and American complaints closely. They found that many charges of cheating made by both governments were poorly substantiated.[1]

Most importantly, in 1988 the arms control process got underway again. This time there was the strong impetus to conclude a treaty limiting Intermediate-range

Nuclear Forces (INF) by the end of President Reagan's tenure in office. The push for an INF Treaty required a de-emphasis on the divisive issue of cheating. At the same time, it produced a better atmosphere in U.S.-Soviet relations. This moved the focus of attention away from concerns about arms control violations and toward cooperation in pursuing security through new agreements.

But the almost complete inattention to questions about compliance and the process of resolving disputes after 1987 is as unrelated to any major changes in the quality of arms control compliance as was the two countries' hypnotic fascination with scouring one another's behavior for real or imagined transgressions in 1981-87. The emphasis on compliance problems emerged in 1981-87 and abruptly subsided thereafter. That fact suggests that both the amount of attention to concerns about compliance and the ability to resolve disputes are extremely sensitive to the political relationship between the superpowers. Furthermore, if other countries have become embroiled in compliance disputes, they are also sensitive to the broader international political climate.

The compliance behavior of states that are parties to arms control treaties may have been poorer to some degree in the 1980s. Yet, it was not significantly worse then than in earlier periods, taking into account the greater number and restrictiveness of the arms control agreements in force in the 1970s relative to previous years. The more significant cause of the compliance crisis of the 1980s was that frustrations and hostility across-the-board in U.S.-Soviet relations were vented through dissatisfactions expressed about compliance.

The process of resolving disputes, that had functioned to the satisfaction of the United States and the Soviet Union during the politically less volatile decade of the 1970s, virtually collapsed under the pressure of U.S.-Soviet estrangement during the 1980s. The superpowers' hostility led to a destructive cycle that, in the end, did decrease arms control compliance and progress toward new treaties. Unresolved disputes, some involving behavior that was indeed questionable, provided the rationale for both countries to move toward non-compliance, as the United States did publicly in the case of SALT II. And accusations of Soviet cheating created public concern in the United States and served to justify delays in progress toward new accords.

In the United Stated in particular, an impulse developed in the early 1980s to make unilateral judgments about the quality of Soviet compliance, to ventilate these concerns publicly without fully exploiting the existing dispute-resolution procedures, and to retaliate against Soviet behavior by threatening or actually embarking upon U.S. non-compliance. On the Soviet side, the internal organization of Soviet society provided inadequate constraints on behavior that stretched the limits of treaty provisions.

Both countries were inhibited by their political polarization from recognizing that it was in their mutual interest and in the interest of continuing to develop an arms-control regime to use appropriate mechanisms to resolve compliance disputes and to avoid the negative cycle of public accusations and tit-for-tat responses.

The rosy glow created in the late 1980s by the INF Treaty, *glasnost* and Gorbachev may wax and wane over time, and political hostilities between the superpowers may surface again. Particularly given the increasing web of arms-control limits, many of which may restrict while not completely banning certain types of practices or weapons, the opportunities for disputes over the interpretation of agreements probably will be as great or greater in the future than they have been in the past.

Table I points out some, but by no means all, of the potential compliance controversies that might arise from the new arms control agreements discussed in this book. If history is any guide, compliance issues are likely to arise primarily from disagreements about the meaning of treaty language, and about whether new technologies or behavior are precluded or allowed by a treaty. These types of disputes are difficult to predict, since the precise content and language of future treaties is unknown. Secondarily, and more predictably, disagreements can be expected to stem from limitations in verification capabilities, that create uncertainty

Table I.   Future Arms Control Agreements: Examples of Potential Compliance Issues

---

Complete Elimination of Nuclear Arsenals

Suspicions about whether a country has a small, virtually undetectable clandestine arsenal of nuclear weapons, that, in the last steps of disarmament, could give that country relatively great political and military power [V]

Limits on Space/Antisatellite Weapons

If *de minimis* thresholds--below which brightness, radar power, etc. activities are of no interest for ABM systems or antisatellite weapons, and above which there must be discussion among the parties--are established as suggested in this book: controversies about whether particular activities are above the thresholds requiring discussion [TL]

Numerical Limits on Nuclear Weapons Systems

Disputes about the range of sea-launched cruise missiles (SLCMs) [V]
Disputes about distinguishing nuclear from conventional SLCMs [V]
Disputes about the permitted degree of modernization, if modernization is allowed [TL]
Disputes about timing or method of dismantling/destruction of precluded systems [V & TL]

[V]= disputes arising from verification limitations
[TL]= disputes arising over the meaning of treaty language

Table I.   (continued)

Comprehensive or Low-Level Threshold Test Ban
   Disputes about distinguishing low-level tests from seismic events [V]
   Charges that cavity decoupling is masking a clandestine testing program [V]
   Disputes about distinguishing low-level tests from industrial explosions [V]
   Lacking on-site sensors, disagreements about whether tests are in excess of permitted levels [V]

Chemical Weapons Agreement
   Disputes about production of prohibited chemicals in the civilian chemical industry [V]
   Disputes about the sources and users of chemical weapons, once use is detected [V]

Biological Weapons Agreement
   Disputes about whether detected presence of toxins is from prohibited uses or natural causes; identifying the sources and users of biological weapons [V]

Conventional Arms Control Agreement
   Disagreements about distinguishing armored personnel carriers and military trucks from civilian vehicles [V]
   Disputes about the presence of helicopters [V]
   Disputes about the behavior of inspectors and the conduct of inspections [TL]
   Disputes about the existence of small unmanned missiles [V]
   Disagreements about the numbers of weapon systems aboard ships [V]
   Disputes about the presence of submarines and the presence or non-presence of nuclear warheads on submarines [V]
   Disputes about the adequacy of prior notification of maneuvers or other restricted activities [TL]

[V]= disputes arising from verification limitations
[TL]= disputes arising over the meaning of treaty language

on one side about the nature of the other party's behavior.
   Table II gives an overview of existing arms control compliance and dispute-resolution mechanisms by treaty.

Change in Approach to Dealing with Compliance Issues

   If the primary engine for the negative cycle of U.S. and Soviet compliance

Table II. Arms Control Compliance and Dispute-Resolution Mechanisms by Treaty

None	Vague/Consultation	Bilateral	Multilateral	International	International Court of Justice
1. Hotline Agreements	1. Outer Space Treaty (refer to "appropriate" int'l org)	1. ABM Treaty (Standing Consultative Commission)	1. Non-Prolif. Treaty (Int. Atomic Energy Agency)	1. Biol & Toxin Weapons Convention	1. Antarctic Treaty
2. Limited Test Ban Treaty	2. Seabed Treaty (refer to UN Security Council)	2. INF Treaty (Special Verif. Commission/Nuclear Risk Reduction Centers)	2. Helsinki Agmt.	2. Environ. Modification Convention	2. [Tlatelolco]
	3. Accidents Measures Agmt (Bilateral consultation)	[3. Threshold Test Ban Treaty/Peaceful Nuclear Explosions Treaties (Joint Consultative Commission)]	3. Stockholm Agreement	3. Geneva Protocol (Post-1982)	3. Convention on the Physical Protection of Nuclear Materials
	4. Incidents at Sea Agmt (Bilateral consultation)		4. West. European Union (Armaments Control Agency)		
	5. Nuclear War Prevention Agmt (Bilateral consultation)		[5. Treaty of Tlatelolco (OPANAL)]		

[Agreement not in force]

behavior in the 1980s was the downturn in political relations between the two countries, then the primary remedy lies in the way both countries approach the issue of compliance, and only to a lesser extent in the content of treaties, in the actual compliance behavior of either side or in the dispute-resolution mechanisms themselves.

The need to insulate the dispute-resolution process from the political climate suggests measures to decrease the likelihood of disputes and to professionalize and routinize the handling of compliance issues when they do arise. A variety of steps could serve this goal:

1. Improving the content and drafting of treaty provisions and broadening the verification measures dedicated to upholding them;
2. Reforming existing institutions for the resolution of disputes;
3. Expanding existing institutions;
4. Creating new institutions for resolving disputes;
5. Multilateralizing or internationalizing existing institutions; and
6. Providing back-up or recourse for existing institutions, if they are unsuccessful in resolving disputes.

Each of these approaches will be discussed below.

Designing Treaty Provisions to Facilitate Compliance and Strengthening Verification Provisions

It has become quite clear that some existing arms control treaties are prone to compliance disputes because the verification provisions incorporated in the agreements were inadequate to deter cheating and to ensure confidence in compliance by the parties. The Biological and Toxin Weapons Convention and the Geneva Protocol, in particular, were agreements concluded prior to an era in which cooperative verification methods were politically feasible. But cooperative verification measures are clearly crucial to the success of multilateral agreements such as these, that restrict activities that are not adequately verifiable by national technical means. The lack of cooperative verification provisions has caused these agreements to be enmeshed in controversy and uncertainty about compliance. Without cooperative verification, these treaties have set important international norms, but cannot be considered verifiable arms control agreements.

More adequately verifiable agreements restricting chemical and biological weapons should obviously supplement or replace the current accords. And no future treaty covering biological, chemical, or other similarly difficult to detect and attribute materials should be accepted by the parties without provisions for thorough cooperative measures. For future chemical or biological weapons treaties, as discussed elsewhere in this book, the necessary measures would include on-site verification of all declarations, dismantling and destruction, and of small-scale production of restricted chemicals or toxins. Other required verification measures would include information exchange and notification of activities relevant to the agreements, challenge on-site inspections, and probably *ad hoc* inspections requested by an inspectorate established by each agreement. Short of such comprehensive measures, adequate verification of such agreements is impossible and compliance controversies are sure to arise.

Another fact that has become clear from experience is that complete bans on particular types of weapons or behavior are much more effective in promoting compliance than partial limitations or qualitative constraints. It was precisely the provisions of SALT II that limited encryption but did not prohibit it completely, and that restrained ICBM modernization but did not close it off entirely, that tempted behavior pushing the limits of the treaty provisions.

The same has been the case with the ABM Treaty provisions that permitted large phased-array radars (LPARs) for certain uses and in certain locations, but prohibited these same radar for other uses and in other locales. The U.S.-Soviet disputes about the Krasnoyarsk radar and about the modernization of U.S. LPARs at Thule, Greenland and Fylingdales Moor, England arose from varying interpretations of these partial ABM Treaty limits on LPARs.

For verification purposes, it is much easier to detect the existence *per se* of a system of a prohibited type than to distinguish a permitted system of a certain type from a prohibited system of the same type. Partial limitations and qualitative restrictions, no matter how carefully constructed, are difficult to verify and open to varying interpretation. Elimination of a complete class of systems facilitates verification and promotes clarity in determining whether compliance is occurring.

Reforming Existing Institutions

The United States and the Soviet Union have not utilized the SCC to the full extent of its charter. The SCC has the mandate to consider trends on the horizon that could affect the treaties under its jurisdiction. One such trend in the late 1970s and early 1980s was the movement of the two countries away from clear compliance with the ABM Treaty in their siting of LPARs. The two countries clearly should have used the SCC to approach this trend in a joint, problem-solving fashion. In the future they should exhibit the foresight to discuss in the SCC and other consultative bodies those military developments on both sides that potentially threaten treaty compliance.

Expanding Existing Institutions

The simple volume of arms control measures that are already in place and will likely be concluded in the next decade dictates against expanding the present consultative bodies to handle new agreements, or creating a single overall consultative body. Rather, the model for new agreements should be that of the INF Treaty, where a Special Verification Commission was created parallel to the SCC to deal with disputes, rather than overloading the SCC with responsibility for another Treaty.

Even with the proper attitudes and the existence of adequate institutional mechanisms for resolving disputes, in periods of poor relations the superpowers' attempts to resolve disputes are likely to be polarized. This suggests the need either for some fundamental change in the structure of dispute-resolution bodies that would increase the incentives for the resolution of disputes, or for some recourse once all the existing avenues for seeking satisfaction about compliance concerns have been exhausted.

Creating New Institutions

At a minimum, every arms control agreement should have provisions for the resolution of disputes. At present, not only do some agreements not have any such mechanisms, but other agreements have only vague provisions that suggest that parties consult about their differences. Table II summarizes the dispute-resolution provisions of existing major arms control agreements.

At the very least, those agreements that do not currently include specialized consultative bodies to address disputes should be equipped with mechanisms on the model of the SCC. The Limited Test Ban Treaty is the most significant agreement that lacks consultation procedures. A number of complaints about venting of radioactive material from underground nuclear tests, that have been raised regarding both Soviet and American practices, could be discussed and hopefully resolved in a consultative body.

The TTBT includes a provision for a Joint Consultative Commission, but it has never been implemented because the Treaty has not been ratified by the United States. During the 1980s, disagreements about compliance with the TTBT were handled in an *ad hoc* and inconclusive manner through discussions between Soviet and American government officials. Any nuclear testing treaty that is a follow-on to the TTBT should certainly include a consultative commission. Those agreements, such as the Outer Space Treaty and the Seabed Treaty, that refer compliance disputes to the UN or vaguely to an "appropriate" international body would be better served if each were equipped with its own consultative body.

Multilateralizing or Internationalizing the Process

A number of proposals have been made for internationalizing the process of verifying compliance with arms control agreements and for resolving disputes. The Soviet Union has proposed a UN\Verification Agency, as well as greater involvement by the UN Secretary General in investigating allegations of violations and in resolving disputes. France has proposed an international satellite verification agency. But most of these proposals concentrate on improving and internationalizing verification procedures and technologies rather than encouraging compliance or improving the dispute-resolution procedures.

The suggestion has been made that internationalizing consultative bodies would enforce discipline on the superpowers by subjecting their charges and behavior to the scrutiny and adjudication of third parties. Two major limitations will discourage the superpowers from routinely dealing with their compliance disputes in multilateral or international fora. These are the questionable effectiveness of multilateral bodies and the need for the superpowers to compromise their concerns about national sovereignty in order to accept the judgments of third parties. The Soviet Union has publicly called for internationalizing verification and compliance dispute-resolution procedures. However, the Soviet Union would certainly "take into account" the opinions expressed by international bodies, but it could not accept a binding judgment affecting national security that would compromise Soviet autonomy and national sovereignty. The same barriers to accepting the judgments of an international authority, and even to sharing sensitive information about national security with such a body, operate just as strongly in the United States.

In any case, as Jim Schear has pointed out, the strongest incentives to resolve disputes are by those directly involved.[2] In other words, the countries most directly involved in a dispute have the most to fear from the lapsing of an agreement and the possible retaliation from the other side, if a compliance dispute is not resolved.

On balance, consultative procedures limited to the parties to specific treaties have proved most successful in resolving disputes. The SCC and the bilateral consultative procedures of the Incidents at Sea Agreement are examples of mechanisms that have productively resolved compliance disputes, except, in the case of the SCC, when political relations have been most hostile. Little progress has occurred in international fora such as the UN when they have been called on to investigate or resolve disputes over compliance.

The problem is not primarily with the mechanisms, but with the approach to the use of the mechanisms that is adopted by parties during periods of poor political relations. Thus, the remedy is to find ways to keep these mechanisms functioning in periods of difficult relations.

Providing Recourse When Dispute Resolution Fails

Phillip Trimble has proposed an international institute for arms control dispute settlement.[3] He calls for non-binding arbitration of all arms control disputes by a new institution that would absorb the SCC, the Special Verification Commission, and all the other current dispute-resolution mechanisms. In Trimble's view, it should involve representation by official personnel of the countries involved; for example, cabinet officers, intelligence officials, diplomats, and general staff members. This agency would be separate from the UN structure.

Such an agency is an excellent idea, providing recourse for the resolution of disputes in periods of political hostility when the existing institutions may be rendered inadequate because they are embroiled in polemics. The need for autonomy and control over national sovereignty by the superpowers is still high. Therefore, and contrary to Trimble's design, such a supranational agency probably should be added to the existing mechanisms as a last-resort recourse for arbitration, rather than replacing them.

Trimble envisions this body being established by treaty. Alternatively, such an agency could be planned by an international conference and modeled on a panel of "Wise Men" or other international commissions. If representation were solely by serving government officials, the risk is too great that in a period of high tension they would simply carry their governments' accusations and frustrations forward into yet another institutional framework. Countries could subscribe to membership in the body, appointing representatives who would be legal scholars, former negotiators, and former diplomats with ambassadorial rank, rather than current officials.

As outlined by Trimble, the functions of such an agency could include treaty interpretation and arbitration, investigation of allegations of non-compliance, and the development of expertise in dispute resolution.

A sanction that would strengthen the influence of a new international arms control compliance agency would be its ability to dramatize the results of questionable or non-compliant behavior for the security of the offending party. The Soviet Union became aware over time that its non-compliant or questionable behavior in cases such as the Krasnoyarsk radar ultimately had indirect but highly negative effects on Soviet security by fueling a stronger American military posture. It would be important for such an agency to be able to release reports on the likely consequences of questionable behavior when first detected. Such reports could highlight the responses to this behavior that would decrease the security of the offender, and perhaps help to deter non-compliant behavior.

As envisioned by Trimble, the agency would have the freedom to undertake examinations and investigations of its own, to analyze impending threats to treaty compliance, as well as to respond to requests for arbitration from the parties. It could do fact-finding, where relevant to specific investigations. Such a body could either have intelligence assets itself, or access to satellites and other capabilities. It may be able to obtain some of them through the UN or other multilateral agencies or commercial sources.

The agency would develop expertise, perhaps through a training institute, in arbitration and dispute resolution. Eventually it could funnel experts to the other subsidiary dispute-resolution bodies attached to particular treaties. It could be funded by assessment of the member states.

Such a body would maintain confidentiality, as long as a dispute were under discussion and being handled. Within some limits it could have the ability to disclose information, if the process of dispute resolution would otherwise fail. A quiescent period in East-West relations is obviously the best time to establish such an agency, when the potential members see a mutual interest in resolving disputes.

Trimble reviews several cases of how such an agency could have worked productively to foster resolution of the compliance disputes of the 1980s. One he does not discuss, but that provides a persuasive example, is how the compliance arbitration agency could have assisted in the resolution of one of the thorniest compliance problems of the 1980s--the dispute over the high level of Soviet telemetry encryption in relation to the non-interference provisions of the SALT II Agreement. SALT II specified that encryption was permitted, but could not impede verification of compliance with the Treaty. The United States argued that nearly total Soviet encryption of telemetry in tests of some ballistic missiles impeded verification of SALT II compliance. The Soviet Union held that the level of their telemetry encryption in ballistic missile flights tests did not impede verification of treaty compliance. The Soviets asked the United States to specify what data from these missile flight tests needed to be received in the clear to verify compliance with SALT II. For intelligence reasons, the United States refused to identify the data required. This dispute ended in stalemate at the SCC.

Had a supranational body for arbitration and dispute resolution existed, the United States could have brought up the issue of Soviet encryption, having failed to obtain satisfaction through the SCC. The agency's personnel could have examined the Treaty provisions, come to a more precise definition of how much encryption in fact constituted "impeding" verification of SALT II, and considered both countries' positions. Perhaps the agency would have recommended that the United States be more specific about its needs for data to verify compliance with the SALT II Treaty. Perhaps the agency would have asked the Soviet Union to justify its high level of encryption. Perhaps it would have proposed a compromise in each party's position.

If neither the position of the United States nor the position of the Soviet Union changed as a result of its recommendation, the agency could have reported on the likely consequences for the security of both sides if the issue were not resolved. The agency might have pointed out for Soviet benefit the role Soviet encryption was playing in mounting U.S. frustrations with Soviet behavior, that could--and in fact, did--lead to U.S. abrogation of the SALT II accord, although that was not the primary motivation of this step.

Conclusion

Dispute resolution will be encouraged if appropriate mechanisms are established with full powers. The ambiguities that lead to disputes can be minimized by negotiating treaties to avoid partial limits and qualitative restrictions, and by providing adequate verification measures to uphold treaties.

Ensuring that every existing and future arms control agreement has a consultative mechanism to resolve disputes is a necessity for dealing with disagreements.

But, even with these improvements, especially in times of international tension the risk will always be high that compliance issues will become a political football. Creating an agency with the express political mission to resolve compliance disputes might well encourage the type of creative solutions of which some diplomats and political leaders are capable, when they are specifically directed to the task.

Notes

1. See Gloria Duffy, Project Director, *Compliance and the Future of Arms Control* (Cambridge: Ballinger Publishing Company, 1988).

2. James A. Schear, "Compliance Diplomacy in a Multilateral Setting" in Michael Krepon and Mary Umberger, eds., *Verification and Compliance: A Problem-Solving Approach* (London: Macmillan, 1988), p. 262.

3. Phillip R. Trimble, "Beyond Verification: The Next Step in Arms Control" *Harvard Law Review* Vol. 102, No. 4, p. 897.

3

The Technical Basis for Verification of a Low Threshold or Comprehensive Nuclear Test Ban Treaty

Charles B. Archambeau[1] (USA), Mikhail B. Gokhberg[2] (USSR), Oleg K. Kedrov[2] (USSR) & Jeremy Leggett[3] (UK)

Summary[4]

Verification of a low threshold or comprehensive nuclear test ban by technical means is quite a mature subject area in the sense that research, focused on the specific scientific issues involved, has been on-going for the last thirty years. However, during the last four years since late 1986, these investigations have taken on a new and important expansion in content in that a US-USSR scientific program has made new kinds of seismic data available for the direct assessment of verification capabilities in each country. That is, new high performance seismic stations in both countries are providing on-site information regarding seismic verification capabilities with the result that many of the uncertainties that arose, because of the lack of in-country access with the required sensing equipment, are being removed. Further, since the equipment is specially designed for the investigation of seismic verification at a very low test threshold, it is possible to systematically test some new methods of monitoring that could not be adequately evaluated before. An objective of the present study is to incorporate some of the

1. University of Colorado, Cooperative Institute for Research in the Environmental Sciences (CIRES), Boulder, Colorado 80309, USA

2. Schmidt Inst. of Physics of the Earth, Academy of Sciences of the USSR, B. Gruzinskaya, 10, Moscow, USSR 123810

3. Imperial College of Science and Technology, Dept. of Geology, Royal School of Mines, London, U.K. SW7 - 2BP

4. The full text of this chapter will probably be published soon in English as a journal article, and will perhaps be included in the Russian version of this book.

results emerging from these studies with those that previously formed the basis for an assessment of verification capabilities to provide an up-dated assessment.

In order to establish a quantitative evaluation of capabilities we summarize the main concepts and methods employed in seismic verification along with the problems that are encountered, particularly those that are encountered in attempting to detect and identify nuclear tests at very low yield levels. In this connection it should be noted that there are different opinions about the possibility to conduct clandestine explosions with decoupling (those detonated in large underground cavities). If one considers it possible to carry out such tests, then one must conclude that there are some problems with the identification of such explosions among a very large number of earthquakes and large industrial explosions. In this context we describe a number of new methods designed to address this particular identification problem. We also supply arguments that demonstrate the great difficulties encountered in conducting tests with decoupling. And we also discuss results implying that an in-country seismic monitoring network, of about 30 high-performance stations, could provide a confident (70 to 90%) probability of identification of any decoupled test having a yield in the range from 1 to 5 kt, and less than 0.1 kt if explosions are conducted without decoupling. We then describe new non-seismic technology and methodology that should be able to provide confident identification to a yield level significantly below 1 kt when combined with current seismic methods. By way of summarizing capabilities for nuclear test ban verification to very low test yields, we have concluded the discussion with an outline of treaty conditions that are desirable if we are to achieve a full reduction of the "verifiable threshold" to levels consistent with our present and likely future capabilities.

4

Verification of Compliance with the ABM Treaty and with Limits on Space Weapons

Richard L. Garwin (USA) & Roald Z. Sagdeev (USSR)

Verifying Compliance with the ABM Treaty

The ABM Treaty (ABMT) of 1972 between the U.S. and the U.S.S.R. is very brief--four pages in *Arms Control and Disarmament Agreements* plus three more of Agreed Statements and Common Understandings. With a protocol of 1974, the ABMT limits each side to a single-site deployment of 100 interceptor missiles and also limits the number of ABM radars or complexes within a 150-km radius. The Treaty also forbids giving ABM capabilities to non-ABM missiles, launchers, or radars.

As regards the ABMT, this chapter is primarily concerned with Article V.1:

Each Party undertakes not to develop, test, or deploy ABM systems or components that are sea-based, air-based, space-based, or mobile land-based.

Agreed Understanding D committed the Parties

...that in the event ABM systems based on other physical principles and including components capable of substituting for ABM interceptor missiles, ABM launchers, or ABM radars are created in the future, specific limitations on such systems would be subject to discussion in accordance with Article XIII and agreement in accordance with Article XIV of this Treaty.

The ABMT permits only those items specified; everything else is forbidden. Thus ABM systems based on other physical principles may not be deployed at all until "specific limitations" are agreed as indicated. If either side does not "agree," such systems are not permitted to be deployed.

After much dispute within and between the U.S. Reagan Administration and the Senate (with its constitutional responsibility in regard to treaty ratification) it is now generally accepted that the Parties are permitted to test ABM components "based on other physical principles" (than rocket-powered interceptors, launchers, and radars) only at the two ABM test ranges permitted each side. But basing these "exotic" components in space, in the air, or on the sea is not permitted in any case. Still, the ABMT will survive only so long as it is in the interests of the Parties. It even contains an explicit provision for abandonment on six months notice if the "supreme national interest" of a Party is involved. In addition, like any treaty, it could in practice be abandoned at any time, without prior notice. The Parties are well aware that the ABMT exists because of the judgment on each side that no damage-prevention ABM system can be built that cannot be countered at lower cost by an expanded or modified offensive force. While this remains true, activities in violation of the ABMT would be countered not by similar ABM activities on the other side but primarily by modification to the offensive force.

The ABMT set the precedent of specifically acknowledging the acceptability of "national technical means" (NTM) of verification of the treaty provisions (imaging satellites, for instance) and banning interference with them. It also banned "deliberate concealment measures that impede verification by NTM of compliance with this Treaty." We have now had 17 years of experience with verification of compliance with the ABMT, and the record is good. One unambiguous act inconsistent with the Treaty is the construction of the early warning radar at Krasnoyarsk first observed by the United States in 1983. The Soviet government maintained for some years that this was a radar for spacetrack purposes and not an early warning radar. However, it is apparently identical with the radar system at Pechora, which is clearly an early warning radar. The Soviet government gave the Krasnoyarsk radar to the Soviet Academy of Sciences with instructions to discover a use for the uncompleted facility in conjunction with international space research. Then, in a remarkable speech by Foreign Secretary Shevardnadze in 1989, they stated that it had taken four years for the leadership to learn the full story of this radar and that it would be destroyed unconditionally.

Other questionable practices have been reported to the offending side, and measures have been taken to stop them, or to destroy the items in question. Unilateral NTM, in conjunction with the ban on "deliberate concealment" have revealed without difficulty the activities in question. Part of the problem has been the determination whether the activity is consistent with the Treaty--for instance, the upgrading of the U.S. radars at Thule, Greenland, and at Fylingdales Moor, England, which the U.S.S.R. maintains are inconsistent with the ABMT. It is difficult to hide ABM-capable radars, and the testing of high-performance ABM interceptors could not readily be concealed from feasible space observation, either, even if there were a will to do so. Furthermore, there is a substantial gap between the capabilities required for effective terminal defense (that is, for destruction of reentry vehicles--RV--during the last minute or so of their flight, as the atmosphere retards the many light decoys that are expected to accompany warheads if a significant ABM system is deployed) and capabilities acquired for other purposes such as air defense or antisatellite activity.

Space-Based Systems and the ABM Treaty

This gap is narrowed if one considers space-based ABM systems, which are clearly banned by the treaty. Observation systems receiving visible or infrared (IR) light can be a key component of a space-based ABM. Such systems are useless in ground-based terminal defense systems because of clouds, or because of dust that would predictably be produced in their area by high-altitude nuclear explosions. If only because such observation systems in the mid-range IR (3-5 μm wavelength) have been in continuous operation in geosynchronous earth orbit (GEO) since well before the ABMT, they are not *per se* ABM components. In fact, their function has been that of early warning of missile attack (or continual assurance that no ICBM or SLBM attack has been launched). Their contribution to the effectiveness of a terminal-phase ABM system is small. The avowed purpose of the U.S. SDI program is to explore and demonstrate effective means of defense against ballistic missiles in the boost, post-boost, mid-course, and terminal phases of their flight. Therefore, satellites observing boost phase may assume the role of a component of an ABM system if there is a capability in existence or under development for boost-phase intercept.

This SDI program for the exploration, perfection, and (if an effective, survivable, and cost-effective defense is found to be feasible) even the deployment of ABM systems presents difficulties for verification of compliance with the ABMT.[1] These difficulties are enhanced by the perplexing but widely accepted argument that SDI (an ABM-oriented program) can test a space-based sensor or interceptor against an orbiting satellite target, when a test against a ballistic missile would clearly be forbidden by the ABMT.[2] The mission of antisatellite weapons (ASAT), in itself, is not in violation of any agreement, recognizing that satellite intercept would occur in wartime or itself be an act of war. In any case most modern arms control agreements are not oriented primarily toward banning specific acts in war or even the initiation of war. Rather they aim toward verifiable limitations on acquisition or development of the capacity to perform those acts--to provide a sufficient delay (buffer time) between the end of compliance with the treaty and even the capability to carry out acts that are banned.

If compliance with the ABMT is to be verified in the present environment in which development and even deployment of ASAT capability is not limited by any treaty, lines must be drawn between ABM-capable components or elements that are built ostensibly for ASAT or other purposes, and ASAT elements that do not have "ABM capability."[3] Let us consider two examples. First, take the

Krasnoyarsk radar, once justified as a spacetrack facility. If the radar beam could not be directed closer to the horizon than about 30° elevation angle, the radar would not be at all useful for early warning. Furthermore, it could readily be destroyed by a normal ballistic missile warhead from the northeast (which it would not even see), even if defended by a farm of interceptors. As a phased-array radar, however, even if the Krasnoyarsk installation after completion were to direct its radar energy skyward, never below 30° elevation, it would require only the typing of a single word on a keyboard to convert Krasnoyarsk to the early-warning mode of the Pechora radar.[4] Nor is the radar oriented or sited suitably for a good spacetrack capability. The earth's rotation ensures that points on the equator can see all low-orbit satellites eventually, while radars at high latitudes (particularly if they do not point south) can see only those satellites with high orbital inclinations.

A second example of the overlap of ABM with ASAT programs stems from the SDI program. Lieutenant General James A. Abrahamson, Director of SDI, argued that the test of a certain SDI satellite capability was not banned by the ABMT because the satellite could not serve as a "component" of an ABM system. Why? Because rather than communicate its observations in real time, it would store them on board the satellite and provide them later for evaluation. If the satellite were to transmit the information by radio, apparently it would be judged by the SDI Organization (SDIO) to be a real ABM component. A similar argument might have been used to legitimize the Krasnoyarsk radar, by ensuring that radar observations obtained when the beam was at low elevation angle were recorded on tape and transmitted later, while spacetrack data could be transmitted immediately by data link. The problem with such artificial "compliance" is that it destroys the buffer time. A data link or a computer program could be energized in a split second or, if not even present, is a small addition to the component or system. Such a change would transform the satellite or other element in a short time from irrelevant to important in an ABM system.

We recognize the real difficulty posed for verification of compliance with the ABMT in a world in which either or both sides pursues a legitimate ASAT capability. Thus, we will attempt to prescribe and evaluate a verification system for this case. We shall contrast this with the much simpler verification problem of the ABMT in a world supplemented by a hypothetical international agreement banning the use or test of Space Weapons or ASAT capability, and banning the deployment of weapons in space.[5]

How to Verify Compliance?

Compliance is verified when one can reliably detect noncompliance. More precisely, significant violations should have large enough probability of detection to deter violations, or to provide timely warning if they do occur. Whether warning is sufficiently "timely" to allow the other side to take actions to maintain its security depends in part on the delay in the verification process, but much more on the nature of the agreement negotiated between the two sides.

There is little need to discuss here detection of possible violations of the ABMT regarding numbers and locations of radars, nuclear-armed interceptors, launchers, and so on. Apparently this is adequate now.

There are, however, potential problems with verification. A difficult task would be to ensure that tiny non-nuclear armed ground-based interceptors are not perfected and made available for replication across the nation in a breakout from the ABMT. However, this is not a credible threat for the following reasons:

1. Exoatmospheric intercept would allow some 10 minutes for intercept. Therefore it would permit use of low-velocity ground-based rockets (thus the launch mass of an interceptor would be only a few times the payload and the necessary acceleration would not be high). There is, however, nothing new in this. It could have been done with many thousands of SPRINT+ missiles.

   The problem is discrimination. No matter how many interceptors one has stockpiled across the nation, if it is known that they exist, there will be millions of decoys among the thousands or ten thousand warheads. There will be large empty balloons, as well as similar balloons enclosing RVs. There also will be close-spaced objects tethered at distances of ~ 10 m from the RV or decoys.[6]

   Of course, there might be too many such decoys for the defense to use nuclear warheads, even if nuclear warheads were inherently sufficiently affordable. But if there are non-nuclear warheads for this exoatmospheric intercept, these (for instance, IR-guided) kinetic-kill vehicles (KKV) would have to be thoroughly tested at high closing velocity against the decoys. Although the low-thrust interceptors themselves might be difficult to see with existing sensors, destruction of these orbiting targets could be observed by the spacetrack net.

2. Endoatmospheric intercept can take place after atmospheric drag retards light decoys sufficiently for them to be discriminated from the RVs. Nevertheless, such a system needs good battle management to assign interceptors to the individual RVs. It would need bulk filtering of radar signals in order to distinguish the RVs that had not slowed from those decoys that have. It would also need high-acceleration, high-velocity, fast-burn interceptors so that the intercept can be made far enough away from the ground to preserve the potential targets of the attack, given that the interceptor launch must wait for the RV to fall below ~ 100 km altitude. Furthermore, all this was achieved in the U.S. SAFEGUARD deployment of 1975-76, with the nuclear-armed SPRINT missile. The interceptor is imagined only to have to intercept real warheads or heavy decoys. Thus,

the use of a low-yield nuclear warhead in the interceptor is not a great burden.

Non-nuclear interceptors might do a better job only if the warheads were lighter than the SPRINT warhead. Nevertheless, the typical 100 m kill radius of a SPRINT warhead within the atmosphere is replaced by the necessity for the interceptor to collide with the RV. If this is to be done with an onboard IR or visible sensor, one requires cloud-free air between the interceptor and warhead, and a lot of testing.

Of course, one could use ground radar illumination of the RV, and a semi-active homing system to guide the interceptor in the final stages of attack, supplementing the command-guided approach used in SAFEGUARD.

In any case, realistic tests of these endoatmospheric non-nuclear interceptors against incoming RVs would be visible at the existing test sites (or elsewhere). Furthermore, at the existing ABM test ranges the tests would be in compliance with the ABMT restrictions.

ABM-Capable KKVs in Orbit? According to a view logically supportable, but in our opinion destructive of the ABMT, verifying compliance with the ABMT would in no way prevent the evolution and refinement of a space-based interceptor (SBI) technology under the guise of ASAT development. For instance, a KKV with near-optimum reach-out speed of 6 km/s could be based in modular fashion on a test satellite, could be provided with self-guiding thermal-IR homing and tested against orbiting decoys or mock RVs in orbit. According to this view, such an act would not be testing "in an ABM mode," because the target is not "in flight trajectory."[7]

A view more respectful of the ABMT (and of those who pay taxes supporting military technology) would lead to lofted tests of KKVs against mock RVs in real flight trajectory--a true ABM test. While the other Party would have a lively curiosity in what was being done, such a test would in no sense be a violation of the ABMT. Assuming a set of successful tests and an analysis that such orbiting KKVs in a deployed system would satisfy the Nitze criteria,[8] a decision might be made to build a defensive system based on orbiting KKVs.

A violation of the ABMT would only occur at the point at which the lofted test was succeeded by a test of the prototype satellite that housed a number of prototype KKVs. A test against mock RVs in flight trajectory (or against targets in boost phase) would then violate the ban on testing space-based systems. A lofted test of the satellite itself would violate the (Article V.2) ban on multiple ABM interceptor missiles.

As we have seen, the natural and economical way to explore, develop, and test ABM weapon capabilities is in compliance with the ABMT.[9] Thus, even perfect verification (as contrasted with unilateral intelligence or bilateral confidence building measures that go beyond verification) would give no indication of this emerging capability, perhaps until deployment began.

Ground-Based ABM Lasers. As a final example of verification of the ABMT in a regime not augmented by other measures, we take the ground-based free-electron laser (FEL). For ABM purposes, the FEL would be used with orbiting relay mirrors to direct 100 MW or more of laser light not against RVs but against boosters a quarter-world away.

The technology itself is enormously challenging--mirrors of 5-m diameter at the laser on the ground and in GEO, as well as replicated numerous "fighting mirrors" in intermediate orbit. If the ground mirror is compensated ~100 times a second for the turbulence of the entire depth of the atmosphere, the laser light might be directed so that 10-20% of it would fall on the mirror at GEO. This light would be available for relay to the fighting mirrors and hence focusing onto the target boosters.[10] Visible light of 0.5 μm wavelength would provide an ultimate divergence angle from a 5 m diameter mirror that is the ratio of the wavelength to the mirror diameter--some 4 m at 40,000 km (GEO) distance. But the atmosphere would normally provide a broadening of this beam in angle by a factor of 30 in each direction, corresponding to only about 1/900th of the light falling on the relay mirror. Therefore, real-time atmospheric compensation will be necessary.

Perfect compensation and no loss of light in the atmosphere would correspond to ~500 W/cm^2 of light incident on the relay mirror.[11] A 5 m diameter mirror in GEO would provide a similar maximum flux against targets near the earth. Considering the propensity for shiny surfaces to reduce absorbed heat, this is totally inadequate for the ABM role. Accordingly a 5 m diameter fighting mirror at a distance of 4000 km (typical) from the target could concentrate the light to provide a potent capability. The same angular spread would correspond to a spot 100 times smaller in area at this 10-fold shorter distance.

Close-In On-Orbit Monitoring Satellites. Verification of non-deployment of such systems could be achieved by in-orbit close monitors for live satellites that might be thought to be ABM related. A capability to launch quickly into various orbits monitoring satellites that would observe from a distance of, say, 10 km would be useful. Furthermore, only very small satellites would be required. For a given resolution of the object--for instance, the ability to observe details as small as 10 cm in extent--a mirror or lens on the monitor could be a factor 100 smaller in diameter from this short distance than from a still-modest distance of 1000 km. Observing in the 1 μm wavelength range, the monitor would need a lens only 10 cm in diameter in order for a normal video camera to yield a real-time image of the satellite under observation with the required resolution. Such an image could be transmitted to a monitoring station on the ground by relay from something like the NASA Tracking and Data Relay Satellite System.

The main point is that without a ban on space weapons and on ASAT tests, "verifying compliance" with the ABMT alone will not stop evolution of technology that could result in a troublesome ABM system. But the deployment of the system in violation of the ABMT could be observed.

A Supplementary Space Weapons Ban

In our opinion, the security of both Parties to the ABMT, as well as of the rest of the world, would be improved by a verifiable, effective ban on space weapons, as well as a ban on ASAT tests. This would include the preannouncement of test launches of offensive ballistic missiles, as well as of ABM interceptor tests. Without such a ban, however, one would have to set numerical limits on mirror diameter, potential brightness, beam power of neutral-particle-beam machines (NPB), capabilities of KKV, and the like. What should guide these limits?

Ashton Carter[12] considers several regimes possible within and outside the ABMT. If the Parties wished to replace the ABMT with a more permissive agreement, the 100-interceptor capability permitted by the ABMT might still serve as a standard for the capability possessed by test devices on an Agreed Orbiting Test Range, for instance. If that were regarded as a negligible capability in 1972,[13] a capability to destroy ten missiles in boost phase, or perhaps 10 in post-boost, or 100 RVs in mid-course would be similarly negligible. The first point, of course, is that the ABMT considered 100 (not 400) interceptors negligible, and so there is no reason to imagine that each of these defensive capabilities should be permitted in addition to the 100 interceptors of the ABMT.

Carter also argues that if such a guideline were adopted, the unmodified offensive force should be used as a standard of defense effectiveness. The ABMT, as signed, did not force continual modification of the strategic retaliatory force in order that the effectiveness of permitted ABM systems be rendered negligible.

For an ABMT supplemented by a ban on space weapons and ASAT tests, the dynamics of verification are very different. Anything that could serve as a weapon in space would be banned. It would be the responsibility of the side wishing to test or to deploy such a thing to explain why it should not be considered a weapon.[14] This would involve a low threshold on power, brightness, etc., above which disclosure would be required, but which would be far below any militarily significant capabilities. No great harm would come from the other side's undetected testing at twice the disclosure threshold.

Is Effective ABM Impossible?

It is generally recognized that effective defense against a very small number of ballistic warheads is technically feasible. So long as security is taken to depend upon deterrence by threat of retaliation, however, such a defense would be destabilizing.[15] Thus, its prospect would result in a growth of the offensive forces on both sides. However, in the discussions surrounding the early days of the SDI program, it was recognized that, in principle, defense might become dominant, in the sense that new discoveries, inventions, or technologies might favor defense against offense of equal or even of somewhat greater cost. Thus, nations may become able to protect themselves against the threat of nuclear-armed ballistic missiles and perhaps eventually against all nuclear weapons. All one can say about this is that it is unlikely, given the understanding brought, in part, by the SDI program. Furthermore, it would not necessarily be desirable, since it might open a society to coercion or destruction from clandestinely emplaced weapons, or the like.

Nevertheless, there is the policy question whether scientific and technical exploration should proceed to determine whether new proposals could lay the basis for such a highly effective ABM system. Could such exploration be done on one side without destabilizing the situation?

In principle, scientific exploration of such questions is very different from a demonstration and still more different from deployment. To take a specific example, in connection with the FEL system, there are uncertainties about atmospheric compensation at these high power levels. As an ABM system, it is fraught with problems of survivability of the mirrors in space, requirement of a clean atmosphere, and the like. However, the least costly and least provocative way to test the critical question of compensation for irregularities of the normal atmosphere would involve the recognition that the system need run for only about 0.2 seconds at high power to test the atmospheric compensation scheme.[16] Such a test installation can be very different from a continuous duty machine.

A similar case holds for an NPB. Here, the maximum possible duration of interest to determine physical propagation questions is the 60 minutes required for the beam to go some 10,000 km.

Thus in a non-space-weapon regime, any activity taking place above the very low disclosure threshold would involve the declaration of the parameters of the particular device or test. Preannouncement would provide an opportunity for the other side to verify the correctness of the declaration. In fact, there should normally be a cooperative monitoring system devised as part of the test, providing information to both sides.[17]

Regulating Conflict in Space?

For many decades, the military use of space in general and space weapons in particular have caught the imagination of novelists and visionaries. Military objects first appeared momentarily in space with the German V-2 during the Second World War. Space only began to be used in a big way for potential military transport with the advent of nuclear-armed ballistic missiles, initially in Soviet and U.S. inventories, in the 1950s.

It has often been suggested to station offensive nuclear weapons in orbit, and to bring them down on their targets on earth by a small rocket that reduces the orbital speed so the warhead reenters the atmosphere. As a way of avoiding vulnerability of land- or sea-based nuclear weapons, this approach does not make much sense. The weapons are far more vulnerable in near-earth orbit than they are on the home territory or in the broad oceans. Further, they are less responsive. Their modest propulsion capability to bring them down on a target results in a wait up to 12 hours until the earth's rotation brings a particular target under the ground track of a particular orbiting weapon. Of course, for many weapons in orbit and for targets more or less uniformly distributed around the earth, one would attempt to assign the nearest weapon to each target, so that the delays would be far shorter. Nevertheless, although the first target in a many-target/many-weapon confrontation would be destroyed very rapidly, more than half the warheads could not strike their targets for 45 minutes, and many weapons would remain unused for hours.

With the launching of the first artificial earth satellites, both civil and military uses of space began to evolve, with many long-duration satellites playing a military role. However, there are several dimensions among which the military activities in space can be assessed, and along which a distinction might be attempted between permitted and forbidden activities. The distinction between offensive and defensive missions is appealing but not very practical. For instance, hydrogen bomb warheads over the years have been deployed by the dozens (and were planned by the thousands) to counter the delivery of nuclear weapons by strategic ballistic missiles. Such defensive weapons could not now be based in space without violating the Outer Space Treaty of 1967 (Article IV). That treaty states

> States Parties to the Treaty undertake not to place in orbit around the Earth any objects carrying nuclear weapons or any other kinds of weapons of mass destruction, install such weapons on celestial bodies, or station such weapons in outer space in any other manner.

Of course, this ban applies equally to offensive and defensive nuclear weapons in orbit.

One might attempt to distinguish civil uses of satellites from military uses of satellites. In general, however, that can't be done without denying the military their legitimate role in society. The use of earth satellites for communication, observation, navigation, and weather observation would contribute to the effectiveness of the military in war. In many respects, however, these capabilities are stabilizing and help to prevent war, in support of the broadened military responsibility to prevent war rather than to attempt to win a war if one should begin.

A further distinction is between weapons-related and non-weapons military applications. But even satellite weather observation has an important weapons-related role. Precision navigation capability via satellite may be extremely useful for blind landing of military and civil aircraft on airfields all over the world. Accuracy not nearly so good would allow impact of nuclear warheads so that the target is within the radius of the crater.

Despite the difficulties with defining harmful uses of space, there is by now a substantial consensus that a useful distinction can be made on the basis of whether there are actual weapons in space. What are the weapons, if not nuclear bombs?

Nuclear explosions in space have not occurred since 1962, and have been banned to signatories by the Limited Test Ban Treaty of 1963. The U.S. deployed for some years two different ASAT systems.[18] Some 20 tests of a Soviet ASAT system were performed by the U.S.S.R. between 1968 and 1982; since which time there have been no such Soviet tests. The Soviet ASAT is a pellet-warhead short-lived satellite that intercepts after one or two orbits, and homes apparently either by an optical seeker or by radar. In the 1980s, the United States has tested a kinetic-kill ASAT in which the satellite destroys itself by collision--in this case not with an interceptor in orbit, but with one launched from an F-15 aircraft and popped up with precise positioning and timing to be in the path of the satellite with an accuracy of a meter or so, for so-called kinetic kill.[19]

Similar KKVs have been proposed for an important role in the SDI defense against strategic ballistic missiles. Clearly, the original SDI goal of a homing head of 5 kg or 10 kg mass was not cost-competitive with the single-warhead small ICBM that would be adopted to counter it.[20]. The lack of viability of SBI was worsened by the extreme vulnerability that derives from clustering the SBI on garages, initially proposed to house 150 interceptors each, and later (in belated partial recognition of the well-known essential need that the defense be survivable) perhaps six interceptors each.

More recently, these "smart rocks" (10 kg warheads propelled to 6 km/s reach-out speed by a 150 kg rocket) have been proposed in doubly exaggerated form and dubbed "brilliant pebbles." One chief proponent (Lowell Wood of the Lawrence Livermore Laboratory) has proposed (abridged version of a speech published in *Aviation Week & Technology*, June 13, 1988, pp. 151-155) that

> Weighing in at around 5 pounds (2.3 kg), including in-orbit support modules, they [each of the brilliant pebbles including rocket propulsion] would cost $25,000-50,000 to launch into orbit . . .

In contrast, the SDIO now shows a model of brilliant pebbles as weighing 40-50 kg and costing perhaps $1,000,000.

Familiar from the beginning of the decade of the 1980s and the first flush of enthusiasm for the SDI, are the space-based chemical lasers, NPB accelerators, fighting mirrors in orbit to be used with ground-based FELs and the like. Less familiar, and more awkward for SDI enthusiasts, is the lowly space mine. In concept, this is a relatively simple explosive-fragment or nuclear warhead for long-duration deployment in space, equipped with close-in sensors to enable it always to keep the quarry satellite within the lethal range of its explosion. The space mine would be put into orbit with the aid of space- or ground-based resources, to provide assessment, tracking, and initial control. The real threat to satellites is from overt space mines. It would, thus, be misleading to suggest that if space mines could not reasonably remain covert one should not worry about them.

The space-mine threat is so serious because, in comparing size and function between the space mine and the quarry satellite, space mines appear to be much cheaper than their quarry. Furthermore, a space mine can be detonated by command of duly constituted authority. Alternatively, it could be arranged to explode if tampered with on-orbit, or if its quarry shows what begins to look like unacceptable capability to evade. If brilliant pebbles are feasible to detect and strike targets initially at a range of hundreds of kilometers, nearby space mines are far simpler.

Weapons based in space may have their targets in space--either visitors or permanent residents. In fact, a system installed to defend against the missiles and nuclear warheads of ICBMs would likely do a much better job of destroying satellites instead, including the "defensive" satellites of the other side. In sum, the sole occupation of space by weapons of one nation would not be tolerated, and the mutual occupation would seem more likely to decrease international security than to improve it.

Some Kinds of Space Weapons Could be Effective Against Aircraft or Ground Targets

Many kinds of weapons in space can have no effect on potential targets on the ground or in the air. For instance, neutral particle beams can't penetrate below 100 km altitude without being gradually stripped to ions and falling prey to deflection and hence gross spreading in the Earth's magnetic field. And the hydrogen-fluorine (D-F) laser beam cannot reach the lower atmosphere because it is absorbed in the air. A D-F space-based laser (SBL) beam could reach the ground in clear air (the steady beam is not much dispersed by atmospheric turbulence on its way down to ground targets). Targets considered for SBL (such as high-flying aircraft) can, however, be destroyed (and probably more readily and cheaply) by ordinary non-nuclear antiaircraft missile homing warheads, delivered to the vicinity of the target by a small specialized ICBM.

There are no weapons in space right now, and the $20 billion appropriated thus far to the SDIO has revealed more problems than promise of a space-based defense against strategic ballistic missiles. Therefore, one should review the prospects for limitation or banning weapons and weapons tests from space. If nations and peoples are to depend upon treaties for their security, the treaty regime must be one that improves that security if the participants actually fulfill their obligations.[21] In other words, the treaty must establish a regime that is desirable; militarily significant deviations from prescribed performance must be detectable (the treaty must be adequately verifiable); and detected violations must still allow sufficient time for counter actions, so that the treaty regime in fact provides more security than does the absence of a treaty. But a perfectly verifiable treaty benefits the participants not at all if its perfect verifiability is due to its affecting behavior not at all.

In any case, it is not our intent to describe technology and verification tools in general--not even those applicable to verifying limitations of space weapons. Space limitations (in this volume), as well as our own preference, suggest that we describe the verification of a particular treaty regime--that which one of us helped present May 18, 1983, to a subcommittee of the Senate Foreign Relations Committee (published, for instance, in *Bulletin of the Atomic Scientists*, p. 10S, May 1984). We reproduce here the first three of 12 articles:

Article I
> Each Party undertakes not to destroy, damage, render inoperable or change the flight trajectory of space objects of other States.

Article II
> 1. Each Party undertakes not to place in orbit around the Earth weapons for destroying, damaging, rendering inoperable, or changing the flight trajectory of space objects, or for damaging objects in the atmosphere or on the ground.
> 2. Each Party undertakes not to install such weapons on celestial bodies, or station such weapons in outer space in any other manner.
> 3. Each Party undertakes not to test such weapons in space or against space objects.

Article III
> 1. For the purpose of providing assurance of compliance with the provisions of this treaty, each Party shall use national technical means of verification at its disposal in a manner consistent with generally recognized principles of international law.
> 2. Verification by national technical means shall be supplemented, as appropriate, by such cooperative measures for contributing to the effectiveness of verification by national technical means as the Parties shall agree upon in the Standing Consultative Commission.
> 3. Each Party undertakes not to interfere with the national technical means of verification of the other Party operating in accordance with paragraph 1 of this Article.
> 4. Each Party undertakes not to use deliberate concealment measures which impede verification by national technical means of compliance with this treaty.

In Chapter 15, "ASAT Treaty Verification," in the book *Arms Control Verification: The Technologies that Make it Possible* (Washington: Pergamon-

Brassey's, 1986), there is a lengthy discussion of this draft Treaty, its meaning, and its significance.

A Treaty Should Provide Buffer Time Against Danger

The purpose of the Treaty is to establish a code of behavior that would benefit the Parties to the Treaty. Some of the provisions of a treaty may have no other function than to aid verification. Other provisions have the purpose of imposing a buffer time between the moment a nation may decide no longer to abide by the treaty and the moment it can physically commit prohibited acts. For instance, in a treaty regime that forbade use but permitted deployment of space weapons, every satellite of considerable value might be subject to destruction within a fraction of a second by the explosion of a space mine previously emplaced by the other side in an orbit similar to its quarry satellite. But with a treaty that bans weapons from space, valuable satellites in GEO will live for at least some hours after the other side rejects the treaty (so long as the regime has not permitted the testing and acquisition of powerful directed energy weapons such as a potential nuclear-explosion-powered x-ray laser). Thus, Article II.1, so long as it is obeyed, builds in a buffer time of hours against destruction of high-altitude satellites by explosion, pellets, or collision. On the other hand, Article I itself (a no-first-use treaty) has a buffer time that may be no more than minutes.

A buffer even of some hours is not very consoling. Such a minimal buffer might well lead the Parties to the competitive manufacture and deployment of exactly those weapons that they fear most. It is Article II.3 that creates a buffer of months, or in many cases, years, if the Treaty is implemented soon enough.

This Treaty does not ban possession of ASAT weapons, but it does ban test of ". . . such weapons in space or against space objects." Since satellites are so much more fragile than are RVs, the ban on testing of "such weapons in space" also would ban the test in space of means to destroy a RV.

Article I of this particular draft Treaty forbids certain harmful acts against "space objects of other States." For verification that one has not been subject to such acts, one party ("A", to be definite) could mount on its important satellites sensors of damaging laser illumination, approaching high-speed meteors, neutral particle beams, and the like. Such sensors need not be very sensitive in order to obtain a record of the actual destruction of the satellite itself. Like emergency radio transmission buoys carried by some submarines, they could broadcast their stored information after it became obvious that the satellite was no longer performing its normal function. In this way, A can verify that B (in fact, any party) is in compliance with Article I, at least as regards the particular satellite.

If there are many Parties with satellites ("space objects") A could not be certain, by instrumenting its own satellites in this way, that B was not destroying satellites of third nations. To a substantial extent, however, verification that B is not violating Article I with respect to other Parties is automatically available from the more difficult task of verifying Article II.3--the undertaking ". . . not to test such weapons in space or against space objects." How can this be verified?

Space Verification Measures Related to the ABMT

The ABMT (*Arms Control and Disarmament Agreements*) pp. 139-147, U.S. ACDA 1980 Edition defines (Article II) "an ABM system" as ". . . a system to counter strategic ballistic missiles or their elements in flight trajectory, currently consisting of . . . ABM interceptor missiles . . . ABM launchers . . . and ABM radars." Article III has the Parties undertaking ". . . not to deploy ABM systems or their components except . . ." within the permitted fixed ABM deployment area, while Article IV exempts from the restrictions of Article III ". . . ABM systems or their components used for development or testing, and located within current or additionally agreed test ranges . . ." In Article V the Parties undertake ". . . not to develop, test, or deploy ABM systems or components which are sea-based, air-based, space-based, or mobile land-based . . ."

The draft ban on ASAT weapons of course bans some actions that would not be prohibited by the ABMT--an intercept of a satellite, for instance. But the Treaty already forbids some acts that would not be prohibited by the ASAT ban. The Article V undertaking not to "develop, test, or deploy ABM . . . components which are . . . space-based . . ." is particularly stringent. For instance, that Article would ban development, test, or deployment of a space-based radar or optical system capable of being a "component of" an ABM system--certainly if it could play the role of or replace an "ABM radar." On the other hand, when the ABMT was negotiated, there were already present launch-detection satellites in high Earth orbit - reportedly the Defense Support Program satellites carrying medium-wavelength IR detectors of the vast heat emitted by the rocket flame in boost phase.[22] The IR early-warning satellites have thus far evidently been judged ABM-incapable and hence no violation of the ABMT. The earliest approach to boost-phase ABM capability sought by SDIO would, however, use orbiting SBI assigned based on data from boost-phase surveillance and tracking satellites (BSTS) or from sensors on the space garages that house multiple SBI. Of course, there is no way that such a system can be compatible with the ABMT, except via its abrogation.

It is necessary to verify that tests of such ABM system components are not taking place (in space) even though such systems can be countered at cost considerably lower and in shorter time than it takes to build them. This is necessary because counter action would be taken only if such violations of the ABMT were detected, since the counters themselves would in general require abandoning the Treaty.

An ABM system using homing SBI with kinetic kill and with homing sensors of small field of view would be dependent on BSTS or its equivalent. Under those circumstances, BSTS could be judged an ABM system component. But more-capable SBI-carrying sensors of large field of view and detection range of thousands of km would need BSTS primarily for early warning and for avoiding duplicate assignments. Then BSTS would be playing the role of the current IR early warning satellites and would not be judged an ABM system component.

Why Not Total Openness?

Compliance with the ABMT would be easily verified if that Party did absolutely nothing. Such inactivity would, however, interfere with goals and activities that have nothing to do with ABM and that have positive benefit for the society. No factories, no scientific research--no possible suspicion about violating the ABMT; but no wealth, security, or progress either.

Some secrecy is also desirable, although secrecy exacts its own costs in implementation and in slowing progress in one's own organization and community. The U.S. patent system, for instance, requires the applicant to disclose the subject invention sufficiently completely that anyone with normal skill in the technology can build the invention, in exchange for a monopoly of use for 17 years. Publication of the invention, or public use (even by the inventor) invalidates a patent if application for a patent is delayed more than a year after first publication. In some other countries, no publication at all is possible before filing an application for patent. In either case, we have here by law an example of what is often prescribed in diplomacy: "open covenants, secretly arrived at."

Another example of secrecy may be more relevant to the present case: a society troubled with crime in a public plaza may put up a prominent sign "This plaza under observation by video camera." This intends both to deter potential criminals on that site and to warn others against potentially embarrassing if not criminal behavior. But the society may take some pains to conceal the location (not the existence) of the camera and may even put up a few dummies or decoys. In undertaking solemn treaties, a nation wants reasonable assurance that the other side will comply (which is likely if the treaty is in its interest and if noncompliance would be detected and result in the demise of the treaty). Compliance is thus dependent on the adequacy of verification, and verification may be enhanced by some secrecy. For instance, it would be desirable to have some tens of credible decoys for the imaging satellites that play such an important role in NTM. The activities banned by the Treaty could not then be confidently scheduled to occur when the few satellites were not in a position to observe. Even as regards behavior not regulated by treaty, although there is no obligation for B to reveal its own activity, it may nevertheless do so to forestall exaggerated counter activity on the other side.

A nation would have substantially less confidence in its ability to detect noncompliance with the ABMT if the other side knew in all detail the capability of its monitoring systems. We learn from the *Scientific American* that white harp seal pups, normally very difficult to detect by airborne observation because of the surrounding white snow, show up black in the ultraviolet. A seal pup violating a deployment limitation would be readily detected if it persisted in ignorance of the capability of the monitoring system, but not if its behavior took into account this peculiarity.

Certain Military Systems can Clearly be Deployed in Space as far as the ABMT and the proposed ban on ASAT and Space Weapons are concerned. One example is a mechanically-scanned radar, or even an orbital synthetic aperture radar. Although these are not large phased-array radars as defined in the ABMT, they could easily detect single RVs. They could not, however, substitute for any components of an ABM system, nor for any combination of them. More quantitatively, as emphasized by Ashton Carter, the "100 interceptor" point defense permitted by the ABMT would not be significantly enhanced or its components replaced by these particular space-based radars. As for the proposed ASAT-Space Weapons ban, a radar is not a weapon and thus would not be limited under that proposal.

Why Insist on Banning ASAT and Space Weapons? The ABMT in itself would not bar the test of SBL as part of an ASAT system (or for that matter their deployment or even their use). The ABMT limits would come into action only if the SBL were or could be a component of an ABM system. It may be necessary to be able to verify compliance with the ABMT even though nations are unable to agree on a form of ban on ASAT and space weapons (just as it is necessary to know how to do the surgery to amputate a limb without desiring to amputate arms or legs). We believe, however, that the ABMT supplemented with an ASAT ban is a far better approach, as well as being much easier to verify. Ashton Carter and John Pike, among others, have proposed quantitative ceilings on permitted space activities, in this way to ban tests of ABM significance. This approach can permit substantial development and demonstration of weapons that would erode the buffer time against ABM deployment. The quantitative limits provide much scope for dispute such as that which has taken place in the U.S. over Soviet compliance with the 150 kiloton limit of the Threshold Test Ban Treaty.

By banning ASAT and space weapons, in almost all cases the quantitative limits could be replaced by *de minimis* thresholds, below which brightness, radar power, etc., activities are clearly of no interest in ABM or ASAT. Furthermore, above the thresholds there must be discussion among the parties, in the context of a total ban on ASAT and space weapons, and in the context of continuing adherence to the ABMT.

In the case of the SBL, for instance, it is easier to monitor that no significant laser energy is generated and projected in space, than to distinguish the 100 J/cm^2 that would damage even fairly robust satellites from the 500 J/cm^2 that might damage current boosters unequipped with even small amounts of hardening against laser energy.

We pass from that one example to a list of functions (and objects) that would be limited and monitored. To buttress the outright prohibition on test of space weapons and on activities in contravention to the ABMT, the regime would mandate presentation for discussion certain activities that exceed "discussion thresholds." Such presentation in the Standing Consultative Commission would allow a Party to explain the nature of the activity, why it is not a prohibited activity, and to provide cooperative self-verification means (onboard cameras, tests performed within view of competent national technical means, etc.).

Discussion Thresholds for Functions and Objects

Space-Based Interceptors. Space tests of SBI are prohibited. In support of this ban, tests in space or objects placed in orbit which contain devices designed to give a mass equal or exceeding 100 g an incremental velocity exceeding 0.5 km/s are subject to discussion and agreement. Rocket propulsion with acceleration below 10 g is exempt from this limitation.

Fast Passage. The passage within 10 km of another space object at a relative velocity exceeding 10 m/s is subject to discussion and agreement.

Lasers. Lasers of potential brightness exceeding 10^{15} W/steradian or pulses exceeding 10^{15} J/steradian may not be directed from space or to space without prior discussion and agreement as indicated above. Potential brightness is defined as the maximum power output of which the laser is capable, multiplied by the area of the exit aperture (mirror) of the laser platform, and divided by the square of the laser wavelength.[23] This limit can be attained through various combinations of fluxes of electromagnetic radiation, wavelength, and diameter of relay mirrors or emitting apertures.[24]

Particle-Beam Accelerators. Particles must not exceed 10 MeV and beam power must not exceed 10 kW without discussion and agreement.

Sensors. Passive sensors are not to be limited. So long as a satellite or probe does not radiate electromagnetic power beyond that reasonably necessary for communication, it is not limited in size or aperture of optics. (Satellites are not limited in their radiation of thermal IR power, nor of reflected sunlight.)

Fissile Materials. Fissile material (U^{235}, Pu^{239}, or U^{233}) in excess of 1 kg may not be launched into space, except in the form of a nuclear reactor intended for power in deep space and which has been subject to non-invasive on-pad inspection.

Discussion

Just about any technology could be developed and tested under the combined permissions of ASAT mission and (discrimination tool in aid of) fixed-site ABM.

On the other hand, the protection of the ABM treaty could be extended to effectively bar space-deployed ABM systems if the unmodified treaty were supplemented by a ban on space weapons. This would avoid the competitive evolution of weapons in the guise of "discrimination aids" and would ease the problems of verification.

Of course, scientific experiments with all results and details to be available to all nations might well warrant an exception from limitations that are, after all, intended to bar the evolution of weapons, and which may unintentionally limit scientific or commercial experimentation that might benefit all. The verification of a commitment to ban all weapons from space, as well as test of weapons in space and from Earth to space is far simpler than the verification of particular limits on space-weapon activities. A primary tool in this verification program is preannouncement of almost all launches and space activities.

On-Pad Inspection in Support of a Ban on Fissile Material in Space

Together with preannouncement comes the possibility of on-pad inspection for certain banned activities or satellite elements. For instance, in support of a ban on the launching of fissile materials, although the verification limit might be no more sensitive than to detect 1 kg of fissile material, the ban would extend to launching any fissile material. This aids verification by eliminating the requirement to determine accurately the quantity if it is present in near-threshold amounts. Very briefly, Pu^{239} and U^{238} can be measured by passive detection of the nuclear gamma rays, if the fissile material is not heavily shielded. Thus, a combination of passive detectors weighing 100 kg and operating at a meter or two from the surface of the launch vehicle for 10 minutes would suffice to verify the absence of such materials, in the absence of shielding. In order to ensure that the fissile material was not shielded and thus hidden, the vehicle would be radiographed according to strict rules and with agreed equipment, while still on the pad.

To preserve secrecy (as might be warranted), the radiographic detector would provide pixel-by-pixel reports on attenuation of the radiographic beam of neutrons or gamma rays to a computer memory. Only those pixels with attenuation greater than 100, for instance, would be reported to the two sides. The side in control of the launch knows perfectly well the distribution of mass and shielding within the launcher and payload.[25] Thus, they could avoid excessive attenuation or could provide explanations, or could ask for skew radiography, so that innocent elements of space launches would not appear like shields. Large fuel tanks for on-orbit propulsion or upper-stage activities could be fueled through normal plumbing on the pad.

Finally, serious attention should be given in the overall verification regime by the human and legal contribution to verification. It would not break new ground to require that a specific treaty be published widely in the nations concerned, and distributed widely to scientific workers and military officers in the fields concerned. As part of the verification regime, these individuals should be required periodically to certify to a responsible body in their nation that their activities comply with the treaty obligations.

Notes

1. Deployment, of course, is clearly incompatible with the ABMT.
2. Indeed, these tests are not in pursuit of an ASAT capability, which can more sensibly be achieved by direct-ascent ground-launched interceptors. Launched from national territory or from ships, such direct-ascent ASAT interceptors can be aided by powerful ground-based radars and would have as their targets large, fragile, isolated satellites with orbits accurately known, unaccompanied by decoys. Furthermore, this ASAT activity could take place in an environment free from nuclear explosions, while ABM space intercepts would be frustrated, if possible, by thousands of nuclear explosions.
3. Indeed, we recommend that each side be required to persuade the other that the item is not ABM capable.
4. A natural or artificial hill 50 m high, 100 m long, and 50 m northeast of the Krasnoyarsk radar transmitter building would have ensured that the radar could have no significant ABM role. An artificial hill might have been removable in weeks rather than the years required to build the radar. Its existence would, however, have been a visible sign of absolute incapacity for ABM, in contrast to the invisible (and instantly removable) impediment of a computer program limiting the radar to high-elevation search.
5. Some valuable but questionable platforms might be permitted if they were "cooperatively mined" by carrying on board explosive devices of the other side, with adequate communications and anti-tamper means.
6. If the attack came at night, some means would be required so that the outside of a balloon containing the warm warhead be about as cold as that of a balloon containing nothing. Multi-layer balloons of aluminized plastic eliminate this sensitivity and would allow effective attacks to be carried out day or night.
7. But compliance with the Treaty requires compliance with every article. If the orbiting KKV were not deemed an ABM component, such a test would violate the injunction of Article VI(a) "not to give missiles . . . other than ABM interceptor missiles . . . capabilities to counter ballistic missiles and their elements in flight trajectory."
8. The requirement that a proposed SDI system must be militarily effective, adequately survivable, and cost-effective at the margin, in order to be considered for deployment.
9. An invaluable contribution to understanding the question of compliance with the ABMT and of verification of compliance is to be found throughout *Defending Deterrence: Managing the ABM Treaty Regime Into the 21'st Century*, A.H. Chayes and P. Doty, eds., (Washington: Pergamon-Brassey's, 1989). Chapter 8 by A.B. Carter "Limitations and Allowances for Space-Based Weapons" is particularly illuminating.
10. A factor of 2 to 4 might be lost to unavoidable scattering in traversing the atmosphere.
11. In fact, 100 MW of light on the 5 m diameter aperture.
12. "Limitations and Allowances for Space-Based Weapons" in A.H. Chayes and P.

Doty, eds., *Defending Deterrence: Managing the ABM Treaty Regime Into the 21'st Century* (Washington: Pergamon-Brassey's, 1989), Chapter 8.

13. But this was in the context of strategic forces that were to grow to 10,000 warheads. In the context of deep cuts, 100 interceptors might not appear so negligible.

14. For instance, laser communications can in no sense be considered a weapon. Since even 10 Gbit/s of data could be transmitted with a received optical signal of 0.5 µW. This could be provided by 3 mW of radiated light at 1 µm wavelength, directed across the diameter of GEO--some 80,000 km--from an optical mirror of 1 m diameter and received by a similar mirror. One certainly has no need for laser communication power above 10 W.

15. Unless it could be unambiguously limited in function and extent, for instance to the defense of missile silos, and did not "lay the basis for" the defense of the national territory.

16. This comes about because a wind of typical speed 25 m/s at altitude takes just that long to displace the air column illuminated by a mirror of diameter 5 m. Thus a system built to explore this question would not need cooling in the FEL and mirrors beyond that required for such a duration, and could save similarly in power supply for the electron accelerator.

17. The *Golden Rule* of behaving (unto the other party) in the manner one would want them to behave has a place in international relations. In *The Evolution of Cooperation*, Robert Axelrod reveals the virtues of "tit for tat" as a strategy, beginning with cooperation, in a system of repeated interaction between two sides.

18. Direct-ascent nuclear-armed ASAT.

19. In June 1985, the U.S. successfully tested a ground-based KKV as part of the Homing Overlay Experiment, destroying an ICBM RV at satellite altitude. Although planned as part of the SDI program, this test certainly demonstrates an ASAT capability far more than it does the ability to destroy meaningful numbers of nuclear-armed RVs in space in a full-scale attack.

20. Several KKV would need to be within about 500 km of the launch site of each missile to have a chance to reach the missile during its boost phase. Even a single 10 kg homing warhead would need an on-orbit mass of 100 to 200 kg to propel it to a 6 km/s reach-out speed. The combination of "absentee ratio" and on-orbit mass means that it is more expensive to launch KKVs than to launch real warheads mixed with credible decoys.

21. Furthermore, security must be imperiled more by the absence of a treaty than by nonparticipants or by the prospect that participants might evade their obligations without detection.

22. The "Report to the American Physical Society of the Study Group on Science and Technology of Directed Energy Weapons," *Rev. Mod. Phys.* Vol. 59, No. 3, Part II (July 1987) details these IR signatures, and the draft paper by D.W. Hafemeister, *Infrared Monitoring of Nuclear Power in Space* is also a good source of data and discussion on the monitoring of nuclear power sources in space and the prospects for reduction of this IR signature.

23. See R.L. Garwin, "How Many Orbiting Lasers for Boost-Phase Intercept?" *Nature* Vol. 315, (May 23, 1985), pp. 286-290.

24. This limitation on potential brightness would correspond to illumination of about 1 W/cm^2 at 300 km distance. It would be reached with 1 kW of laser light at 1 µm wavelength, into a mirror of 1 m^2 area.

25. In fact, they could do preliminary radiography on their own.

5

Verified Elimination of Nuclear Warheads and Disposition of Contained Nuclear Materials*

Theodore B. Taylor (USA) & Lev P. Feoktistov (USSR)

Introduction

This chapter sets forth possible procedures for verified dismantlement of nuclear warheads, destruction of their non-nuclear components, and disposition of their contained fissile materials in ways that make them inaccessible for use in making new warheads.

No nuclear warheads (as opposed to missiles and other parts of delivery systems) have yet been eliminated by treaty. After warheads have been removed from missiles, the INF treaty allows each country to retain them, without restrictions.[1] Similar conditions are expected to apply to the START treaty to reduce the numbers of deliverable Soviet and American strategic nuclear warheads. Nevertheless it is reasonable to hope and expect that dismantlement of strategic and tactical nuclear warheads, not just the means for their delivery, will be called for sometime in the future. This possibility has prompted a number of studies, including the one reported in this chapter.[2]

The focus in this chapter is on procedures to verify the elimination of nuclear warheads that, under treaty, have been specified and made available for dismantlement and rendering of their contained fissile materials useless for making other nuclear warheads. It does not deal with methods to assure that all the warheads specified by treaty have actually been disclosed, however. Nor do we discuss possible methods to disclose production of new warheads of the types specified for

---

*   This is a slightly modified version of T. B. Taylor, *Science & Global Security* **1**, 1 (1989); data on nuclear weapons and materials are from US sources, and are the responsibility of T. B. Taylor.

elimination, using undisclosed stockpiles of fissile materials. Such assurances will require additional verification methods. These can be expected to become more important as deep cuts in nuclear arsenals increase the strategic importance of any hidden stockpiles of nuclear warheads or fissile materials.

A major constraint on the procedures we describe here is that they not reveal secret information about the design of the warheads as they are dismantled. We assume that two levels of secrecy must be maintained. The first involves information that nuclear weapon states do not want to reveal to each other. The second is information that may be well known to two or more nuclear weapon states, but is not generally public. This category includes information that, if made public, would substantially assist non-nuclear-weapon states in their efforts to acquire nuclear weapons. Public disclosure of such information could be regarded as violating the Non-proliferation Treaty, which calls for nuclear weapon states that are signatories not to transfer nuclear weapon technology to other countries.

The World's Nuclear Warheads

Estimates of the present worldwide numbers of nuclear warheads, as well as numbers of US and Soviet nuclear warheads of various kinds, are shown in Table 1.[3] Estimates of the total quantities of highly enriched uranium, plutonium, and tritium associated with the warheads are also included. More than 90% of these materials are accounted for, roughly equally, by the United States and the Soviet Union.[4] These estimates are uncertain, especially the quantities of nuclear materials in Soviet warheads. Nevertheless they are helpful in setting the scales of operations needed to dismantle large fractions of the world's present stockpiles of nuclear warheads.

There are only three fundamentally different types of nuclear warheads. Pure fission warheads derive their explosive energy entirely from rapid fission chain reactions. "Boosted" fission warheads incorporate small quantities of deuterium and tritium that release large numbers of neutrons when they react at the temperatures produced by a fission explosion. These neutrons then speed up the rate at which the fission chain reaction proceeds, and increase the overall yield of the explosion considerably above what it would be without boosting. Thermonuclear warheads require pure fission or boosted fission explosions to produce the conditions needed to ignite sufficient quantities of thermonuclear fuels to account for a substantial fraction of the overall yield of the warhead.

Warhead weights range from less than 50 kilograms to more than 4,000 kilograms; diameters range from less than 20 centimeters to more than 1 meter; yields range from much less than 1 kiloton to at least 20 megatons (TNT equivalent).[5]

There are several types of physical couplings between nuclear warheads and their delivery systems. Warheads for land- and sea-based strategic missiles are

Table 1.   The World's Present Nuclear Warheads

The World's Nuclear Warheads

United States	23,400
Soviet Union	33,000
United Kingdom	700
France	500
China	300
Israel	50 - 200
South Africa	?
Pakistan	?
India	?

World total   *about 58,000*

U.S. and Soviet Nuclear Warheads

Number of Warheads

	United States	USSR
Strategic		
Land-based missiles	2,470	7,630
Submarine-launched missiles	5,850	3,970
Bombs	5,170	1,400
	13,490	*13,000*
Nonstrategic		
Aircraft bombs & missiles	3,500	6,370
Land-based missiles	1,805	4,700
Submarine-launched ballistic missiles	0	50
Submarine-launched cruise missiles	150	400
Anti-ballistic and surface-air missiles	385	4,200
Artillery	2,010	2,000
Antisubmarine	1,760	1,860
Demolition (ADM)	300	?
	9,910	*19,580*

Table 1.   (continued)

Nuclear Materials in U.S. and Soviet Nuclear Warheads

Material	United States	USSR	*Total*
Plutonium	100 tons	100 tons	200 tons
Highly enriched uranium	500 tons	400-800 tons	900-1,300 tons
Tritium	100 kg	100 kg ?	200 kg ?

usually mounted on the missiles, although some warheads may be in storage separately at any given time. Other delivery systems, such as artillery, tactical aircraft and ships, have associated storage facilities for nuclear and conventional warheads. Although such differences can affect some of the details concerning physical means for identifying and containing warheads at specific deployment sites before they are dismantled, the basic principles explored here apply to all cases.

The effect of nonmilitary disposal of fissile materials from dismantled warheads would be more symbolic than substantive if further production of these materials for weapons were allowed to continue. But such symbolism may be important politically, contributing to public support for nuclear disarmament. Furthermore, joint development of safe and verifiable procedures for dismantling warheads and transferring recovered materials from military to peaceful use can accelerate confidence in verification aspects of future, more stringent disarmament agreements, including a ban on further production of fissile materials for nuclear warheads.

Alternatives for Disposal of Warheads

There are many different ways in which warheads specified under a treaty can be disposed of. Three are considered here.

1. Each nation removes the specified warheads from deployment sites and periodically provides negotiated quantities of fissile materials (plutonium and highly enriched uranium) to an inspection authority. These quantities might be the same for the US and the Soviet Union, and smaller for any other parties to a treaty. Alternatively, they might be proportional to the total numbers of removed warheads of several types. In any case, these quantities should probably be negotiated in the original treaty. The quantities need not reveal the real amounts of fissile materials in each type

of warhead, and may correspond to significantly more or less of these materials than are actually present.

2. Each nation removes and retains all fissile materials and thermonuclear fuels (tritium and deuterium, in compounds or as elements) from the warheads for unrestricted use, and the remaining components are verifiably destroyed.

3. Each nation separates the fissile materials and tritium from the other warhead components. The fissile materials are committed for use as fuel supplements for non-military power reactors or for direct disposal in forms that would not be practical for subsequent recovery for use in weapons. The remaining components are verifiably destroyed. Their material residues, including tritium, may or may not be returned to the owner nation.

A variation of this last option would be to negotiate amounts of fissile materials greater than the quantities to be extracted from the warheads to be committed for nonmilitary use or direct disposal. The excess would be supplied from other sources, such as warheads not yet subject to dismantlement by treaty or material stockpiles. The negotiated minimum quantities may differ from country to country, to account for differences in total quantities of weapons materials in national stockpiles. The purpose of such an approach would be to help ensure parity in depletion of fissile materials, considered as fractions of total national stockpiles, as well as parity in giving up specific types of warheads or nuclear weapon systems.

The first option achieves reductions in theoretical maximum numbers of nuclear warheads by reducing the accessibility of key materials that are absolutely required to make nuclear warheads. It is the easiest to implement technically, since it does not require verification of any warhead dismantlement operations. But it offers no verifiable guarantee that all the fissile materials contained in the warheads are relinquished, or that the other parts of the warheads are destroyed. Nor is it likely to disclose the remaining quantities of fissile materials in a country with enough accuracy to prevent a strategically important imbalance in quantities of these materials from eventually developing between countries that are parties to the treaty. Note that an uncertainty of 10% in the initial quantities of fissile materials in the United States or the Soviet Union, after a bilateral ban on their further production, could correspond to enough fissile materials for several thousand nuclear warheads.

The second option ensures that the specified warheads are destroyed, but does not deal with the components that are most difficult to produce--the plutonium and enriched uranium.

The third option is the most difficult to carry out technically, but is also the only one that ensures that the specified weapons are destroyed and their contained fissile materials are made inaccessible for weapons. It is considered here in some detail, not because it is evidently the most attractive, but because it raises some

Table 2.   World Nuclear Power Plant Capacity

| | Capacity GWe | |
	1988	**2000**
United States	100	111
France	49	64
USSR	28	85
Japan	27	50
West Germany	19	24
Canada	12	16
United Kingdom	11	11
	------	------
Subtotal	246	361
All other	51	99
	------	------
Total	297	460

especially interesting technical questions that need to be answered in any comparative assessment of these options. Adding fissile materials to those extracted from the warheads to be dismantled, a variation mentioned above, is not analyzed here. Its inclusion would require some minor modifications of the dismantlement process, to allow for safeguarded flows of materials from sources other than the specified warheads.

Use of Warhead Fissile Materials in Nuclear Power Plants

A worldwide tally of present and projected nuclear power capacity is shown in Table 2.[6,7] More than 95% of the fuel for power reactors is uranium of low enrichment (typically about 3% uranium-235) or natural uranium. The rate of loading uranium-235 in a 1,000-megawatt-electric light water reactor fueled with uranium only is about 1,000 kilograms per year. A few reactors are beginning to use recycled plutonium to supplement the uranium-235 (but not in the United States).[8] In such cases, the fuel is in the form of mixed oxides of plutonium and uranium, with plutonium accounting for a few percent of the mixture. The annual loading rates of uranium-235 and plutonium in the mixed-oxide reactors are about 670 kilograms of uranium-235 and 350 kilograms of plutonium per 1,000 megawatt-electric-year. Higher plutonium concentrations are possible, but may cause unacceptable reactivity-control problems. The demand for reactor fuel converted from fissile materials taken from weapons will probably be for uranium-235, rather than plutonium, for at least a decade.

The uranium-235 in the world's stockpiles of nuclear warheads is a potential energy resource worth more than $30 billion.[9] This total contributes about 0.5 cents/kWhr to the cost of electric power produced by typical nuclear power plants. Most of this cost could be avoided if highly enriched uranium from warheads were used to supply the uranium-235 needed for power reactors.[10]

The Plutonium extracted from warheads can be stored for eventual use as a supplement to uranium-235 in low enrichment reactor fuel, use in plutonium breeder reactors, or direct disposal, without using it for fuel, in ways that would make it very difficult to retrieve for use in warheads.[11] Government decisions and inter-governmental negotiations will be required to determine which of these options is actually used for disposition of the warhead plutonium. In any case, the extracted plutonium should be subject to bilateral or international safeguards to assure it is not used for making warheads.

Process Steps for Eliminating Warheads

Overview

A system for verifying the elimination of nuclear warheads must ensure that:

1. All warheads and associated payload hardware identified by the owner country and earmarked for elimination are what they are claimed to be.
2. All items earmarked for elimination are destroyed.
3. None of the nuclear material from the warheads to be dismantled is diverted to unauthorized uses.

These guarantees must be provided without the need to disclose sensitive information about design of the warheads or other associated equipment, such as re-entry vehicles, penetration aids, or shielding against radiation.

All detailed information about the design of specific nuclear warheads is now classified. This includes yields and total weights; quantities of contained materials, including but not restricted to tritium, highly enriched uranium, and plutonium; and dimensions, configurations, and weights of fabricated components. Such information cannot be derived with any confidence from information that is now public. It is therefore assumed here that countries will be unwilling to reveal this information in the warhead dismantlement process.

Two key assumptions about secrecy are inherent in the process descriptions that follow.

The first is that the aggregate quantities of uranium-235, uranium-238, and plutonium of any isotopic composition that are contained in a mix of several different types of warheads can be declassified in the course of future treaty negotiations. This would allow accurate systems for accounting for fissile materials to be set up, without revealing information about the fissile material content of any particular kind of warhead.

The second assumption is that *upper limits* to some of the material quantities, component weights, and dimensions associated with warheads and other payload items can be declassified without national security concerns, provided that the upper limits are sufficiently large compared with their *actual* values. Then each owner nation could mask the true value of quantities it wished to keep secret by adding appropriate items, in unrevealed amounts, to the objects to be dismantled. An example would be the addition of a large weight of sand to each of the containers for some type of warhead, without ever revealing what that weight was.

Having made these assumptions, we can describe a verification system which ensures that all fissile materials in the warheads are accounted for (and made available for inclusion in reactor fuel or direct, permanent disposal) without revealing sensitive design information about specific warheads.

The main steps in the warhead elimination process are shown schematically in Figure 1. Broadly speaking, the process provides the following assurances:

1. All materials in the warheads are contained within well-defined boundaries from the time they are placed in shipping containers at the deployment sites until they have been dismantled.
2. Any attempts to divert any of the warhead components to unauthorized purposes will be detected.
3. All major components of the warheads or other payload items are destroyed, in the sense that they would require refabrication to be used in other warheads.
4. All uranium-235, uranium-238, and plutonium in the warheads is accounted for in the measured output of these materials from the dismantlement facility.
5. Substitution of fake warheads for real ones at the deployment sites, before dismantlement operations begin, is likely to be detected.

"Fingerprinting" is a key concept related to detection of substitutions. It covers any method for observing indicators that the contents of all the warhead containers claimed to be the same type are, in fact, the same. Since these indicators must not reveal sensitive information about the warhead designs, it may be necessary to encrypt them in such ways that they can be compared accurately enough to reveal significant *differences* between the contents of containers without disclosing restricted data.

The process steps and ways to achieve the above assurances are described briefly in the following sections.

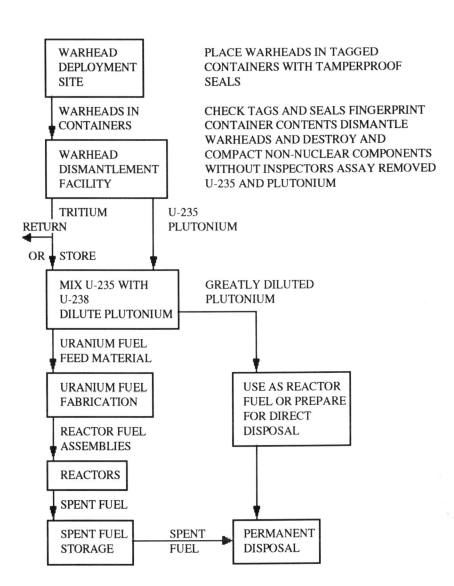

Figure 1. The main steps in the warhead elimination process.

Tagging, Sealing, and Shipment of Warheads to Dismantlement Facility

When the dismantlement operations start at a deployment site, all nuclear warheads to be eliminated--possibly along with other attached payload components such as re-entry vehicles and guidance packages--are placed inside shipping containers. The containers are provided by the owner country, which is also responsible for removal of the payloads/warheads from delivery vehicles or storage facilities at the site. The containers are not subject to internal inspection on arrival at the site, since they may contain materials that have been added off-site to mask actual weights of warheads or some of their components (see below). Transfer of payloads/warheads from delivery vehicles or storage to the shipping containers is observed by inspectors. The units may be temporarily covered while being transferred to the shipping containers, to avoid revealing sensitive information about their external appearance.

The inspectors then tag and seal each container. The tags are for unique external identification of each container. The seals are designed to reveal any unauthorized opening of the containers.

Methods for tagging the containers include microscopic photography of parts of the outside surfaces or use of spray paint to produce photographed "signatures" that are almost impossible to change or reproduce without detection.

One method of sealing the containers is wrapping them with bundles of optical fibers. Illumination of one end of such a bundle produces a unique and complex pattern at the other end. Before-and-after photographs of these patterns will reveal attempts to remove or cut the bundles of fibers. Such techniques have been used routinely by the International Atomic Energy Agency for safeguarding purposes.[12]

Another sealing option is the spot welding of any removable covers for access to the containers, using the welds themselves as seals. Such seals have unique patterns that can be photographed before and after to reveal unauthorized opening of the containers.[13]

The tagged and sealed warhead containers, which may temporarily be stored at the deployment site, are then shipped to a warhead dismantling and destruction facility in the owner country. At this facility all tagged containers are examined by inspectors to ensure that they have not been tampered with. Inspectors would not need to accompany the shipments in transit, as long as careful accounting for each container is maintained at the deployment sites and the dismantlement facility. After shipment and inspection of the tags, significant numbers of unopened containers would typically be kept temporarily in storage at the dismantlement facility.

Dismantlement of Warheads and Other Parts of Payloads

The announced nuclear weapon states have facilities for dismantling obsolete nuclear warheads to recover nuclear materials or other components to be used in new types of warheads. It is possible that these facilities could be modified to meet the conditions needed for verified dismantlement under a disarmament treaty, especially the need to preserve secrecy concerning some of the warhead design details. This may be difficult in dismantlement facilities that are used both for handling warheads that are not subject to a treaty and ones that are.

This option cannot be assessed without access to detailed information not now public. However, it is possible to describe, in general, proposed process steps in a warhead dismantlement facility, and ways to ensure that the dismantlement and verification objectives are effectively met, whether or not new facilities or modified existing ones are used.

The descriptions provided here are not based on any conclusion that new dismantlement facilities would be preferable to existing ones, even though the latter might have to be significantly altered to allow for appropriate inspection. Decisions whether to modify existing facilities or build new ones for this purpose should follow intensive unilateral and bilateral assessments of the alternatives. Lacking access to descriptions of existing facilities, a hypothetical one is described here.

A schematic illustration of such a facility is shown in Figure 2. Enclosures within which inspectors would not be allowed during dismantlement operations are indicated by double lines. These areas could be inspected between dismantlement operations, to ensure that there are no hidden stockpiles of nuclear materials or other sensitive components.

A well-defined boundary surrounds the entire dismantlement facility or area (if it is situated within a production facility). Portals with access through this boundary are all monitored visually and with appropriate equipment to ensure no passage of unauthorized objects, materials, or people. The main function of the portal-monitoring equipment is to detect unauthorized removals of fissile materials from the facility, or introduction of unauthorized items into the facility. The portal to be used for incoming shipping containers with warheads inside is the only one authorized for incoming fissile materials. The only portal authorized for outgoing fissile materials is the one used for removal of fissile materials after extraction from the warheads, for transfer to an adjoining facility for isotopic dilution of uranium-235 (if needed) and chemical dilution of the plutonium.[14]

The principal inputs to the facility are the tagged and sealed containers with warheads and other payload hardware. All other inputs, such as process materials or new equipment needed for dismantlement operations, are kept to a minimum.

The principal outputs are the following:

- Accurately measured quantities of uranium-235 and uranium-238 mixtures and plutonium (both probably in metallic forms that do not reveal warhead design features), for secure transfer to an immediately adjoining site for dilution.

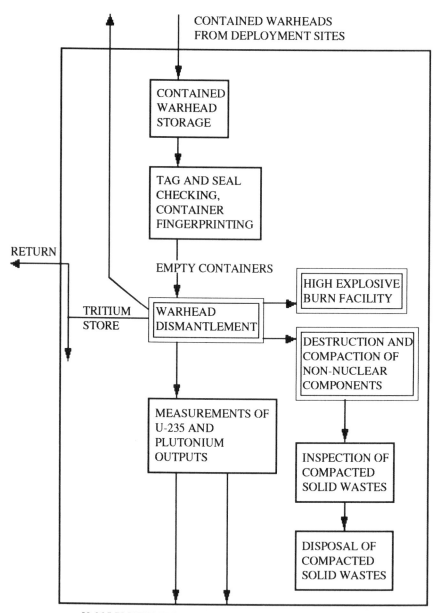

CONTAINED WARHEADS
FROM DEPLOYMENT SITES

CONTAINED
WARHEAD
STORAGE

TAG AND SEAL
CHECKING,
CONTAINER
FINGERPRINTING

EMPTY CONTAINERS

RETURN

TRITIUM
STORE

WARHEAD
DISMANTLEMENT

HIGH EXPLOSIVE
BURN FACILITY

DESTRUCTION AND
COMPACTION OF
NON-NUCLEAR
COMPONENTS

MEASUREMENTS OF
U-235 AND
PLUTONIUM
OUTPUTS

INSPECTION OF
COMPACTED
SOLID WASTES

DISPOSAL OF
COMPACTED
SOLID WASTES

U-235 PLUTONIUM (both to adjoining facility for dilution)

Figure 2. Schematic diagram of a dismantlement facility.

- Tritium, in amounts not to be revealed to inspectors, to be returned to the owner nation or disposed of in a safeguarded manner.
- Small containers of radioactive materials used for warhead chain-reaction initiators or functions other than directly releasing explosive energy.
- Residues of compaction or incineration of all other components of the warheads or other payload items.

Warhead containers intended for re-use could also be considered as facility outputs. After their contents have been removed for dismantlement, the containers are weighed and inspected, to ensure they are empty. The owner nation is then allowed to place into the containers an undisclosed weight of some common material, such as water or sand, to mask the overall weights of warheads. The containers are then sealed by inspectors (but not weighed), and scanned by an external radiation source to ensure that there is no uranium or plutonium inside.[15] The containers remain sealed until they are externally inspected at a warhead deployment site before they are opened to receive more warheads.

The solid and liquid waste outputs from the site are kept to a minimum and subjected to detailed visual and instrumental inspection before they are removed from the site. A radiation scan of the residue output from each batch of dismantled warheads would ensure that this stockpile of residues did not contain significant quantities of fissile materials.

If the high explosives in the warheads are burned, the waste product is mostly gas. This can be vented from the site after passage through an appropriate gas cleanup system for removing objectionable pollutants.

Vehicles entering or leaving the outer boundary of the facility are kept to a minimum. This can be done by using specialized equipment for transfer of the warhead containers or other materials or equipment to the inside enclosures where they are authorized to go. Similar equipment can also be used for all outputs, so that vehicles leaving the site need not be inspected.

The warhead components are dismantled by nationals of the owner nation inside a facility subject to the containment principle that all the outputs from the facility are observed. The high explosives and other non-nuclear components are destroyed in appropriate facilities inside the containment area. The plutonium and uranium are converted, without inspection of the process, to forms (such as metallic "buttons") that will not reveal warhead design features. Equipment appropriate for melting or dissolving the fissile materials and any low-enrichment uranium in the warheads, and then mixing them, are required, along with standard criticality and other safety procedures used in fissile-material processing plants.

Accurate measurements of the quantities and isotopic compositions of the recovered uranium and plutonium are made by inspectors, to obtain the initial data needed for accurate materials-accounting in all subsequent phases of handling the uranium and plutonium until their ultimate disposal.

In initial stages of nuclear disarmament any tritium might be returned to the owner nation, to avoid having to maintain production to make up for tritium decay (with a 12.5 year half-life) in warheads not yet subject to a disarmament treaty. In this case, the amounts of tritium removed from the warheads need not be revealed to inspectors, since, even for mixtures of warheads, their overall tritium content is likely to be especially sensitive information. Alternatively, the tritium might be placed under safeguards, for possible future use in thermonuclear fusion reactors, or simply allowed to decay. In this case it may be necessary, at least eventually, to reveal the quantities to inspectors.

If the removed tritium is not returned to the owner nation, and a ban on further tritium production is in effect, the number of remaining warheads will tend to decrease at a rate in the vicinity of 5% per year, corresponding roughly to the decay rate of the tritium. This is because most modern nuclear warheads require some minimum quantity of tritium to function reliably. If warheads are dismantled at a rate greater than about 5% per year, however, and the removed tritium is returned to the owner nation, the decay of tritium in remaining warheads can be compensated for without having to produce any new tritium.

Tritium containers leaving the site would be scanned to ensure they contain no fissile materials.

Radioactive materials used in the warheads for generators of neutrons for initiating fission chain reactions would be separated from other components and treated as small quantities of high level radioactive wastes to be disposed of at an appropriate facility. The relatively small shipping containers would also be scanned, before leaving the dismantlement facility, to ensure that they do not contain fissile materials.

Deterrents to Substitution of Fake Warheads for Real Warheads

The procedures just described can ensure that objects claimed to be warheads are dismantled, their components destroyed, and all contained fissile materials accounted for. By themselves, however, these procedures cannot completely ensure that fake warheads may not have been substituted for real ones before the dismantlement operation began at the deployment sites.

Objects substituted for the warheads before they are tagged and sealed, might include any of the following:

1. Objects similar in all respects to the real warheads, except that natural or depleted uranium has been substituted for some or all of the plutonium and highly enriched uranium that would have been in the real warheads. The purpose of this substitution would be to withhold significant amounts of fissile materials from the dismantlement process. The fake warheads might or might not be capable of producing a nuclear explosion, depending on the amounts of fissile materials withheld.

2. Objects that might or might not closely resemble the real warheads. In any case, they are much easier to fabricate, to less demanding tolerances, than real warheads. Such objects might include some fissile materials, but substantially less than in the real warheads. The fake warheads might or might not be capable of producing a nuclear explosion. Their function would be to allow unauthorized withholding of complete real warheads.

3. Complete warheads that are being retired from stockpiles and that have much less fissile material than the warheads that are supposed to be eliminated.

Several measures can be used to help verify that such substitutions have not occurred, without revealing any secret warhead design information:

1. The specified warheads are tagged and sealed as early as possible, starting with warheads at a few deployment sites randomly chosen from sites specified in the treaty, with a very short time (for example, less than 24 hours) between choice of each site and the arrival of on-site inspectors. Complete substitutions for all warheads would have to be accomplished before the initial tagging and sealing operations begin.

2. Verification techniques are used that will reveal significant differences between the contents, especially in amounts of fissile materials, of any containers for warheads that are claimed to be of the same type. Thus, if illegal substitutions were made, they would have to be made for all warheads of the same type, rather than for some selected fraction. (Specific ways to carry out this type of verification are discussed below.)

3. Inspectors measure accurately the total quantities and isotopic compositions of mixtures of plutonium or uranium extracted from batches of more than one type of warhead in each dismantlement campaign. Use of this procedure will require that total plutonium, uranium-235, and uranium-238 extracted from several (e.g. three) types of warheads be declassified. But it is difficult to see how this could reveal information that is critical to the national security of any announced nuclear weapon states.

4. A few sealed warhead containers of each type are randomly selected for safeguarded storage for an unspecified time. This will preserve evidence of compliance (or non-compliance) with a treaty, in case more effective verification techniques are developed in the future. Present uncertainty about such possibilities could act as a major deterrent to cheating under a current treaty. Furthermore, the selected warheads could be used as standards against which to match very detailed fingerprints. These fingerprints consist of encrypted data preserved in tamper-revealing data processing systems. The only information output is what the comparisons revealed, without disclosing any of the raw data.[16] The number of warheads selected for these purposes might be two or three of each type.

5. The possibility of "whistleblowing" (reporting of treaty violations to a verification authority by nationals of a country whose government orders the violations) is a deterrent that cannot be assessed quantitatively. It may become increasingly important as the universal benefits of nuclear disarmament become more generally apparent and publicized worldwide. Ways to ensure that individuals or groups who report violations can remain anonymous need to be further developed and assessed.
6. None of these measures would reveal restricted information, especially if each owner nation is allowed to add unrevealed weights of common materials, such as sand or water, to the warhead containers, to disguise the warhead weights or some aspects of their composition. Uranium would not be allowed for this purpose, since introduction of unknown quantities of it into the process would invalidate checks of independent estimates of total quantities of highly enriched uranium that have been produced.[17] The total weights and configurations of any such added materials must be the same for all warheads of a particular type, to ensure that the total contents of all fully loaded containers for each warhead are the same.

Fingerprinting Contents of Warhead Containers

As previously indicated, measurements that will reveal differences between the contents of containers of warheads that are claimed to be of the same type, without revealing secret information to the inspectors, can play key roles in providing assurance that fake warheads have not been substituted for real ones. The term "fingerprint" is used here to mean the totality of all measurements.

There is a wide variety of possibilities for such measurements. They fall into two categories: external measurements before the warhead containers are opened, and measurements of residues from the dismantlement process. In either case, allowable differences between measured quantities that are nominally for the same type of warhead would have to be negotiated, since such measurements may vary somewhat between warheads of the same type. Examples are the isotopic composition of plutonium and uranium, or weights and configurations of fusing and firing components.

Possibilities for the elements of a fingerprint include the following:

1. Total weight of the contents of each warhead container before it is opened for dismantlement. This weight is derived from the difference between the weight of the loaded container before it is opened, and the weight of the empty container (after its interior has been inspected, but before unknown amounts of materials have been added by the owner nation). It is specified that the total weight of the contents should always be the same (within negotiated limits) for the same types of warheads. This does not preclude

the possibility of substituting fake warheads and changing the weight of added materials to keep the total weight the same.
2. Precise measurements of the aggregate quantities and isotopic compositions of plutonium and uranium extracted from each batch of dismantled warheads consisting of known numbers of several specified types. Isotopic composition of plutonium, especially, can vary significantly between different warheads of the same type, however. Allowable differences in average isotopic compositions, from batch to batch, would therefore have to be negotiated.

The measurements applied to the fissile material outputs are taken here to be the principal basis for fingerprinting. They would reveal use of fake warheads that contain less plutonium, uranium-235, or uranium-238 than in the real warheads, unless fake warheads are substituted for all warheads before they are sealed at the deployment sites. Although they would not necessarily reveal differences in the non-nuclear components of warheads that are supposed to be of the same type, such violations would risk being detected eventually by fingerprinting techniques that might be developed for probing the randomly selected sealed containers that have been placed in safeguarded storage.

Among the many other fingerprinting techniques that might be developed and used in the future are an entire class that would produce extremely detailed raw data concerning the configurations, compositions, and masses of materials in the warheads. The raw data would be withheld from inspectors, but combined in a sealed data processing system that would produce scrambled output data that would reveal no classified information, but reveal significant differences between objects inside the containers. Examples of such measurements include weight distributions along several axes and high-resolution scanning with external sources of gamma-rays, x-rays, or neutrons.

If external radiation sources are used for active scanning of the warheads, care must be taken to make sure that the radiation cannot accidently cause detonation of any contained high explosives. This assurance could be provided by extensive testing, by each owner country, of the response of its high explosive systems to more powerful sources of radiation than proposed for fingerprinting. As for possible radiation induced other damage to the warheads, this should not be a problem since the warheads are to be eliminated anyway.

Some preliminary analysis has shown that passive radiation scanning could also produce a reliable fingerprint, especially if the radiation levels are measured at different angles to an axis of the warhead. Substitution of other radiation sources for plutonium or uranium is likely to produce external radiation fields around fake warheads that are different from those around real warheads. In our view, a combination of passive and active methods for obtaining radiation fingerprints would be most effective for deterring substitution of fake warheads or warhead components, especially if the detailed nature of the fingerprint scanning methods and areas to be scanned cannot be foreseen.

Disposal of Warhead Uranium and Plutonium

After accurate measurement of their masses and isotopic compositions by inspectors, the uranium and plutonium would be transferred from the dismantlement facility to an adjoining facility for further processing to prepare them for their ultimate disposal. This facility would also be enclosed by a containment perimeter.

The uranium-235 and uranium-238 mixtures from the warhead dismantlement facility are further diluted as necessary with depleted or natural uranium, to provide uranium with about 3% uranium-235 that could be used for fuel in light water power reactors. For use in heavy-water or graphite reactors fueled with natural uranium, which account for a small fraction of the world's nuclear power, the uranium-235 could be diluted with depleted uranium (about 0.3% uranium-235) to a concentration near 0.7%. In either case this dilution renders the uranium incapable of sustaining a fast-neutron chain reaction, for which the minimum enrichment required is about 6%.

Assuring that the plutonium is rendered useless for making weapons is more problematical. Plutonium from warheads can be rendered less desirable for making new warheads by using it as fuel in reactors or by addition of plutonium removed from spent reactor fuel. The reason is that plutonium irradiated or produced in typical power reactors contains mich higher concentrations of even-numbered plutonium isotopes, especially plutonium-240. This isotopic dilution can substantially increase the critical mass, compared with "weapons grade" plutonium (more than 94% plutonium-239). Plutonium-240 also releases neutrons

Table 3.   Preliminary Parameters for U.S. Nuclear Warhead Dismantling Facility.

Capacity	8 warheads/day
	(25,000 in 10 years)
Average U^{235} output	160 kg/day
Average plutonium output	32 kg/day
Average tritium output	32 grams/day
Storage capacities (100 days throughput)	
Undismantled warheads	800, in containers
U^{235}	16,000 kg
Plutonium	3,200 kg
Tritium	3.2 kg

from spontaneous fission at a high enough rate to cause premature initiation of a chain reaction during the assembly of a substantially supercritical mass. Unlike uranium-235 diluted with uranium-238, however, reactor grade plutonium can, if necessary, be used for making some types of nuclear explosives[18]. Such nuclear warheads should have to be tested. A comprehensive nuclear test ban would therefore be a mayor obstacle to diverting irradiated or reactor grade plutonium for making new warheads. In any case, plutonium extracted from warheads should be greatly diluted and either irradiated directly in reactors or mixed with reactor-grade plutonium and fission products before its ultimate irretrievable disposal.

Possible Parameters for a Warhead Dismantlement Facility

Possible parameters for a large warhead dismantlement facility in the United States are listed in Table 3. Its capacity for dismantling 8 warheads a day is about as large as may be credibly required for implementing future nuclear disarmament treaties. That is, it would be capable of dismantling all US warheads in less than 10 years if operated 6 days a week. The main characteristics of a corresponding facility in the Soviet Union might be similar.

The average daily outputs of uranium-235, plutonium, and tritium correspond to averages of 20 kilograms, 4 kilograms, and 4 grams, respectively, per warhead (see Table 1).

The average weight of a warhead now in the US stockpile is about 350 kilograms.[20] This corresponds to an average daily input of 2,800 kilograms of total warhead weight. The weight of other objects, such as re-entry vehicle structures and guidance packages, in the warhead shipping containers is unlikely to exceed that of the warheads. Additional material in the warhead containers, added to mask the weight of the warheads, might also be as much as another 2,800 kilograms per day, for a nominal total of about 8,400 kilograms removed from the containers each day.

If half the average warhead weight is assumed to be high explosive, the corresponding high explosive input is 1,400 kilograms a day. Most of the residue from burning this will be gaseous products vented, after scrubbing, to the atmosphere.

The remaining average of about 7,000 kilograms per day of non-nuclear materials and thermonuclear fuels not containing tritium could be separated into valuable materials (such as deuterium or beryllium) to be returned to the owner country, and waste materials for direct disposal. In any case, if all these materials were compacted into slabs with a bulk density in the vicinity of 4 grams per cubic centimeter, their total volume would be 1.8 cubic meters per day. A reasonable actual size for each slab might be 1 square meter, with a thickness of 4 centimeters corresponding to an average weight of about 160 kilograms. Each of these slabs (about 40 per day), supported horizontally, could then be conveniently scanned with gamma rays and neutrons to ensure they contained no fissile material or uranium-238.

The warhead and nuclear material storage capacities shown in Table 3 correspond to 100 days of average throughput. This is a rough estimate that allows for process holdups and fluctuations.

At less than 10 tonnes per day, the facility's daily total input of materials to be processed is similar to that of commercial mixed uranium and plutonium oxide reactor fuel fabrication plants. The capital costs of such plants are several billion dollars. Since none of the final products of a warhead dismantlement facility are components fabricated to exacting tolerances, it seems reasonable to expect that the capital cost of a new dismantlement facility would be lower.

Labor costs for operating such a facility are unlikely to be greater than 10 or 20 million dollars per year. A full-time work force of 100 direct labor employees, at $100,000 per person-year (including overhead), would amount to $10 million per year.

It is therefore unlikely that the total costs of dismantling the world's nuclear warheads, and providing the contained fissile materials for use as nuclear fuel or for direct disposal would exceed a few billion dollars.

Timing

It is possible that detailed design and construction of facilities needed for eliminating large numbers of warheads may be the pacing items that determine when the complete elimination process can actually begin.

If a treaty calling for elimination of large numbers of warheads comes into force before the needed facilities exist, the warheads could be tagged and sealed in containers, and placed in storage to await completion of the dismantlement facility.

In any case, optimism about new treaties calling for elimination of many warheads should carry with it a considerable sense of urgency about the means for eliminating the warheads. If it is determined that modification of existing dismantlement facilities in the two countries is not appropriate, designing and building new facilities may be necessary.

Next Steps

The concepts and analyses presented in this chapter indicate that elimination of identified nuclear warheads that are specified in a nuclear disarmament treaty can be verified with high confidence, without revealing national secrets about warhead designs. Much remains to be done, however, to specify procedures for accomplishing this objective in sufficient detail to provide the basis for negotiated formal protocols and the means for carrying them out.

Two consecutive next steps are therefore proposed.

The first is the establishment of an official joint US-Soviet working group to design and assess specific procedures and corresponding facilities for verified elimination of nuclear warheads. Work by this group should be given high priority by both nations and not require negotiation of further treaties.

The second step is to carry out joint US-Soviet demonstrations of the techniques identified in the first step. These demonstrations would be expected to include some field testing of parts of a warhead dismantlement and verification system. Initial tests could be performed using unclassified mockups of warheads. These could be followed with complete system tests, using warheads from each nation.

Results of these two steps could then be incorporated into negotiated protocols for verification of new treaties.

Notes

1. INF Treaty, protocols for verification, December, 1987.

2. See, for example, J. Taylor, J. Barton, and T. Shea, "Converting Nuclear Weapons to Peaceful Use," *Bulletin of the Atomic Scientists,* February 1985; James de Montmollin, "Some Considerations Involving Verification of New Arms Control Agreements," unpublished report, December 1985, and "Value of Fissile Material from Dismantled Warheads as Reactor Fuel," unpublished report, June 1986; and E. Amaldi, U. Farinelli, and C. Silvi, "On the Utilization for Civilian Purposes of the Weapon-grade Nuclear Material that May Become Available as a Result of Nuclear Disarmament," report of the Accademia Nazionale dei Lincei, Rome, 23-25 June 1988.

3. Robert S. Norris and William M. Arkin, eds., "Nuclear Notebook," *Bulletin of the Atomic Scientists,* June 1988 and July/August 1988. Estimates of the numbers of warheads are much more uncertain for the Soviet Union than for the US. The estimated number of Israeli warheads is based primarily on revelations by Mordechai Vanunu in the London *Sunday Times,* 5 October 1987.

4. Frank von Hippel, David H. Albright, and Barbara G. Levi, "Fissile Materials in US Warheads and Plutonium in Soviet Warheads," *Quantities of Fissile Materials in US and Soviet Nuclear Weapons Arsenals* (Princeton: Princeton University, July 1986), PU/CEES Report No. 168. We have assumed that the uranium-235 and tritium in the Soviet stockpile are each the same as those in the US. Either or both of these assumptions may be far from correct.

5. Derived from Thomas B. Cochran, William M. Arkin, and Milton M. Hoenig, eds., *US Nuclear Forces and Capabilities* (Cambridge, Massachusetts: Ballinger, 1984).

6. For Western capacities: *The Nuclear Power Plant Capacity of the Western World,* (Alzenau, West Germany: NUKEM, April 1987), NUKEM special report.

7. For capacities of USSR, Eastern Europe, and China: "World Survey," *Nuclear Engineering International,* June 1987, pp. 28-39.

8. David Albright, "Civilian Inventories of Plutonium and Highly Enriched Uranium," in Paul Leventhal and Yonah Alexander, eds., *Preventing Nuclear Terrorism* (Lexington,

Massachusetts: Lexington Books, 1987), pp. 265-297.

9. We base the estimate of uranium values on the assumption that the value of uranium-235 (in uranium enriched to about 3% in uranium-235) to be used for fuel in the world's nuclear power plants during the next decade is about $38,000 per kilogram. Of this total, $19,000 is accounted for by an assumed price of $66 per kilogram for unenriched U_3O_8; $2,000 per kilogram by conversion to UF_6 prior to enrichment; and $17,000 per kilogram for enrichment to 3% uranium-235 (with 0.3% in the depleted "tails"). Enrichment costs correspond to $150/SWU. All these costs are consistent with recent average costs presented in *NUKEM Market Report on the Nuclear Cycle* (Alzenau, West Germany: NUKEM, April 1987). Separative work requirements for uranium enrichment as functions of enrichment of product and tails are from *Standard Table of Enriching Services* (Washington DC: DOE).

10. This presumes that worldwide use of nuclear power will continue for several decades and show at least moderate growth. If, for whatever reasons, this should not be the case, and international markets cannot absorb the uranium-235 from nuclear warheads dismantled in the course of vigorous nuclear disarmament, it could be rendered useless for nuclear explosives by dilution with natural or depleted uranium.

11. The estimated global weapon plutonium inventory is about 20% of the weapon uranium-235 inventory. Since plutonium-bearing fuel costs much more to fabricate than all-uranium fuel, the value of plutonium per kilogram, as feedstock for reactor fuel, is less than for uranium-235.

12. W.A. Higinbotham, Brookhaven National Laboratory, private communication, July 1988.

13. Alex DeVolpi, Argonne National Laboratory, private communication, 1988.

14. For a summary of portal monitors for detection of fissile materials, see David Albright, "Portal Monitoring for Detecting Fissile Materials and Chemical Explosives", in *Reversing the Arms Race*, edited by F. von Hippel and R. Z. Sagdeev, Gordon & Breach, 1990.

15. Fetter et al., "Detecting Nuclear Warheads," *Science & Global Security* **1**, 225 (1990). The best approach is probably to use an external, pulsed 14-MeV neutron source to stimulate fissions in plutonium or uranium, and observe delayed fission neutrons or gamma rays emitted from the object being scanned.

16. Richard L. Garwin, private communication, March 1989.

17. Such estimates can be derived from published or estimated aggregate separative work units applied to uranium enrichment, provided the enrichment of tails and products is known. It is possible that sometime in the future further releases of national data of this kind will make such estimates more accurate than they can be today. See Frank von Hippel, "Warhead and Fissile Material Declarations", *ibid.*, Ref. 14.

18. J. Carson Mark, Theodore B. Taylor, Eugene Eyster, William Maraman, and Jacob Wechsler, "Can Terrorists Build Nuclear Weapons?" in Leventhal and Alexander, 1987, pp. 55-65.

19. *ibid.*

20. Derived from data in Cochran et al. See note 5.

6

Verifying a Production Cutoff for Nuclear Explosive Material: Strategies for Verification and the Role of the IAEA

Lawrence Scheinman (USA) & Irakli G. Gverdziteli (USSR)

1

This chapter addresses the verification of a cutoff of production of fissionable materials for nuclear weapons purposes with particular attention to the possible role of the International Atomic Energy Agency (IAEA). The point of departure is the assumption that Moscow and Washington are agreed that a fissile material production cutoff is an appropriate and mutually acceptable arms control measure. While the focus is on a Soviet-American agreement, it is assumed that the importance of achieving a comprehensive agreement by extending a production cutoff to all the nuclear weapon states is well understood.[1]

Given this perspective, there is no discussion of the merits of a stand-alone production cutoff compared with one linked to other nuclear arms control and disarmament measures. Such measures include a freeze on further nuclear weapon production, reduction and dismantlement of existing nuclear warheads, a comprehensive test ban, or restrictions on delivery systems. On the one hand, we acknowledge the contribution that a production cutoff of fissile material for nuclear weapons can make in placing a ceiling on Soviet and U.S. nuclear forces by foreclosing expansion of fissile material inventories. Further, we acknowledge its potential importance in advancing the cause of nuclear non-proliferation by terminating an activity that the weapon states seek to prevent in non-nuclear weapon states. Both or either consideration could well justify a stand-alone production cutoff agreement. On the other hand, without underestimating the political value of continued progress in arms control, we recognize that because a cutoff *per se* does not foreclose weapons research and development, eliminate nuclear testing, nor result in a reduction in the superpowers' strategic nuclear arsenals--three arenas of possible future agreement--it can be argued that a production cutoff alone brings relatively little in the way of arms limitation. For present purposes it is assumed that these considerations either will have been taken into account while negotiating a production cutoff, or will have been placed on the agenda for subsequent consideration.

A second boundary condition for the following analysis is that the production cutoff discussed is limited to termination of production of fissile material--highly enriched uranium (HEU) and plutonium--for nuclear weapons. It is more an end-use limitation than an absolute prohibition on the production of those materials. The production of fissile materials for non-proscribed purposes, both military (e.g., naval propulsion) and civil (e.g., research reactors), presumably would be permitted to continue.[2] This of course has implications for verification. Monitoring a comprehensive cutoff in which all production facilities and activities are shut down is easier than monitoring limited production arrangements. In the former case, any production of prohibited material would *ipso facto* raise a presumption of violation of a cutoff agreement, placing the burden of proof squarely on the shoulders of the offending state to prove that its actions did not violate its undertakings. In the latter case, it becomes necessary to sort out legitimate from illegitimate activity and to establish verification arrangements that would permit verification authorities to reach conclusions regarding compliance. This could include reaching agreement on permissible amounts of production.

Most nuclear material destined for nuclear weapons is produced in dedicated military facilities. Other sources for such material exist, however. They include facilities that produce weapons-grade material for non-weapon purposes, and civil nuclear facilities that normally are not operated in a manner to produce weapons-usable material, but can be altered (at a cost) to do so.

As noted above, fissile material of weapons-grade quality is produced for naval reactors and some military as well as civilian research reactors. While France runs its naval reactors on uranium enriched to about 10%, the United States uses HEU (>90%) for its extensive nuclear submarine fleet. Precise information on the level of enrichment used in the Soviet submarine fleet is not known. There are, however, indications that it may be less than that of the United States. In any event, the amounts in question are significant. According to one recent study U.S. navy purchases of enrichment services during fiscal 1983-1985 "corresponded to a demand of approximately 5 tonnes of U^{235} per year."[3] Knowing much less about Soviet requirements, but using the comparable shaft horsepower of the Soviet and U.S. navies, this study assumed that Soviet requirements are roughly equivalent to those of the United States. While the number and location of Soviet enrichment facilities is not known, it is known that the United States operates two enrichment plants to produce needed HEU. Since the United States has not produced HEU for nuclear explosive purposes since 1964, it is assumed that almost all U.S.-produced HEU is allocated to non-weapons purposes, primarily naval, and that the Soviet requirements would, at a minimum, be roughly the same. These production activities presumably would continue under a cutoff agreement, but measures would have to be agreed to verify that they do not serve as a source of warhead material.

Unless otherwise agreed, a cutoff agreement also would not include a ban on production of tritium that, due to its relatively short half-life (12.4 years) must be periodically replenished to maintain warhead operational readiness. Tritium is an essential ingredient in nuclear warheads that is used as a booster in fission weapons and in fission triggers in thermonuclear weapons. Since tritium production reactors also could be used to produce plutonium, measures would have to be identified and agreed to safeguard against such misuse. It has been estimated that "the production of 6 kilograms of tritium would require an amount of production reactor capacity equivalent to that required to produce about 0.5 tonnes of weapons-grade plutonium [or] approximately the average production rate of one of the Savannah River reactors."[4] A half ton of plutonium could provide about 100 nuclear warheads. A major uncertainty at this time is whether it is possible to safeguard adequately against plutonium production in a tritium production reactor in view of the unlikelihood that such facilities would be available for on-site inspection because of their security significance. Inclusion of tritium in a nuclear materials production halt would cause eventual reductions in the nuclear arsenals of the superpowers. It also would simplify verification by leading to a complete shutdown of facilities able to produce weapons-grade plutonium. However, we assume, for our purposes, that such an agreement remains on the agenda of future actions.

These contingencies suggest that to be credible, a production cutoff would have to incorporate measures to ensure that production of weapons-grade fissile materials is limited to the requirements of the civil or non-proscribed military activity. Further, the parties must be agreed in respects such as production, possibly including agreed quantitative limits or even arrangements for storing and monitoring materials produced in excess of declared requirements. If it could be agreed, end-use verification of declared amounts of weapons-grade material would add even greater credibility.

Attention also must be given to the civil nuclear sector. A cutoff agreement would not affect production of fissionable material in civil nuclear activity. The mainstream civilian nuclear fuel cycle is in light water reactors using low enrichment uranium (LEU) and high fuel burn-up in the reactor core. Spent fuel assemblies are subsequently stored rather than being reprocessed, at least at present in the United States and apparently also in the Soviet Union. This cycle does not normally involve access to weapons-grade material. LEU (typically 3%) is not itself a weapon material, and light-water-reactor fuel assemblies normally are subjected to irradiation levels (25,000-30,000 MWD/t) that produce plutonium containing more Pu^{240} than considered desirable by weapons designers for explosive purposes.

To avoid the performance penalty ordinarily associated with high Pu^{240} content, power reactor-produced plutonium either would require further treatment to reduce the proportion of Pu^{240}, or there would have to be recourse to more sophisticated warhead design. Further treatment involves laser isotopic separation of Pu^{239} from other Pu isotopes. This entails an advanced technology available in very few nuclear weapon states. The United States, for example, does not presently have a plutonium laser isotopic separation facility on line although one is planned for construction in Idaho.[5]

Weapons design capabilities are more widespread. The main point is that non-weapons-grade plutonium cannot be discounted as a source of explosive material. Indeed, the United States has produced and successfully tested a nuclear explosive device made with reactor grade plutonium. Furthermore, one cannot ignore the possibility of altering the operation of civilian power producing reactors to yield weapons-grade plutonium. This alteration pays substantial economic penalties because of the frequent shutdowns required for refueling.[6]

Within the civilian nuclear fuel cycle still other avenues of access to weapons-usable material exist. Enrichment facilities designed to produce LEU could be altered or operated to produce higher levels of enrichment. Plutonium produced in fast breeder reactor blanket assemblies could provide weapons-usable material that would be accessible through reprocessing in facilities able to handle such assemblies. And, if they were to be constructed, plutonium laser isotopic separation plants would provide a means of acquiring high-purity plutonium ideal for explosive use.

In addition, some reactors are designed to produce both electricity and weapons-grade plutonium. The N-reactor at Hanford, Washington, which could be partially refueled in a very short period, although now out of operation, is a case in point. The Soviet RBMK reactors are theoretically capable of dual use activity, and some were initially used primarily to produce plutonium,[7] although it appears that their fueling machines are designed to reload at a slower rate than appropriate for genuine dual-use reactors. Nevertheless, reactors of this type as well as on-load fuelled reactors such as Magnox (UK) and CANDU (Canada, Korea, Argentina), can be continually refuelled without reactor shutdown. They thus pose the problem of shifting missions and the possibility of clandestine production of strategically useful plutonium. They therefore represent an area of concern in the effort to achieve an effective and credible fissile material production cutoff.

This enumeration, that is neither comprehensive nor exhaustive, offers a perspective on the scope of the task of verifying a cutoff of production of fissionable material for nuclear weapons. Verification must address:

1. Facilities dedicated to the production of fissile material for nuclear weapons. Facilities include places that produce, process, or store significant quantities of fissile materials.
2. The risk of diversion of significant quantities of fissile material from

    dedicated facilities serving non-weapon military purposes.
3. The risk of diversion of significant quantities of fissile material from the
    civilian nuclear fuel cycle.

Not discussed above, but clearly of relevance especially in the context of an arms control/disarmament situation involving significant reductions in the levels of nuclear weapons is the possibility of clandestine production facilities. A further question is not addressed here because it is not part of a *production* cutoff agreement. This concerns verification of declared starting inventories of fissionable material useful for weapon purposes including materials deliberately not declared, and stockpiles of depleted uranium. Verification of these inventories would nevertheless be a critical separate measure.

2

The task is substantial, but by no means daunting. Indeed, a model system for dealing with important aspects of this task is already in place. Although verification has been a major stumbling block in post World War II efforts to secure arms control agreements (INF notwithstanding), important progress has been made in verification of non-production of nuclear explosives in non-nuclear weapon states. The 1970 Treaty on Non-Proliferation of Nuclear Weapons (NPT) aimed at foreclosing further spread of nuclear weapons. It requires non-nuclear weapon state parties to renounce nuclear weapons, and not to receive, manufacture or seek assistance in manufacturing nuclear weapons or other nuclear explosive devices. It also requires those states to accept safeguards "on all source or special fissionable material in all peaceful nuclear activities"[8]. It entrusts to the IAEA the task of implementing safeguard measures to verify compliance by non-nuclear weapon state parties with their undertaking not to divert nuclear energy from peaceful purposes to nuclear weapons or other nuclear explosive devices.[9] For their part, the nuclear weapon states undertake to "pursue negotiations in good faith on effective measures relating to cessation of the nuclear arms race at an early date and to nuclear disarmament . . . . ."[10] This undertaking is directly relevant to efforts to achieve a cutoff of production of fissile material for nuclear weapons.

There are several differences between an agreement seeking to avoid the further spread of nuclear weapons and one seeking to achieve a cutoff of production of fissile material for nuclear weapons by nuclear weapon states. There are also some strong similarities or parallels, however, in particular the focus on accounting for the production, use and storage of nuclear material. A brief overview of IAEA safeguarding activity is useful before considering its possible relationship to verification of a cutoff agreement.

IAEA safeguards are based on statutory authority to ensure that assistance with which the Agency is involved is not used to further any military purpose.[11] The

IAEA also applies safeguards at the request of a state to any of that state's nuclear activities, or at the request of the parties, to any bilateral or multilateral arrangement.[12] It is under the latter provision that the IAEA has assumed most of its safeguarding responsibilities.

Safeguards are applied pursuant to safeguards agreements negotiated between the IAEA and the state involved. Those agreements are negotiated under the aegis of either of two IAEA safeguards documents--INFCIRC/66 or INFCIRC/153. These documents and several others, such as the Inspectors Document,[13] and the safeguards agreements negotiated between the IAEA and individual states or groups of states form the basis for the agency's international safeguards system. INFCIRC/66, the first of the two documents developed, applies to cases where the agreement is limited to specific materials, equipment facilities information or services listed on a special inventory. This is the case for states not party to the NPT (or not having otherwise accepted safeguards on all their nuclear activities) with respect to nuclear assistance from a supplier who has required safeguards on that assistance. Almost all suppliers-- even those not party to the NPT--appear to require IAEA safeguards on their exports, even if they do not require that their trading partners accept full-scope safeguards.[14] Most safeguards agreements, as noted above, have been negotiated pursuant to NPT undertakings by which the safeguarded state accepts full-scope safeguards. These agreements therefore provide for comprehensive safeguards on all source and special nuclear material in all peaceful nuclear activities in the state. These are the so-called INFCIRC/153 agreements.

The purposes and approach of the two safeguards document differ in several ways. The purpose of INFCIRC/153 is to verify that safeguarded nuclear material is not diverted to nuclear weapons or other nuclear explosive devices. Under the NPT it is possible for nuclear material for non-proscribed military use to be withdrawn from safeguards (if the material is not subject by the supplier to a no-military use condition). Procedures prescribing how this can be done are specified in INFCIRC/153, paragraph 14. Currently there has been no request to invoke this provision.[15]

INFCIRC/66, that includes this language in agreements negotiated under its auspices in recent years, also is intended to ensure that any supplied item is not used for any military purpose. INFCIRC/66, as mentioned, is item specific while INFCIRC/153 focuses on flow of nuclear material through the fuel cycle, using the idea of key points at which measurements should be taken or samples drawn. Unlike the NPT-related safeguards document, INFCIRC/66 does not specifically provide for the use of containment and surveillance measures in conducting safeguards, resulting in some differences in approach in the two cases. In practice, however, there is little real difference in how safeguards actually are applied by the IAEA under either document.

The IAEA now has 168 safeguards agreements with 99 states including four nuclear weapon states, France, the United Kingdom, the Soviet Union and the

United States, all of whom have voluntarily submitted all or limited parts of their peaceful nuclear activities to IAEA safeguards. The People's Republic of China that made a voluntary safeguards offer in 1988, has negotiated a similar agreement. Altogether this accounts for about 95% of nuclear material in peaceful use in all non-nuclear weapon states, and some material in nuclear weapon states. This includes separated plutonium (10.4 tons, of which 0.6 tons have already been recycled); plutonium in spent nuclear fuel (254.4 tons); HEU (13.1 tons); LEU (31,704 tons); source material (natural and depleted uranium--54,514 tons); and thorium.[16]

Seventy-nine of these states have concluded agreements under INFCIRC/153. Four of the five nuclear weapon states, pursuant to "voluntary offers" made to meet political concerns of non-nuclear weapon states, have also concluded agreements that largely follow the wording of INFCIRC/153 but differ in terms of stated objective. About half the remaining 15 states are parties to the NPT but have not yet concluded the necessary safeguard arrangements and continue to be safeguarded under earlier INFCIRC/66 agreements. The remaining 8 states, that are not parties to the NPT or an equivalent treaty (such as the Treaty of Tlatelolco establishing a nuclear weapon free zone in Latin America and requiring its parties to accept full-scope safeguards) are subject to INFCIRC/66 safeguards.[17] In addition several NPT states have yet to meet their obligation to negotiate a safeguards agreement with the IAEA, but in none of these states are there any nuclear activities of safeguards significance. Pursuant to these agreements the IAEA in 1988 carried out 2128 inspections at more than 600 installations using a field staff of about 190 inspectors, a professional support staff of another 250 persons, and a budget of approximately $50 million. These inspections vary in intensity from a single visit once a year by a single inspector, to week-long inspections by teams of 15 or more inspectors, to round-the-clock coverage of highly sensitive facilities during operation. The inspection activities vary correspondingly, depending on the types, forms and amounts of material present.*

IAEA safeguards are a system of technical measures designed to achieve political objectives. The main political objective is to provide assurance of compliance with agreements. Just what this means has been a matter of some debate. Some emphasize verification of peaceful use, meaning confirmation of non-diversion; others stress detection of diversion. Still another political objective frequently mentioned is deterrence of diversion or of non-compliance. In recent years assurance of compliance has been on the ascent and deterrence has been played down. To an extent these are semantic differences, but emphasis on one or the other approach can affect perceptions of the utility and effectiveness of international safeguards. It is clear that to provide assurance there must exist a capability to detect non-compliance. However, undue emphasis on detection of

---

* See Appendix I for a synopsis of inspection activities carried out by IAEA at natural and low enriched uranium conversion and fabrication plants.

diversion suggests detection of a diversion in progress and in the mind of some the ability to interdict the illicit action. It also implies an assumption of dishonesty on the part of the state or operator that can and has exacerbated tensions between the verifying agency and the inspected party.[18]

IAEA safeguards are capable of detecting diversion in the sense of providing information that material cannot be accounted for, but as they are in the nature of an auditing procedure, detection is virtually certain to be *ex post facto*. The situation is different in the case of a continuing diversion scheme aimed at diverting a large quantity of material. In such a case safeguards may detect a diversion in process.

INFCIRC/153 provides not only a political objective (assurance of non-diversion) but also a technical objective. This objective is the "timely detection of diversion of significant quantities of nuclear material."[19]   This formulation provides the Agency a framework for criteria to evaluate the degree to which it is achieving its political objective. However, it also has contributed to some extent to the differences of view noted above. Significant quantities (i.e., quantities of a material needed to make a nuclear explosive) and detection times (i.e., time between a diversion and its detection, that is in turn related to the time needed to convert diverted material in a given form to a form required to make a nuclear explosive) have been agreed upon on a provisional basis (Table 1, Appendix II). They have also been used to establish the desired frequency of verification. Thus, materials involving one significant quantity or more of unirradiated direct use material are assigned detection times ranging from 7-10 days to one month depending on its form. On the other hand, detection time for indirect-use material is one year.[20]

Questions of significance and timeliness are, of course, ultimately matters for political decision. However, it may be noted that in many situations where none exist, the introduction of even a single nuclear weapon can be very destabilizing. On the other hand, in the case of nuclear weapon states with large arsenals, the concept of significant quantity is quite clearly different. Use of these concepts in a production freeze situation presumably would yield considerably different numerical values.

Safeguards comprise a set of on-site activities intended to verify that the way in which material is used conforms to the provisions of the safeguards agreement. A number of elements are involved including design review to enable the IAEA to devise effective safeguards strategies; examination of records and reports; and on-site inspection. The objective is effective safeguards and on the whole the system is sufficiently flexible to permit modification or make allowance for enhanced containment, improved operator measurement and accounting systems, and provisions for installation and use of agency measurement systems integrated into plant material handling systems. Whether the flexibility can be implemented depends on the extent of cooperation between operator, state authority and the IAEA. This is not uniform.[21]

The essence of IAEA safeguards is the independent verification by the agency of state reports of the presence and movement of nuclear materials subject to safeguards. Nuclear material accountancy is the principal safeguards measure supplemented by containment (to define and control movements or access to nuclear materials) and surveillance (to confirm declared movement and detect undeclared movements of nuclear material and to maintain continuity of knowledge or information). Nuclear material accounting involves tracking inventories and transfers of nuclear material, using defined areas (material balance areas) and defined accounting periods. The end result of a verification exercise is a material balance statement indicating whether and how much nuclear material cannot be accounted for. What is involved is in fact a two-tiered verification system consisting of an annual material balance verification, and conclusions at shorter intervals for strategically sensitive materials, for example, monthly intervals for plutonium and HEU.[22]

The states under INFCIRC/153 safeguards are obligated to establish state systems of accounting for and control of nuclear material.[23] Plant operators are required to provide the IAEA with information necessary for the agency, the national authority and the facility operator to agree on a safeguards plan for the facility. They also must keep accounting and operating records. They also submit detailed data to the state authorities so the latter may provide periodic reports reflecting changes in material inventory, physical inventory and material balances for prescribed periods for defined material balance areas. As for those states that are under INFCIRC/66 safeguards, they are in essence obligated to provide the agency with similar information and to facilitate the conduct of the agency's safeguards activities.

The IAEA carries out independent fact-finding and measurements (including record examination and physical verification) to verify reports submitted by the state. Thus, they can confirm whether safeguarded material can be accounted for. The key element of this activity is on-site inspection by designated international inspectors. Among other things, they check facility operating and accounting records, verify calibration of equipment, make independent measurements of nuclear material, obtain samples of material for independent analysis, and apply and inspect agency seals affixed to selected items or places in a facility.

Most inspections are routine (i.e., carried out on an announced basis in accordance with a frequency previously agreed to between the IAEA and the state). The agency system also provides for both unannounced and special inspections, and in the case of centrifuge enrichment plants, unannounced inspections at a limited frequency.

Verification extends to discrete items such as fuel assemblies (using item counting and non-destructive assay techniques) and to materials in bulk form (using sampling and chemical analysis or non-destructive analysis). As soon as these activities are completed, the IAEA evaluates the results and assesses and seeks to resolve any anomalies discovered, i.e., unusual observed conditions that might occur during a diversion. An anomaly does not imply a diversion, but signals the need to reconcile the observed condition with the material to be accounted for. Unresolved anomalies can lead to action by the agency's governing board or even be referred to the UN Security Council.

For each state, conclusions drawn by the IAEA for a material balance period are reported directly to the state, and a more general Safeguards Implementation Report is issued annually to the governing board and to all Member States. The summary of the safeguards implementation report findings are published in the IAEA's Annual Report.

To summarize: IAEA verifies the presence and movement of nuclear material subject to its safeguards and, in the case of INFCIRC/66 (non-NPT) arrangements, may extend to other materials, equipment facilities, services and information. Verification is based on the principle of material accounting, supplemented by containment and surveillance. The nuclear fuel cycle is divided into a number of 'material balance areas.' Inputs and outputs of material in these defined areas are measured in given periods of time, and periodically subject to physical inventory with a view to reaching a material balance and determining whether any material is unaccounted for. The system is anchored in on-site verification by IAEA inspectors who verify, by independent means, state reports on the accounting for and control of nuclear materials. Unexplained losses are examined to the point where the IAEA is satisfied that any significant anomalies can be satisfactorily explained. If the inspectorate cannot satisfactorily resolve an anomaly it may be reported to the Board of Governors and if necessary to the UN Security Council.

It is not the purpose of this chapter to assess and evaluate the effectiveness of IAEA safeguards, but it would not be appropriate to leave this discussion without some observations about how the system has functioned. The most comprehensive judgment rendered thus far is found in the Final Document of the Third (1985) NPT Review Conference where it is stated that:

> IAEA safeguards provide assurance that States are complying with their undertaking and assist States in demonstrating this compliance. They thereby promote further confidence among States and, being a fundamental element of the Treaty, help to strengthen their collective security. IAEA safeguards play a key role in preventing the proliferation of nuclear weapons and other nuclear explosive devices.[24]

If this is the current consensus it does not go, and has not gone unchallenged. There is concern in some quarters about the adequacy of IAEA safeguards to detect diversions quickly enough to permit effective countermeasures to be invoked, especially in the case of separated plutonium. The IAEA's annual Safeguards Implementation Report, a document provided by the Secretariat to the Board of Governors and Member States offers a frank assessment of the extent to which internally set objectives are met in the context of achieving technically defined goals. Some critics have drawn upon the report to ask whether the incompleteness in attaining those objectives does not tarnish the value of the system as a whole. Others point to Israel's attack on a safeguarded research reactor in Iraq in June, 1981 as evidence that states lack confidence in international safeguards.

It is not feasible to undertake a detailed analysis of these various concerns. The easiest retort is to refer to the NPT Review Conference statement quoted above. It also may be noted that the Israeli attack reflected a limiting case situation and considerations peculiar to that country's security perceptions and circumstances. The other criticisms reflect the difficulties involved in marrying technical operations with political objectives, The criticisms also reflect the reality that, whatever the merits of the conceptual approach, implementation reveals problems and gaps, and that verification is a dynamic learning process in which one seeks to build constructively on experience, strengthening the system where appropriate, and adding supportive measures where necessary. Most importantly, the system has improved over time, becoming more efficient and effective, and clarifying what problems exist and how best to seek their remedy.[25] If the system has revealed imperfections, it also has come to be accepted by those it serves as essential to international nuclear cooperation and to nonproliferation. In the final analysis, its viability depends on the commitment of the international community to the norm of nonproliferation and to maintain a verification regime to provide assurance of compliance.

3

A production cutoff, as we noted, involves verification of three things. The first is non-production of fissionable material at dedicated weapons-material production facilities. The next is non-diversion of fissionable material from legitimate uses to illicit purposes (including diversion from peaceful nuclear activities or from facilities producing or fabricating fissile material for non-proscribed military purposes). The third is that clandestine production or separation of plutonium (or U^{233}) or enrichment of uranium does not occur.

The experience and attributes of IAEA safeguards meet many, though not all, these verification requirements. This alone does not suffice to recommend assigning to the IAEA responsibility for verifying a cutoff agreement. The benefits and costs of such a decision are discussed below. But from the point of view of technical capacity as well as administrative and legal competence, there is little reason to doubt that the existing IAEA safeguards system could be extended to verify a fissile material production cutoff agreement. The statute of the IAEA authorizes it to apply safeguards to any bilateral or multilateral arrangement in the field of atomic energy if requested by the parties.[26] The arms control measure discussed essentially extends to nuclear weapon states a system applied in non-nuclear weapon states to cover all nuclear material in all their peaceful nuclear activities.

Such an extension has been a subject of international discussion for several years. In 1969, at the Eighteen Nation Disarmament Committee, the United States proposed a fissionable material production cut-off, compliance of which was to be entrusted to the IAEA. The IAEA would be "asked to safeguard nuclear material in each State's peaceful nuclear activities and to verify the continued shutdown of any facilities for production of fissionable material that are closed."[27] This represented a change from earlier U.S. cut-off proposals that were tied to bilateral verification. Over the past several years a number of Soviet spokesmen, including Ambassador Timerbaev (Soviet representative to the IAEA), and General Secretary Gorbachev, have remarked positively on the potential role of the IAEA in nuclear arms control and disarmament.[28]

At the 1984 annual General Conference of the IAEA, Sweden renewed an earlier proposal that the nuclear weapon states fully separate their civilian and military nuclear activities and submit all civilian nuclear fuel cycle activities to safeguards.[29] The Swedish proposal was made with the view that eventually a weapons material production cutoff might be negotiated and verification consigned to the IAEA, a notion that has received support from a number of non-nuclear weapon states party to the NPT.[30]

The IAEA, as noted earlier, already applies safeguards in four of the nuclear weapon states pursuant to voluntary offers to submit all (in the case of the United States and Great Britain) or some (in the case of France, the Soviet Union and now China) civilian nuclear activities to international safeguards. (The agreement with China was expected to be in force before the end of 1989.) In practice, due largely to resource limitations, the IAEA conducts only modest safeguards activities in any nuclear weapon state.[31]

As far as political confidence in IAEA safeguards is concerned we already have seen that the most recent NPT Review Conference strongly endorsed their nonproliferation and security value. But as we noted, by no means should this be taken as a sign of lethargic acceptance of safeguards as they are. Virtually nobody seriously questions the adequacy of IAEA safeguards insofar as reactors and spent-fuel storage facilities are concerned. Yet doubts have been expressed-- sometimes quite forcefully--about the ability of safeguards to verify that plutonium in large throughput facilities such as reprocessing or fuel fabrication plants has not been diverted. It bears emphasis that for nonproliferation purposes, very rigorous targets are set. The minimum amount of material (significant quantity) that must be detected in a given time (the time needed to convert nuclear material to the chemical and physical form necessary for nuclear explosives) is 8 kg for plutonium and 25 kg for HEU. These are taken to approximate the amount of such materials needed to make a nuclear explosive.[32]

Establishing a detection threshold (i.e., the sensitivity required of a verification system) is a political question. In the case of a production cutoff involving the superpowers with their very substantial nuclear weapon arsenals, no reasonable purpose would be served by setting the detection threshold at the amount required to make a single nuclear device, or even several. The only plausible criterion would be that level above which cheating would be strategically significant, a criterion that would have to be politically negotiated. It could be argued that given the size of the existing superpower nuclear arsenals, no amount of cheating would be strategically significant as long as there was survivable retaliatory capability. Not only would this not pass muster with the politically influential arms control community, but it would be regarded as tantamount to no agreement at all by most of the world. Another approach might be to estimate what deployment of what weapons systems could alter the strategic balance, to determine what amount of fissile material would be required to arm that system, and to set the detection threshold accordingly. Still another approach might be to arbitrarily take a percentage of current stockpiles as a level of clandestine production that would not be significant in terms of strategic balance, but would be a realistic verification target. Studies that have been done along these lines seem to settle on 1000-1600 kg/yr plutonium and 5000-6500 kg/yr HEU. These levels are well within the detection capability of current international safeguards.[33] A reduction in the size of nuclear arsenals--as presumably would result from a successful negotiation of START--would obviously have an impact on assessments on the level of sensitivity required for adequate verification.

IAEA experience with verification of uranium enrichment plants is limited, and in the case of gaseous diffusion non-existent (all large operating diffusion facilities are in nuclear weapon states and still highly classified, while an Argentinean pilot facility has not been submitted to safeguards). The agency has, however, developed and put into operation a verification regime for gas-centrifuge-type enrichment plants. This regime is based on the principle of unannounced access to the cascade areas with a limited frequency, enabling inspectors to verify, in a timely manner and with high confidence, that the production of significant quantities of uranium at an enrichment level higher than declared has not taken place.[34]

Although the IAEA has not had direct experience with dual-purpose reactors, verification of their operations falls within its technical capability and is consistent with its mandate to ensure that items subject to safeguards remain in peaceful use. These reactors are capable of on-load refuelling permitting short-term exposure of target fuels without reactor shutdown. IAEA currently applies safeguards to on-load refuelling reactors in several countries including Canada, Argentina, Korea, India, Pakistan (CANDU) and Japan (MAGNOX). Parties to a production cutoff agreement would have to agree not to produce plutonium for weapons purposes in such facilities, and to establish appropriate verification arrangements including refuelling activities, storage and subsequent treatment of discharged fuel assemblies.[35]

Some tasks critical to acceptable verification of a production cutoff either involve activities that the IAEA has not yet dealt with, or lie beyond its capability and mandate. For example, IAEA experience with uranium enrichment verification has been limited to facilities based on the ultracentrifuge process. A production cutoff agreement could entail continued HEU production for civil and/or non-proscribed military uses. Presumably the parties would have agreed on production limits and it would be necessary to verify that production did not exceed those limits. Access by international inspectors to certain sensitive areas might be precluded because of the sensitivity and classified nature of the technology, and because of the proliferation implications of providing access to international inspectors.[36]

Measurement of receipts and shipments from the production facility might be entrusted to international inspectors, and perimeter monitoring could be used in this case, but the access problem would still exist. One alternative would be reciprocal inspection by nationals of the parties to the agreement with some provision for authentication by the international verification authority.

Two other matters critical to a production cutoff agreement are the risk of clandestine production/fabrication facilities and the risk of undeclared material stockpiles. IAEA does not have the authority or the capability to verify that production of fissionable materials for weapons purposes is not being carried out clandestinely in undeclared facilities. Nor does it have the authority to search for undeclared stockpiles of material in a state. However, where an agreement provides for comprehensive safeguards on all peaceful nuclear activities, the state subject to safeguards is obligated to report *all* nuclear material in peaceful nuclear activities within its territory, or under its jurisdiction or control anywhere. Declared materials may be exempt from safeguards under agreed circumstances (e.g., for use in non-proscribed military activities), but this does not absolve the state from responsibility for making a comprehensive initial declaration. While nothing prevents the IAEA from raising questions or seeking explanations, there is no authority for agency inspectors to do searches or similar investigations to determine the possible presence of undeclared materials in a state. To ascertain the existence of undeclared production facilities or material stockpiles, parties to a cutoff agreement would have to rely on national technical means and/or procedures for challenge inspections, a technique for which the IAEA lacks authority and experience but that is incorporated in the Treaty of Tlatelolco establishing a Latin American Nuclear Weapon Free Zone and is under discussion in other arms control negotiations such as the Chemical Weapons Convention.[37]

4

Presuming the technical capacity and authority of IAEA to verify a production cutoff agreement, is it the preferred institution for implementing this responsibility? One can envision three levels of verification arrangements:

1. bilateral

2. international
3. hybrid arrangements combining elements of bilateral and international verification.

Each has benefits and costs.

Bilateral Arrangements

Such arrangements, as the INF verification agreement demonstrates, can be achieved fairly quickly and can provide for considerable scope and depth. Their negotiation is isolated from extraneous agendas. They are also likely to be viewed by the parties directly affected as more credible than alternative arrangements. This is not only because their nationals have direct responsibility for implementing verification, but also because they can respond more quickly and directly to cheating.[38]

INF contains some of the most far-reaching and comprehensive verification provisions ever agreed. In particular, it allows for short-notice challenge inspections of agreed sites. Inspectors may demand an inspection and be admitted to a point of entry without identifying beforehand the particular site they wish to visit. The agreement also contains provisions for resident inspectors at agreed sites (the Votkinsk and Hercules plants). INF provides for a significantly larger inspectorate than IAEA, and allows for no restrictions by either party on the designation of inspectors. Both parties appear satisfied that the verification arrangements ensure timely detection of militarily significant violations. It is questionable whether an international body would be vested with so extensive an authority.

On the other hand, bilateral verification may have less credibility for third parties than international verification. The importance of third party credibility depends upon how the arms control agreement in question relates to other arms control or political objectives. One objective of a production cutoff is surely to help reduce the discriminatory aspects of the NPT by delegitimizing further production of fissionable material for nuclear weapons. NPT non-nuclear weapon state parties may, therefore, feel strongly that the non-production undertaking, being comparable to their undertaking not to divert fissionable material from peaceful use, be submitted to the same verification safeguards. The discrimination issue should not be underestimated, especially since there is no real difference, either with respect to the undertaking to be verified or the scope of verification activities to be performed, between what the IAEA does today in non-nuclear weapon states and what would be required in a production cutoff. The latter would be widely viewed as merely an extension of the former.

International Verification

International verification could involve the IAEA or a newly created organization. It certainly is not that IAEA should (or even could) be considered for verification responsibilities in all arms control agreements, or even all nuclear arms control agreements. Yet there are some compelling reasons for considering using IAEA in the case of a fissionable material production cut-off. The strongest of these, noted above, involves the issue of discrimination. It would be politically difficult to justify turning to another verification authority to monitor compliance with an agreement involving the non-diversion to weapons use of nuclear material under safeguards. At the very least it would imply lack of confidence in IAEA safeguards, raising the question of why non-nuclear weapon states should continue to submit to those safeguards if they don't purchase an adequate degree of assurance in the eyes of the weapon states. It would be remarkable if under such circumstances non-nuclear weapon states did not ask: If IAEA safeguards are not good enough for the weapon states, why should we accept the costs and burdens of safeguards for ourselves? Worse still, it could suggest a permanent discrimination between weapon and non-weapon states and reinforce criticisms of the non-proliferation regime as a whole.

Another important reason for international verification is that while a production cutoff would, at its inception, most likely apply only to the two superpowers, in the longer term the objective clearly would be to extend the cutoff to other nuclear weapon states, and possibly even to threshold non-NPT states. A multilateral commitment of that sort would require invoking a multilateral verification arrangement.

On the other hand, international verification raises substantial problems. States jealously guard their sovereignty and do not easily transfer authority or autonomy to international institutions. The IAEA has been granted relatively substantial authority, but still lacks an independent political base for enforcement. Finally it must depend on the good will and cooperation of the states subject to safeguards to fulfill effectively its responsibilities. Many of the latter, even while supporting international verification, instinctively press for narrow interpretation of IAEA authority and rights.[39]

Other questions also arise in the case of IAEA. Political responsibility in IAEA is exercised by a Board of Governors of 35 member states. One must question how acceptable it would be to the United States and Soviet Union to have political authority in the hands of a heterogeneous board, or to what extent those two states would feel compelled to exert even greater influence in the agency than they do today and what effect that would have on other states many of whom see the IAEA's primary value in facilitating broader access to nuclear technology rather than in safeguards. Furthermore, the *modus vivendi* of IAEA has been to maintain some degree of equilibrium between development and control and to have that reflected in the budget. A substantial increase in verification responsibility, even if funded exclusively by the superpowers, could lead to new pressure to augment development resources to maintain at least a semblance of statutory balance. At a minimum, the addition of new responsibilities would have some impact on existing activities, competition for resources and political decision-making. That impact potentially would have both positive and negative aspects.

A final difficulty with international verification is that some responsibilities may not be amenable to direct implementation by an international institution. We have referred to several earlier. They are access to parts of facilities employing classified technologies, the risk of facilitating proliferation by allowing access to certain facilities, and dual use facilities producing materials for use in non-proscribed military activities. It is here that the third, *hybrid* type arrangement becomes potentially relevant. There is nothing in the IAEA statute to prevent delegation of some responsibilities to subsidiary organs, or vice versa. One could imagine an arrangement involving bilateral/ international or multilateral (nuclear weapon states only)/international. Even more complex arrangements such as bilateral and/or UN Disarmament Verification Agency for military aspects, and IAEA for peaceful elements of an arms control/disarmament agreement are imaginable. It is instructive to look at an existing, operating example of the coexistence of two multinational safeguards systems--one global (IAEA), the other regional (EURATOM)--to see that novel arrangements can be agreed, and that they have both costs and benefits.

EURATOM and IAEA both have responsibility for applying safeguards in several countries in Western Europe. Beyond that common responsibility there are many differences between the two organizations. EURATOM was established as a supranational institution with extensive rights to act for its member states and to bind them by laws and regulations. IAEA is an international institution whose safeguarding rights and responsibilities are based on contractual relationships between the agency and the state concerned. EURATOM's safeguards responsibilities are more extensive, starting with uranium ore (not covered by IAEA safeguards), and verifying not only that safeguarded materials are not diverted from their declared uses, (that in the EURATOM case could, but for the NPT obligation assumed by its non-nuclear weapon state members, be for peaceful or military purposes) but also that any specific obligations incurred vis-à-vis external suppliers also are fulfilled.[40] IAEA safeguards focus on ensuring the peaceful use of safeguarded nuclear materials. Furthermore, EURATOM has a direct relationship with plant operators throughout the member states of the European Community rather than relying on the establishment of national systems of accounting and control as does the IAEA.[41]

Political considerations related to the commitment to building a European Community led to the inclusion in the NPT safeguards requirement of language permitting non-nuclear weapon state NPT parties to conclude the required safeguards agreement called for in Article III of the Treaty either "individually or together with other states." There followed a lengthy negotiation aimed at organizing the coexistence of both safeguards systems in a way that ensured EURATOM's integrity while IAEA could fulfill with confidence its objective of independently verifying that all material under safeguards could be accounted for.

It is not surprising that two highly structured bureaucratic organizations confronted with this challenge would have to sort out many problems. Major concerns included avoiding imposing unacceptable burdens on operators by duplication of multinational safeguards activities; allocating responsibilities to establish efficient safeguards without affecting the integrity of either system; and establishing mechanisms for resolving such differences as might arise without compromising safeguards in the interim. It took nearly three years to conclude an agreement and another four years to bring it into full implementation. Even today, eighteen years after initial negotiations began, some facility attachments have not been completed. The intrusion of political dogma into technical discussions caused some of these delays. Others can be explained by the mere fact that the blending of two functionally similar systems with sharply overlapping responsibilities but a need for independent judgment had to be achieved.

If these are some costs associated with establishing the simultaneous operation of two safeguarding bodies, some arrangements agreed demonstrate how hybrid systems, if deemed necessary or appropriate, can be fashioned. Three features of the IAEA/EURATOM arrangement deserve mention. One is the mechanism of *joint teams*--inspection teams of inspectors from both systems. They conduct on-site verification activities, primarily at sensitive facilities that require inspector presence whenever the facility is in operation. Responsibilities are allocated among inspection team members; data is collected in common; but analysis, evaluation and reports are made independently. A mechanism of this nature could be honed to allocate particular responsibilities between bilateral and international inspectors in a case where bilateral and international verification both were essential to an arms control agreement.

A second device is the principle of *observation* in which activities such as item counting or examination of records are carried out by EURATOM inspectors with IAEA inspectors observing the items and records but not repeating the inspection operation. Observation does not restrict the right of the IAEA inspector and is not limited to EURATOM inspector activities but extends to plant operations themselves. The criterion of acceptability is the ability of the IAEA inspector to reach independent conclusions. It is possible to conceive this mechanism operating in situations in which for one reason or another international hands-on inspection is neither appropriate nor acceptable, but international verification is necessary.

Third is the establishment of *technical liaison committees* to reconcile differences and settle concrete problems pragmatically. The principle is not very different from the Standing Consultative Committee established in the context of SALT I except that, in this case, the objective is to reconcile acceptably conflicts or coordination problems between two verification systems.

Based on the above one can visualize an arrangement involving two verification authorities in which certain activities were carried out under bilateral auspices and others under international auspices with criteria and procedures for authentication determined by political agreement. A hybrid arrangement involving a two-tiered verification system in which selected activities beyond the authority or experience of the IAEA were delegated to a subsidiary organ that was formally part of and politically responsible to the international institution could have two values. On one hand, by allowing bilateral verification it could meet concerns of the immediately involved states regarding the integrity of the safeguards system. On the other hand, by providing for authentication and an appropriate degree of independent international verification, it could go far toward meeting the discrimination problem while reinforcing the principle of international verification. A hybrid arrangement involving independent authentication would have somewhat less international credibility, but perhaps be more politically expedient at least in its initial phases.

Whatever verification arrangements might be agreed certain problem areas will persist and require appropriate measures. One is the uncertainty of the initial stockpile of fissile material. There is the risk of an undeclared and consequently unverified stockpile of weapons-usable material. While this would not be a significant issue at the outset, when what is involved is essentially a freeze on production and nothing more, it would become progressively important as and when agreements were reached and implemented regarding the reduction of nuclear arsenals.

This is directly related to the second problem area--the defining of the quantity of nuclear material, diversion of which must be detected if confidence in the verification system is to be maintained. Alone, this is less of a problem than it is when linked to uncertainty regarding an undeclared and unverified stockpile of fissile material.

A third, and related question is that of clandestine production facilities. National technical means may go far toward determining whether there exists sufficient evidence of clandestine activity to warrant the invoking of some form of challenge inspection. This is not a problem with respect to reactors or reprocessing plants, but may be a problem with respect to enrichment by laser isotopic separation.[42] One issue that may have to be addressed at an early stage is whether an effort should be made to monitor production at uranium mine sites to better comprehend the probability and dimension of clandestine nuclear activity.[43]

5

Each verification approach provides opportunities and has limits. None entirely satisfies all objectives and values of those principally concerned. It is our view that, on balance, the optimal approach is a bilateral strategy. On the one hand, it would facilitate bilateral inspection of elements of the arms control agreement considered essential by the parties most directly affected, and open the possibility for reserving to bilateral inspection sensitive military-related activities involving classified information.   On the other hand, it would confirm the principle of using international institutions already involved in verification activities in non-nuclear weapon states to verify similar activities in nuclear weapon states. This would go far toward meeting existing concerns of discrimination in the NPT environment that would undoubtedly intensify if separate arrangements were established to deal in the weapon states with responsibilities identical with those carried out in non-nuclear weapon states by the IAEA.

Verification arrangements of the nature described above would provide the credibility necessary to facilitate arms control progress. It is, however, appropriate to ask for how long incremental arms control agreements based on the current world nuclear structure can endure and whether, in the longer term, global security and stability would not be better served by seeking to introduce structural change.

The problems associated with the taming of the atom do not stop at the borders of today's nuclear weapon states. Nuclear science is already embedded in many states, several of whom have translated that scientific knowledge into technological programs designed to support national energy economies. Assuming, as we must, continued world economic and social growth, requiring increased energy resources, and increased sensitivity to the environmental and ecological impact of fossil fuel burning to meet that demand, it is reasonable to postulate a continued and possibly growing role for nuclear energy.[44] Satisfactory resolution of problems associated with nuclear safety and waste management could result in a significant increase in the role of nuclear energy in the decades ahead.

However, because of its dual character, nuclear technology and nuclear material produced for peaceful purposes also can be used for destructive purposes. The widespread dispersion of nuclear technology and material increases the possibility of it being used destructively either because of national malevolence or because it falls into the hands of terrorists.   Furthermore, technology is not static, raising possibilities for producing weapons-usable materials such as those that a fissile material production cut-off would seek to control by means that will be more and more difficult to monitor and control--for example, uranium enrichment by chemical, plasma or laser isotopic separation any of which could lead to the capacity to produce HEU.   Not only will new technologies be developed, but they also will spread from country to country. Similar problems also exist at the other two points in the nuclear fuel cycle that are particularly vulnerable from the point of view of acquisition of nuclear material suitable for explosive purposes--fuel fabrication and plutonium separation.

These considerations suggest the need to revisit current ideas of international nuclear cooperation with a view to identifying means by which to reduce further the risk of diversion of produced nuclear materials or the switching of nuclear production capabilities from peaceful to non-peaceful uses. This is not to demean the role of the IAEA; quite the contrary, it is to build on and strengthen its already significant responsibilities. The IAEA today provides assurances regarding peaceful purposes and it plays a central and critical role in nonproliferation. The Agency has developed a substantial verification system based on such concepts as significant quantities and the timely detection of diversion of nuclear material. It is a dynamic system, based on modern technology and a highly qualified staff, both of which are constantly improving.[45] It has justifiably earned widespread credibility and support and a substantial degree of legitimacy.

As good as it is, the IAEA does have its limits. For example, it cannot seek out undeclared facilities. It is incomplete since not all states in the world fully participate in the system. As long as it is not globally applied, the information base on which the IAEA makes determinations and judgments regarding the accountability of nuclear material remains incomplete. In addition, it has limited sanction powers in the event of a violation. It is based on the principles of monitoring and of voluntary participation. That is, where full-scope verification is concerned, states participate either because of an obligation assumed under a treaty such as the NPT or due to national policy to place voluntarily all nuclear activities under IAEA safeguards. Partial safeguards result from requirements of nuclear suppliers that supplied nuclear material or facilities be subject to IAEA safeguards. The IAEA, thus, cannot prevent diversions, but only serves as a restraint, even though that restraint is admittedly strong and important.

For nuclear energy to play its full role in economic development in the future there is a need to increase qualitatively the level of assurance that nuclear plant and material is being used for exclusively peaceful purposes. An elevated level of assurance regarding peaceful use is extremely important to international society. But that level of assurance can be achieved only in the circumstance that the international system of control becomes an organic part of the organization for producing, using and storing nuclear materials. For one thing this means that participation in international institutions dealing with nuclear technology should be based on obligatory principles regarding use of nuclear material. For another, it means that violations must be regarded and treated as unqualifiedly illegal and subject to strict response by the international community at both the economic and political levels.

To this end consideration should be given to establishing an international system for production and use of nuclear materials based on the experience and authority of the IAEA. Measures to move from autonomous national nuclear activity to international development of nuclear energy for peaceful purposes should become a consensus objective of the global nuclear community. Based on the principles that all peaceful use should be open to all interested countries, that the development of safe nuclear reactors is a joint responsibility of all nations competent in nuclear technology, and that all users of nuclear energy are obligatorily committed to peaceful use only, a regime should be contemplated in which nuclear fuel cycle activities are structured and operated based on an international rather than a national framework. This would include revisiting earlier ideas of international (or regional) nuclear fuel cycle centers providing for joint production of nuclear materials for peaceful purposes and international fission material storage centers for managing sensitive nuclear materials not actively in use for production of nuclear energy.[46]

Internationalization of the nuclear fuel cycle cannot be done by the stroke of a pen. As a first step toward shifting from autonomous national nuclear activity to international nuclear development, consideration could be given to adopting the principle that new fuel cycle activities should be structured and operated on an international rather than a national framework. There would be some utility in reexamining the assumptions and recommendations of the Baruch Plan, not only for its objective of breaking new ground in the organization of human activity in the field of nuclear development, but also with respect to abolishing nuclear weapons from the face of the earth.

In the current era of mutual confidence and appreciation of the catastrophic consequences that could flow from the use of nuclear weapons, there arises the possibility of achieving this objective that was not attainable in an earlier time. Incremental measures such as reflected in SALT, the INF, a fissile material production cutoff, and the projected START and related measures in both the nuclear and other fields must continue and retain the unswerving commitment of political leadership around the world. But we also must think in new dimensions and strive to move toward global agreements and structures consistent with the objectives of international security and stability and world peace. The suggestion made to move beyond autonomous nuclear development to an international regime is a small step in that direction. It is possible that such an agreement cannot be achieved for any of a variety of reasons, but it would be unforgivable not to try to attain that goal.

Appendix I

Synopsis of Inspection Activities for Natural and Low Enrichment Uranium Conversion and Fabrication Plants

Uranium conversion and fabrication facilities that handle LEU are inspected six times per year and those handling natural uranium are inspected four times per year. At one of these inspections in each case the annual Physical Inventory Verification (PIV) is conducted by the Agency. At the PIV the presence of all items declared to be present in all material strata is confirmed. A statistically-determined sample of the items in each stratum is inspected by weighing (in some cases by volume and density measurements), by using instruments, and by the withdrawal of samples for chemical analysis. The number of items measured and the measurements applied are such that there is a high probability that an abrupt or protracted (over the year) diversion of a significant quantity of nuclear material will be detected.

Associated with each PIV, activities are performed that confirm that nuclear material from elsewhere has not been borrowed for presentation at the inventory verification to conceal a diversion.

The other inspections during the year (five for LEU handling facilities and three for natural uranium handling facilities) take place on a normal schedule throughout the year. Some modifications of that schedule may take place based on the transfer schedule provided in advance by the facility operator because one purpose of such inspections is to verify receipts and shipments and other inventory changes. Finished fuel pellets are sampled several times a year to quantify any differences between the operator's measurement system and the Agency's to limit the effect of any such systematic difference on the Agency's ability to detect protracted diversion.

Throughout the year monthly reports of inventory and inventory changes are examined for consistency and at inspection the facility records and reports are audited. The accumulated results of these activities, including the Agency's measurements, and any difficulties between the quantities of transferred material as reported by the shipper and the receiver are evaluated for safeguards significance.

Source: Developed with assistance of IAEA Safeguards Staff

Appendix II

Table IA. Estimated Material Conversion Times for Finished Pu or U Metal Components

Beginning Material Form	Conversion time
Pu, HEU, or U^{233}	Order of days (7-10)
PuO_2, $Pu(NO_3)_4$ or other pure compounds; HEU or U^{233} oxide or other pure U compounds; MOX or other non-irradiated pure mixtures containing Pu, U (U^{233} + U^{235} >=20%); Pu, HEU and/or U^{233} in scrap or other miscellaneous impure compounds.	Order of weeks $(1-3)$[a]
Pu, HEU. or U^{233} in irradiated fuel	Order of months (1-3)
U containing <20% U^{235} and U^{233}; Th	Order of one year

Source: IAEA Safeguards Glossary, IAEA/SG/INF/1 1980, p. 214

a. This range is not determined by any single factor but the pure Pu and U compounds will tend to be at the lower end of the range and the mixtures and scrap at the higher end.

Table IB. Significant Quantities

Material	Significant Quantity	Safeguard apply to:
Direct-use nuclear material		
Pu[b]	8 Kg	Total element
U^{233}	8 Kg	Total isotope
U (U^{235}>=20%)	25 Kg	U^{235} contained
Indirect-use nuclear material		
U (U^{235}>=20%)[c]	75 Kg	U^{235} contained
Th	20 t.	Total element

Source: IAEA Safeguards Glossary, IAEA/SG/INF/1 1980, p. 21

b. For Pu containing less than Pu^{238}.
c. Including natural and depleted uranium.

Notes

1. The idea of a fissile material production cutoff is not new. A well developed literature on the subject already exists, much of which furnished background for this chapter. See H.A. Feiveson, F. von Hippel and D. Albright, "Breaking the fuel/weapons connection" *Bulletin of the Atomic Scientists* (March 1986) p. 26; F. von Hippel and B.G. Levi, "Controlling Nuclear Weapons at the Source: Verification of a Cutoff in the Production of Plutonium and Highly Enriched Uranium for Nuclear Weapons" in K. Tsipis, D.W. Hafemeister and P. Janeway, eds., *Arms Control Verification: The Technologies that Make it Possible* (Washington: Pergammon-Brassey's, 1986); F. von Hippel, D.H. Albright and B.G. Levi, "Stopping the Production of Fissile Material for Weapons" *Scientific American* (September 1985), p. 26; William Epstein, "A Ban on the Production of Fissionable Material for Weapons" *Scientific American* (July 1980), p. 31; D.W. Wainhouse et al., *Arms Control Agreements*, (Baltimore: Johns Hopkins Press, 1968), ch.1. An important, unpublished, source is Thomas E. Shea and John H. Barton, "Verification of Arms Control on U.S. and Soviet Fissionable Materials," Report prepared for Electric Power Research Institute, June 29, 1984.

2. The following discussion benefitted from the report by Shea and Barton cited in note 1.

3. F. von Hippel and B.G. Levi, "Controlling Nuclear Weapons at the Source," in Tsipis, et al., *Arms Control Verification: The Technologies that Make it Possible*, note 1, p. 367.

4. *Ibid.*, p. 368.

5. At the time of writing, the U.S. Congress is reviewing a Department of Energy proposal to construct a special isotope separation facility in Idaho. Strong opposition has been registered in the non-proliferation community because, as this might purify plutonium derived from commercial nuclear fuel, this would breach a long-standing policy to maintain strict separation of civil and military applications of nuclear energy. Although Congress in 1982 passed the Hart-Simpson-Mitchell amendment to the Atomic Energy Act prohibiting the military use of commercial plutonium or enriched uranium, DOE officials have stated that commercial fuel is regarded as a potential source for an eventual special isotope separation facility. A congressional declaration of national emergency under s.108 of the Atomic Energy Act could waive the ban on the military use of commercial spent fuel.

6. See Shea and Barton, note 1.

7. Based on information provided by the Soviet Union to IAEA officials.

8. Treaty on the Non-Proliferation of Nuclear Weapons, A.III.1.

9. *Ibid.*

10. *Ibid*, A. VI. More precisely, A. VI calls on *all* parties to the Treaty to pursue such negotiations. But it is widely understood that the main burden falls on the weapon states. While not establishing a formal legal obligation, this is the only treaty provision establishing a *political* obligation to proceed in good faith with arms control negotiations, making it an exceptionally important provision.

11. Statute of the IAEA, A.II.

12. *Ibid*, A.III.A.5.

13. IAEA, GC(V)/INF/39.

14. While all NPT parties are obliged to require IAEA safeguards on any source or

special fissionable material, or equipment or material especially designed or prepared for processing, use or production of special fissionable material exported to any non-nuclear weapon state, they are not obliged to require that the receiving state place all its peaceful nuclear activities under international safeguards (so-called full-scope safeguards). Earlier, the parties to the Treaty debated whether the requirement to ensure that exported materials "shall be subject to the safeguards required by this article" (A.III.2) meant full-scope safeguards or not. Those favoring the narrower interpretation prevailed.

15. For an introduction to this issue see Tariq Rauf & Marie-France Desjardins, "Canada's Nuclear Submarine Program: A New Proliferation Concern," *Arms Control Today* (December, 1988) p. 13; Ben Sanders and John Simpson, *Nuclear Submarines and Non-Proliferation: Cause for Concern*, Occasional Paper Two, Centre for International Policy Studies, Department of Politics, University of Southampton (July, 1988).

16. For up to date information on IAEA safeguards coverage consult IAEA *Annual Report*.

17. Argentina, Brazil, Chile, Cuba, India, Israel, Pakistan, and South Africa.

18. Unlike the IAEA safeguards system that calls for timely detection, the U.S. Nuclear Non-Proliferation Act of 1978 speaks in terms of "timely warning" meaning in sufficient time to take diplomatic or other measures to prevent *consummation* of the intended diversion. For separated plutonium, this could be a matter of days, and defeating such a diversion before it is completed is not really plausible even under the best assumptions.

19. INFCIRC/153, para. 28.

20. The agreement is one among experts on the Special Advisory Group on Safeguards Implementation, and has been noted by the IAEA Board of Governors, but never formally approved. The figures in Table IA and IB represent the agreed conversion times and significant quantities and are used by the Safeguards Division in planning and implementing safeguards.

21. Implementation problems are discussed in Peter Tempus, *Problems and Progress in International Safeguards*, IAEA, International Symposium on Nuclear Material Safeguards, Vienna, Austria, 10-14 November 1986 (IAEA-SM-293/160); Lawrence Scheinman, *The International Atomic Energy Agency and World Nuclear Order*, (Washington: Resources for the Future, 1987).

22. For a discussion of safeguards methods and procedures see David Fischer and Paul Szasz, *Safeguarding The Atom: A Critical Appraisal*. A SIPRI Book, J. Goldblat (ed.) (London: Taylor and Francis, 1985).

23. A special situation exists for EURATOM (discussed in Part IV). The NPT permits states to negotiate safeguards agreements with the IAEA separately or with other states. EURATOM is effectively the state system of accounting and control and EURATOM states themselves do not have separate systems.

24. Final Declaration of 1985 NPT Review Conference, NPT/CONF. III/64/I (Article III and preambular paragraphs 4 and 5, paragraph 2).

25. For example, there has been steady improvement in the attainment of inspection goals over the past several years. Inspection procedures and safeguards approaches are continuously revaluated in the interest of improved efficiency and effectiveness. Further, new and improved safeguards equipment (e.g., non-destructive assay instrumentation) has become available and implementation of safeguards goals, willingness of facility operators to permit use of new equipment, inspector designation and the like. Each year has,

however, seen progress in ameliorating or resolving these issues.

26. IAEA statute, A.III.A.5.

27. U.S. Arms Control and Disarmament Agency, *Documents on Disarmament,* 1969, p. 159.

28. While leaving open whether new arms control measures would result in a new verification organization or in expanding IAEA responsibilities, Ambassador Timerbaev noted in a press briefing that "We have stressed on more than one occasion, including at the General Assembly of the United Nations, and here also in the International Atomic Energy Agency that the rich experience that the Agency has in terms of guarantees can be usefully implemented and applied to control many phases and processes of disarmament." (Press Briefing for UN Correspondents Association, 21 February 1986.)

29. The United States already has a largely separated civil and military fuel cycle and there is some indication that the Soviet Union, whose fuel cycles are more integrated, is contemplating moving in the same direction.

30. See note 24.

31. For a discussion of this issue see Adolf von Baeckmann, "IAEA Safeguards in Nuclear-Weapon States," *IAEA Bulletin,* v. 30, no. 1 (1988), p. 22.

32. See Table 1.

33. Von Hippel, Albright and Levi in their article cited in note 1 took 1 %/yr of the current U.S. stockpiles as a level of clandestine production that could be considered insignificant and also a realistic target for verification, to arrive at figures of 1000 kg Pu and 5000 kg HEU. Shea and Barton, in their study cited in the same note, focussed on the notion of a strategically significant violation and linked this to a specific major deployment, such as MX or SS-18, arbitrarily selecting 20% of a new major deployment as a threshold that verification should be designed to meet. The figures of 1600 kg Pu and 5000 kg HEU represent the amount of material needed for a 20% deployment.

34. This applies to the centrifuge enrichment plant at Almelo in the Netherlands and to any other such facilities built in the participating states. More precisely, the principle has been demonstrated, but application to some facilities such as URENCO may be difficult because of small diameter piping that is used. Some research and development is still required to ensure effective application of the agreed principle.

35. It probably would not be feasible to insist that no low-burnup fuel was discharged from a reactor since fuel develops defects and is removed and the first fuel discharged from on-load refueling reactors is low-burnup.

36. It should be recalled that before the U.S. Portsmouth centrifuge enrichment facility was cancelled, perimeter monitoring and input-output materials-balance accounting arrangements had been worked out. A comparable approach presumably could be devised for other enrichment facilities, preserving and protecting classified national security information.

37. The Treaty of Tlatelolco, which came into force in 1967, prohibits not only the testing, use, manufacture, production or acquisition of nuclear weapons, but also their receipt, storage, installation, deployment and any form of possession of nuclear weapons. The latter provisions distinguish it from the NPT that does not foreclose a nuclear weapon state that maintains ownership and control of nuclear weapons from deploying them on the territory of an allied non-nuclear weapon state party to the Treaty. A second regional treaty, the Treaty of Raratonga, established a nuclear weapon free-zone in the South Pacific. It entered into force in December, 1986. Although no final agreement has been

reached, negotiators of the proposed chemical weapons convention have given considerable attention to the IAEA safeguards system, drawing upon it institutionally, administratively and technically in an effort to achieve agreement on a credible and acceptable verification regime for chemical weapons.

38. The Israelis, for example, feel this way and one must wonder how the Israelis would have acted had the safeguards team for Iraq involved an Israeli national.

39. For a discussion of this problem see Fischer and Szasz, *Safeguarding the Atom*, cited in note 22, chap. 11.

40. That is to say EURATOM has to assure itself on the internal level that safeguarded materials are not diverted from their declared purposes and assure third parties that conditions for supply are being fulfilled. EURATOM entails a supranational relationship between the operator and the community at the regulatory, executive, and judicial levels, not at a contractual one as in the case of the IAEA.

41. For some detail on EURATOM, see *Safeguards in Europe*, IAEA, (April, 1985) IAEA/P1/A.12E 85-01123, prepared for the Agency by Peter Kelly a former British representative on the IAEA Board of Governors.

42. For a discussion of the technical parameters of verification by laser isotopic enrichment see U.S. Arms Control and Disarmament Agency, FY 1989 *Arms Control Impact Statements* (July, 1988), s.III.E--"Atomic Vapor Laser Isotopic Separation."

43. An alternative would be to consider using perimeter-portal controls at uranium mills to monitor production.

44. This issue is discussed by the Director General of IAEA, Hans Blix in *The World's Energy Needs and the Nuclear Power Option*, The David Rose Lectureship, Massachusetts Institute of Technology, October 23, 1989; and in Hans Blix, *Nuclear Power and the Environment*, Conference on Nuclear Power and the Changing Environment, British Nuclear Forum, (London) July 4, 1989. More generally see IAEA, *The IAEA's Contribution to Sustainable Development* a Report Prepared at the Request of the IAEA General Conference for Presentation to the UN General Assembly. (Vienna, May, 1989).

45. Improvements are discussed in V. Schuricht and J. Larrimore, "Safeguarding Nuclear Fuel Cycle Facilities"*IAEA Bulletin* v. 30 n.1 (1988).

46. For further discussion of these points consult Azkchangelskava, I.A., Etmakov, C.S. et al., *International Control System on Atomic Energy Peaceful Uses* (Enezgoizdat, 1986); and Babaer, N.S., Semenov, B.A. and Mezsesian, I.A., *International Atomic Agency* (Energoizdat, 1987); and Scheinman, Lawrence, *The International Atomic Energy and World Nuclear Order* (Resources for the Future, Washington D.C., 1987).

7

Verifying START

Steve Fetter (USA) & Stanislav N. Rodionov (USSR)

The recently signed treaty on intermediate-range nuclear forces (INF) has sanctified the "zero option." It has long been understood that it is easier to verify a complete ban on a weapon system than it is to verify a numerical limit. Under a complete prohibition, the sighting of a single banned weapon would constitute clear evidence of a violation. Moreover, a complete ban would eliminate training, testing, and repair activities that could serve as a cover for clandestine weapon deployments or could support a sudden breakout from a treaty.

Although a total ban may be easiest to verify, this is not realistic for many weapon systems. The rhetoric of Reykjavik aside, we will have to live with sizable numbers of several types of nuclear weapons for the foreseeable future. In past agreements, such as the SALT I Interim Agreement and the unratified SALT II Treaty, numerical limits were keyed to objects or practices that could be readily monitored with national technical means (NTM) of verification (e.g., photoreconnaissance and electronic-intelligence satellites). The deployment of new weapons, such as mobile missiles and cruise missiles, will be difficult to monitor using NTM, however. This paper explores various options for verifiably limiting the strategic nuclear arsenals of the superpowers in the context of the current Strategic Arms Reduction Talks (START).

The START proposal would limit the total number of strategic nuclear delivery vehicles (SNDVs)--ballistic missiles and bombers--to 1600. The total number of warhead "points" on these SNDVs would be limited to 6000. (Due to various counting rules to be described later, the actual number of deployed warheads would be substantially greater.) Of these 6000 warhead "points," a maximum of 4900 would be permitted on ballistic missiles.[1]

The Rationale for Verification

Verification is the process of determining the degree to which parties are complying with the provisions of an agreement. Three reasons are often given for verification: (a) to build confidence between parties by verifying treaty compliance, (b) to deter cheating by raising the costs and lowering the benefits of cheating, and (c) to detect militarily significant cheating early enough to protect national security. Each of these plays an important role in treaty verification.

Building confidence

The role of verification in building confidence is often emphasized by advocates of arms control, who see the arms race as caused at least partly by mutual misunderstanding and action-reaction dynamics. Thus, the verification process itself can reduce the apprehensions of both parties by dispelling residual suspicions of noncompliance and by showing ongoing support for the treaty regime. This effort should be cooperative, since parties would have strong incentives to prove that they were observing the terms of the treaty. To serve this purpose, verification systems must have very low false-alarm rates, or else they might have the effect of increasing, rather than decreasing, confidence.

Deterring cheating

Many analysts doubt that parties automatically comply with a treaty just because it is in their interest. Although an agreement as a whole may serve a nation's interests, certain treaty provisions may prove onerous or unattractive, or an unilateral military advantage could be obtained by clandestinely violating the agreement. To deter cheating, a verification system should make the costs of covert activities and the risks of discovery greater than the expected benefits of cheating. If, for example, missiles produced in a covert facility would cost ten times as much as missiles produced in the open, then a country might decide that the marginal military benefits were not worth the cost, just as they might forgo an expensive system in the absence of an agreement. It is important to note that if the penalties for being caught cheating are high enough, then a verification system must merely deny a country high confidence that it could cheat without discovery, rather than provide high confidence that cheating could be detected. The problem with applying these concepts to superpower arms control is that they depend on estimates of costs and benefits which are unknown to the other party.

Detecting cheating

Although some analysts feel that any cheating, no matter how trivial, is significant because it shows dishonesty, the majority feel that it is most important to be able to detect militarily significant cheating soon enough so that the nation's security would not be jeopardized. This is the most common standard against which verification systems have been measured in the past. But what level of cheating is militarily significant?

The answer to this question must take into account the nuclear strategies of both sides, or how and under what circumstances nuclear weapons would be used. If, for example, both superpowers view nuclear weapons solely as deterrents to nuclear attack, then the job of verification would be relatively easy--it would only have to be capable of detecting deployments that could threaten a second-strike retaliatory capability. This might require, for example, a capability to detect the clandestine deployment of thousands of ballistic missiles, as would be needed for successful barrage attacks against mobile missiles, bomber bases, and submarine patrol areas.

If either superpower relies on nuclear weapons for more than just simple deterrence, the job of verification becomes more demanding. For example, NATO currently depends on nuclear weapons to deter a Warsaw Pact invasion. If, on the eve of an invasion, the Soviet Union rolled out hundreds of secretly deployed mobile missiles, some fear that NATO's political will to resist would evaporate, along with the credibility of NATO's threat to escalate to the nuclear level. Another example is the counterforce or "window of vulnerability" scenario, in which one nation uses a fraction of its nuclear missiles to destroy most of the other's intercontinental ballistic missiles (ICBMs) and bombers, leaving the attacked nation with a choice between suicide and surrender. In both of these scenarios, a nation can "lose" even though it retains the ability to destroy the opposing society in a retaliatory blow. Although most such scenarios have serious logical flaws, detecting activities that might make them theoretically possible is a prudent basis for verification requirements.

Cooperative Verification

Verifying numerical limits on objects that cannot be adequately counted with NTM requires a considerable amount of cooperation between the monitored and the monitoring parties. Cooperation is not new--even SALT verification was cooperative in the sense that parties agreed not to interfere with NTM. The degree of cooperation required for START, however, is vastly greater. The verification system for START, which must build ambitiously on the foundation laid by the INF Treaty, would include data exchanges, provisions to enhance NTM, on-site inspections of various types, perimeter-portal monitoring, and perhaps a tagging system of some sort.[2]

Data exchange

The Soviet Union had long refused to disclose the number and location of its weapons. Under pressure from the U.S. Senate, the Soviet Union agreed to divulge the number of weapon systems for the SALT II Treaty. Data exchanges were expanded greatly by the INF Treaty, which required that the location of all weapon production, final assembly, storage, testing, and deployment facilities be declared, as well as the number of weapons at each declared site. The data base is to be updated each time a missile is transferred from one facility to another. The START agreement can be expected to require similar exchanges of data on all limited weapon systems.

On-site inspection

Until recently, the Soviet Union had been even more adamant in refusing to permit on-site inspections (OSIs), claiming that OSIs were unnecessary to verify compliance and that they would be used to gather intelligence. The Peaceful Nuclear Explosions Treaty proved, however, that the Soviet Union would permit OSIs if they were necessary to obtain an agreement that was in its interest. The INF Treaty, which permits several different types of OSIs, illustrates this dramatically.

Immediately after the signing of the INF Treaty and the exchange of data, "baseline" OSIs were conducted by both sides to verify the accuracy of the data exchange. In just three months, every declared site was visited--a rate of about two inspections per day. The elimination process is also subject to on-site inspection to verify that legitimate missiles are actually being destroyed. During this three-year process of elimination, up to 60 short-notice inspections can also be requested to verify the updated data base. The destruction of all missiles at a particular site is verified during "close-out" inspections. A START agreement, which would encompass many times more declared sites and missiles to be destroyed, would also require many more OSIs than INF.

Suspect sites

The INF Treaty lacks provisions for inspecting sites other than those that are declared. This was considered reasonable for INF, since the missiles were banned completely; any remaining stocks could not be tested and would therefore not be considered reliable. In a START treaty, however, legal missiles will remain to mask the possible presence of a covert stockpile of missiles. To deter the possession of secret stockpiles, it would be valuable to be able to request a short-notice inspection of any facility that is suspected of covert activities banned by the treaty. There are two problems, however: there are many highly sensitive facilities that neither side would want inspected, and such inspections are highly unlikely to turn up evidence of a violation.

The first concern is that suspect-site OSIs would be used at pretext for gaining entry to secret facilities. Some analysts claim that parties would be deterred from such behavior because they would fear reciprocal requests; others are not so sure. This problem could be ameliorated by allowing inspections of suspect sites only when evidence is first presented of a possible violation. The request would then be like the request for a search warrant in the United States, for which the police must present evidence of possible illegal activities before they are allowed to conduct a search. This would be unacceptable, however, because the nature of the evidence might reveal how it was obtained (thereby jeopardizing intelligence sources), and no impartial court is available to judge the worth of the evidence. Alternatively, one could set rules for sites that would be open to inspection. For example, only buildings that are large enough to hide treaty-limited items need be inspected. The United States and the Soviet Union could make a list of an agreed number of sites (perhaps 100) that would not be open to inspection. This list could be confidential; indeed, the list need not even be revealed to the other party unless an inspection was requested at one of these sites. One could, for example, deposit the lists in a safe that would require both parties to open. Critics could, of course, claim that all the cheating would occur in sites that are off-limits.

The second concern is that inspections of suspect sites would never turn up evidence of a violation, because inspections that could turn up such evidence would be refused, perhaps by claiming that the suspect site was a sensitive military facility. Although this is undoubtedly true, there are still two excellent reasons to do OSIs: the granting of inspection requests builds confidence by showing that cheating is not taking place (at least at those sites), and the possibility of having to refuse a request--which would be tantamount to a confession of guilt in the eyes of many--would help deter cheating.

Perimeter-portal monitoring

A "perimeter" is a fence around a facility that forces all traffic through a "portal," where the traffic is monitored for treaty-limited items. Perimeter-portal systems are usually associated with production monitoring, but they could be used to monitor the flow of treaty-limited items through any facility. Consider, for example, monitoring the production of missiles. When a missile stage leaves the production facility, the monitored party could declare it and the missile count would be incremented. If an object large enough to be a missile stage passes through the portal but the monitored party does not declare it, inspections would be permitted to ensure that the object was not a missile stage.

One of the stages of the SS-20 intermediate-range ballistic missile (IRBM) that was banned by the INF Treaty is similar to a stage of the SS-25 ICBM. Because of this similarity, a perimeter-portal monitoring system was established at Votkinsk, where SS-25s are assembled, to verify the absence of SS-20 assembly. For purposes of reciprocity, a similar system was also built in Magna, Utah, where the solid-rocket motors for the U.S. Pershing II had been produced. The perimeter-portal system at Votkinsk is of direct significance for START, since the rate of SS-25 assembly will inevitably be monitored.

Enhanced NTM

NTM are constantly becoming more powerful: photoreconnaissance satellites can resolve smaller objects, more wavelengths are being collected, and so on. The usefulness of NTM can be enhanced even more if the monitored party cooperates by making treaty-limited items and activities available for observation. SALT II did this in a modest way by banning deliberate interference with NTM (camouflage, encryption of certain data, etc.) and by specifying procedures to make the destruction or dismantling of certain items easily observable with NTM. The INF Treaty expanded on this by allowing each side a fixed number of opportunities to request that the other side openly display its missiles at a given site. START will undoubtedly adopt these procedures, and future treaties could extend these techniques still further. One could, for example, request that a particular attack submarine surface within a given amount of time to verify that it was not operating in agreed "keep-out" zones. Requests would be limited, and the response time would be long enough so that exact deployment patterns need not be revealed.

Tags and seals

Tags and seals are not used in the INF Treaty, but they might find several uses in a START agreement. A tag is an unreproducible label that is affixed to a treaty-limited item.[3] Tags need not be unremovable, but they must indicate that they have been moved or tampered with. Tags can be unique, like a fingerprint or serial number, or they can be identical, and simply indicate that a particular item is part of the allowed inventory. Tags have the virtue of converting a numerical limit into a ban on untagged items: the observation of a single untagged item would be *prima facie* evidence of a violation. Seals could be used with or without tags to indicate, for example, that a cruise-missile canister had not been opened.

Table 1. **U.S. and USSR strategic nuclear forces in 1989, using the proposed U.S. START counting rules**

Type of SNDV	Delivery Vehicle	Number of SNDVs	Number of Warheads
United States			
ICBMs		**1000**	**2450**
Silo-based	Minuteman II	450	450
	Minuteman III	500	1500
	MX (Peacekeeper)	50	500
SLBMs		**640**	**5632**
16 Poseidon	Poseidon C3	256	2560
12 Poseidon	Trident I C4	192	1536
8 Trident	Trident I C4	192	1536
Bombers		**360**	**1872**
ALCM-carriers	B-52G/H (98/70)	168	1680
Penetrating	B-52G/H (69/26)	95	95
	B-1B	97	97
	TOTAL	*2000*	*9954*
Soviet Union			
ICBMs		**1386**	**6412**
Silo-based	SS-11	420	420
	SS-13	60	60
	SS-17	138	552
	SS-18	308	3080
	SS-19	350	2100
Rail-mobile	SS-24	10	100
Road-mobile	SS-25	100	100
SLBMs		**934**	**3372**
16 Yankee I	SS-N-6	256	256
1 Yankee II	SS-N-17	12	12
22 Delta I & II	SS-N-8	280	280
14 Delta III	SS-N-18	224	1568
4 Delta IV	SS-N-23	64	256
5 Typhoon	SS-N-20	100	1000
Bombers		**175**	**805**
ALCM-carriers	Bear H	70	700
Penetrating	Bison/Bear	105	105
	TOTAL	*2495*	*10589*

Table 2. **Hypothetical U.S. and USSR strategic nuclear forces in the late-1990s after START reductions**

Type of SNDV	Delivery Vehicle	Number of SNDVs	Number of Warheads
United States			
ICBMs		**565**	**1445**
Silo-based	Minuteman III	215	645
Rail-mobile	MX (Peacekeeper)	50	500
Road-mobile	SICBM	300	300
SLBMs			
18 Trident	Trident I/II	432	3456
Bombers		**193**	**1057**
ALCM-carriers	B-52H	96	960
Penetrating	B-1B	97	97
	TOTAL	*1190*	*5958*
Land-attack SLCMs			
Nuclear	TLAM-N	758	758
Conventional	TLAM-C/D	2643	----
Soviet Union			
ICBMs		**714**	**3000**
Silo-based	SS-18	154	1540
Rail-mobile	SS-24	100	1000
Road-mobile	SS-25	460	460
SLBMs		**324**	**1896**
5 Typhoon	SS-N-20	100	1000
14 Delta IV	SS-N-23	224	896
Bombers		**200**	**1100**
ALCM-carriers	Bear	100	1000
Penetrating	Blackjack	100	100
	TOTAL	*1238*	*5996*
Land-attack SLCMs			
Nuclear	SS-N-21	?	?
	SS-N-24	?	?

Strategic Nuclear Delivery Vehicles

At present, there are three basic types of strategic nuclear delivery vehicles: ICBMs, submarine-launched ballistic missiles (SLBMs), and intercontinental bombers. In addition, long-range sea-launched cruise missiles (SLCMs) could be used for strategic attacks. Although START may impose some restrictions on SLCMs, they will not be counted as SNDVs under the agreement. Several other methods of weapon delivery--ballistic missiles based on airplanes or surface ships, ground-launched cruise missiles, and de-orbited satellites--are banned by existing treaties.

Table 1 gives the approximate strategic balance as of 1989, and Table 2 presents a hypothetical strategic force for the United States and the Soviet Union that would be consistent with START. The reductions required by START are substantial: a total of about 3,000 ballistic missiles and 80 submarines would have to be destroyed or dismantled. Even after these reductions, the superpowers would retain a total of nearly 2,500 SNDVs, a sizable fraction of which may have to be inspected periodically to verify warhead loadings. This section reviews the key verification problems for each type of delivery vehicle and evaluates possible solutions.

Intercontinental Ballistic Missiles

ICBMs are land-based ballistic missiles with ranges usually in excess of 10,000 km. ICBMs are big: even the smallest (the proposed U.S. Midgetman missile) is 12 meters long and weighs about 15 tons. The largest missiles, each of which is armed with up to ten multiple independently targetable reentry vehicles (MIRVs), are over 30 meters long and weigh more than 150 tons. ICBMs are produced and assembled in large, distinctive facilities that are easily identified by photoreconnaissance; it would be very difficult to produce ICBMs in a covert facility. Moreover, ICBM tests are readily detected and monitored by various satellite systems; full-scale clandestine testing is impossible.[4] ICBMs are now based in three ways: in silos, on roads, and on railroads.

Silo-based ICBMs

Until recently, all ICBMs were deployed in silos. Silos are heavily reinforced concrete missile launchers that are flush with the surface of the ground; they are easily spotted by photoreconnaissance. Since they take more than a year to build, the rapid deployment of a large number of additional silos is unlikely. Although silos are easily counted, they may not provide a good measure of the strength of the ICBM force for two reasons: (a) the number of ICBMs that could be launched in an attack may not be equal to the number of silos, and (b) the capabilities of silo-based missiles might be increased secretly.

Nondeployed missiles

The first worry is the possible existence of extra missiles that could be launched in an attack. The number of missiles produced is normally much larger than the number employed; the extra missiles are used for tests or for spares. For example, of the 220 MX missiles that have been built by the United States so far, only 50 are deployed; 21 are for tests, 99 are spares, and 50 are for a still-unauthorized later deployment.[5] Soviet practices are not well known; many analysts think that they build fewer spares than the United States because they replace their missiles more often.[6] The number and location of nondeployed missiles must be declared under START, but they will not be counted against the treaty limits.

The reuse of silos was a concern in the 1970s. SALT II banned the storage of extra missiles near silos and the testing of rapid reloading and firing of ICBMs. These provisions are verifiable using NTM. If significant quantities of extra ICBMs are stored away from silos, it still may be possible, in the first weeks of a crisis, to erect extra missiles on open ("soft") launch pads for use in a first strike. (Since the missiles would be very vulnerable, they could not be used for much else.)

One possibility is that declared stockpiles of nondeployed missiles could be launched from soft pads. This possibility is most troubling for solid-fuel, cold-launched, canisterized missiles such as the Soviet SS-24 and SS-25 and the U.S. MX and Midgetman missiles. If declared storage sites are monitored under the treaty, however, prompt warning of any attempt to use these missiles could be obtained. It would take at least several days--and probably several weeks--to assemble a significant force from such stocks. A remotely-monitored perimeter-portal system around each storage site would be more than sufficient to provide the necessary warning.

Another possibility is that nondeployed missiles at certain secret locations would not be declared under the treaty. An OSI might be requested at such a site, but only if the monitoring party knew where to look. It should be noted that ICBMs cannot simply be piled up in warehouse like a cord of wood - one small fire could blow the building and it contents sky high. But special storage for ICBMs would be recognizable; these sites undoubtedly have already been identified. Deceptive storage is possible, but size of ICBMs (especially Soviet silo-based ICBMs such as the SS-18) makes this difficult. Deceptive storage may also increase the chance of an accident that would reveal such cheating.

A third possibility is that new ICBMs could be produced covertly, although the production of ICBMs would be very difficult to hide, and full-scale flight-tests

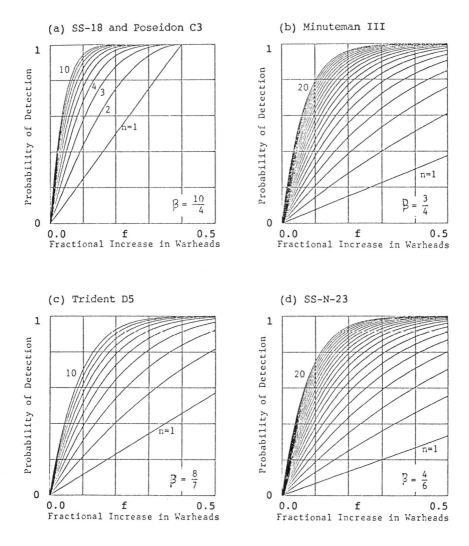

Figure 1. The probability of detecting a given increase in the number of missile warheads as a function of the number of OSIs.

would be essential to ensure their reliability. The test-flights of covertly produced missiles might be hidden among those of legal missiles; if this was sufficient cause for concern, legitimate missiles could be tagged and random on-site inspections of tests performed to verify that the missile stages to be tested had valid tags. The United States and the Soviet Union have already agreed to prenotification of ballistic missile launches;[7] it would only be necessary to send an inspection team at random intervals to observe a fraction of the tests. Observing 20 percent of ICBM launches would, for example, give a 90 percent probability of detecting at least one in a program of ten illegal test launches.[8] Even four such inspections per year would prevent high confidence in escaping detection.[9]

It is relatively easy to verify a reduction in the number of silo-based ICBMs. As mandated by the SALT II Treaty, the silos are simply destroyed by an explosion. And, as specified by the INF Treaty, the missiles can be crushed, burned, exploded, or destructively tested in the presence of inspectors. The magnitude of the elimination program dictated by START would probably require special environmental controls to limit pollution.

The problem of nondeployed missiles exists independent of START. In the absence of an agreement, the United States would face, as it has for decades, the possibility that substantial numbers of nondeployed missiles could be erected on soft pads during a crisis. It is not clear how the START reductions would make this possibility more ominous, for although the U.S. force would be smaller under START, the risk of such deployments presumably would be made smaller as well.

Fractionation limits

The second worry is that the number of warheads on a missile ("fractionation") could be increased surreptitiously, or that less-capable missiles could be exchanged for a more-capable variety. These problems were resolved in SALT II by counting each missile as having the maximum number of warheads that the missile had been tested with, and by assuming that each silo contained the most capable missile ever deployed in that type of silo.[10] If there were any doubts about the type of missile stored in a particular silo, these could be easily resolved by a few random OSIs or by enhanced NTM (pulling a randomly selected ICBM from its silo under the observation of photoreconnaissance satellites).

The counting rule for fractionation may present future problems for both sides. The SALT II and proposed START counting rules credit the Soviet SS-18 ICBM as having 10 warheads, although some U.S. analysts claim that it could be deployed with as many as 14 warheads without additional flight testing.[11] If the entire SS-18 force were so equipped, the number of SS-18 warheads would be increased by 40 percent, but the total number of ICBM warheads would be increased by only 20 percent.[12] The U.S. Minuteman III ICBM, which is credited with three warheads under the counting rules, has been tested with up to seven warheads.[13]

The probability of this relatively modest increase can be made negligible by permitting a few random OSIs to verify fractionation limits. For example, just one inspection per year would detect a 20 percent increase in SS-18 warheads 50 percent of the time (assuming that it would take about one year to upgrade the SS-18 force). Three inspections per year would detect such small increases with almost 90 percent confidence. Figure 1a shows the relationship between the fractional increase in the number of warheads, the number of inspections, and the probability of detection.[14]

In the simplest scheme, one could pick a missile at random, remove the shroud, and count the number warheads on the bus. Since the environment inside the shroud is carefully controlled to protect delicate equipment inside, some feel that the shroud could not be removed without seriously disrupting the normal operation of the missile force. Surely one or two such inspections could be permitted without too much trouble. Some analysts claim that sensitive information about the warheads, decoys, penetration aids, and the bus might be revealed during an OSI; if so, the bus could be draped with cloth and the warheads counted through the cloth. If one bus is stacked on top of another, however, the problem of determining the number on the bottom would remain.

If removing the shroud is too intrusive, portable radiation detectors probably could be used to count warheads by detecting radiations emitted by the fissile material in the warheads.[15] Such techniques could also be used to verify the number of warheads on stacked buses. Although it would be much more complicated, radiography could also be used to determine the number of warheads, or fissions could be induced in the fissile material with a neutron or photon source.

The problem of verifying fractionation could become particularly acute if the superpowers agree, in a subsequent agreement, to reduce the number of MIRVs on existing missiles to decrease first-strike incentives. "De-MIRVing" would be much cheaper than building new single-warhead missiles (at least in the short term). But even if de-MIRVing could be verified, a substantial reduction in the number of warheads on existing missiles would not be a good idea, because the warheads could be replaced rapidly. Richard Garwin has suggested using seals to ensure that dummy weights remain in unused bus positions, but these could, of course, be removed whenever the monitored party decides to abrogate the treaty.[16] The old MIRVed buses might be destroyed and replaced by smaller buses, but covert storage or production of the old bus would not be difficult. One would presumably want to flight-test samples of the covertly produced buses, and this would be nearly impossible without observation. Still, we believe that de-MIRVing is acceptable only when the maximum possible increase in the number of warheads is not militarily significant, as would be the case with the SS-18 force after START.

Mobile ICBMs

Mobile ICBMs are exactly like their silo-based counterparts, except that they are carted about the countryside by truck or train to avoid surprise attack. Because there is no fixed silo to use as a surrogate measure of the number of missiles, production and inventory controls are vital to mobile ICBM verification. The Soviet Union has produced both road- and rail-mobile ICBMs, and the United States has plans to build a road-mobile or a rail-mobile system (and perhaps both). Because mobile missiles are relatively new, few have been produced and intelligence about production rates should be good. The Soviet Union is proposing a limit of 800 mobile launchers and 1,600 mobile-missile warheads for START, but the United States is likely to insist on a lower number--probably 500 to 800 warheads.[17]

Road-mobile ICBMs

Since 1985, the Soviet Union has deployed about 100 road-mobile single-warhead SS-25 missiles. The United States is developing a similar road-mobile system, the Midgetman or small ICBM (SICBM), but deployment is uncertain. Road-mobile ICBMs are carried on large transporter-erector-launchers (TELs). Upon receiving warning of an attack, the TELs would disperse from their operating bases. To be effective (and not to cause undo alarm during a crisis), dispersal should be practiced regularly.

In the START talks, the United States and the Soviet Union have agreed on several aspects of mobile-missile verification. First, they have agreed that road-mobile ICBMs would normally be kept at relatively small main operating bases, each containing a limited number of missiles. The United States has suggested an area of 25 square kilometers for the operating bases; the Soviet Union has suggested 100 square kilometers. The SS-25 missiles are stored in garages with sliding roofs; the number of such shelters at an operating base would be limited to the number of missiles based there. A limited fraction of the missiles could be dispersed outside the main operating base at any given time. A larger fraction could leave the base for military exercises or training, but advance notification would be necessary and an OSI could be requested after the exercise. In addition, each party would have a limited number of requests for enhanced observation with NTM that the monitored party could not refuse. Under the INF Treaty, the United States can request that the Soviet Union remove the roofs from such garages at a given site for observation by photoreconnaissance satellites. The request must be fulfilled within six hours, and the missiles must remain exposed for twelve hours.

The verification of numerical limits on mobile ICBMs could be accomplished through controls similar to those developed for the SS-20 and Pershing II IRBMs in the INF Treaty. First, the initial inventory would be established with a data exchange that declared the location of all missiles and TELs. As mentioned above, the United States should be able to have higher confidence in the initial inventory of SS-25s than it had in the number of SS-20s, since the SS-25 is newer, fewer are deployed, and the assembly of SS-25s is being monitored at Votkinsk. Baseline OSIs at each declared facility would then verify the initial inventory. Thereafter, the monitoring party would be notified of all movements of missiles from one facility to another. Elimination of excess missiles and TELs could be accomplished through OSI or enhanced NTM.

Second, perimeter-portal systems would be installed at all solid-rocket-motor production plants. Production controls would be very effective for missiles not yet produced (such as the SICBM) or that have been produced in relatively small quantities (such as the SS-24 and SS-25). Since the covert production of ICBMs would be difficult, the problem is mainly one of verifying that all missiles produced before production controls began were declared.

The usefulness of any undeclared stockpiles could be limited by tagging all declared missiles. Short-notice OSIs could verify that declared facilities contained only legitimate, tagged missiles. Undeclared missiles would then have to rust away in storage or risk exposure. Tags might even reduce the need for on-site inspections. If, for example, perimeter-portal systems were installed at deployment areas, objects large enough and heavy enough to be a missile would have to have to display a valid tag to pass through the portal without further inspection. Large objects that are not missiles would be subject to further inspection using video cameras or radiography, all of which could be done remotely or with minimal on-site presence.

Rail-mobile ICBMs

The Soviet Union has just begun deployment of the SS-24 rail-mobile missile, which can carry up to ten warheads. The United States has plans to deploy 100 rail-mobile MX missiles, each with ten warheads. Verification of limits on these missiles could be accomplished in much the same way as limits on road-mobile ICBMs: missile trains would be restricted to main operating bases; the number of shelters per base would be no greater than the number of declared trains per base; shelters would not be longer than a normal train; a fraction of trains could leave the bases for exercises, training, and maintenance; there would be opportunities for enhanced monitoring with NTM; and perimeter-portal systems would be installed at missile production and assembly facilities.

Verification may be easier for rail-mobile missiles as compared with road-mobile missiles. The location of all rail lines is well known, and the missile-carrying cars can be distinguished from normal cars (they have twice as many wheels). Sensors, such as a light beam perpendicular to the track or seismic sensors, could be placed at choke-points in the rail network to detect missile cars.

Every time a missile car was detected, a valid tag would be expected on the missile car. The tag could be read without stopping the train by using an infrared transceiver. Storage, maintenance, and testing facilities could be monitored in the same way. To be useful, missile storage facilities would have to be located on a rail spur, which makes the detection of covert facilities relatively easy.

Submarine-Launched Ballistic Missiles

Numerical limits on SLBMs are relatively easy to monitor. The number of nuclear ballistic missile submarines (SSBNs) is well known, and the number of launch tubes on each SSBN is easily verified by photoreconnaissance. Moreover, unlike ICBMs, the number of SLBMs that could be used in a nuclear attack is limited to the number of launchers, since SSBN cannot be reloaded quickly.

The START limits will require both superpowers to reduce the number of SLBM warheads they deploy. There are three ways to do this: (a) reduce the number of submarines; (b) reduce the number of missiles per submarine; or (c) reduce the number of warheads per missile.

The first option--reducing the number of submarines--is the easiest to verify and would result in the greatest decrease in operating costs. It is the least desirable option for strategic stability, however, because the survivability of the SLBM force is roughly proportional to the number of SSBNs at sea. Under the START proposal, only 17 or 18 fully loaded Trident submarines could be deployed, of which 10 to 12 would be at sea at any one time--about half the number deployed and at sea today.[18] Although the U.S. Navy decided upon a force not much larger than this (20 Tridents) in the absence of arms control restrictions, going to an even smaller number of SSBNs in a future agreement would not be prudent.

The second option--reducing the number of missiles per submarine--could be easily verifiable. One could, for example, fill some fraction of the launch tubes with concrete and weld the covers shut under the observation of photoreconnaissance satellites or on-site observers. Better still (although much more costly), a section of the submarine containing several launch tubes could be removed, and the two halves of the submarine welded back together. In this way, the survivability of the SLBM force would not be reduced by arms limitations, and rapid breakout from treaty restrictions would be eliminated.

The third option--reducing the number of warheads per missile--is harder to verify, but it is cheaper than removing launch tubes and might be less destabilizing than reducing the number of SSBNs. A reduction in fractionation could be verified as discussed above for ICBMs, except that SLBMs would have to be lifted from their launch tubes and probably removed from their canisters for inspection. This should not be too objectionable, however, because the number of inspections would be limited.

Three SLBMs--the U.S. Poseidon C3, the U.S. Trident D5, and the Soviet SS-

N-23--are capable of carrying more warheads than the proposed START counting rules allow. The proposed START counting rules credit the Poseidon C3 with ten warheads, the Trident D5 with eight warheads, and the SS-N-23 with four warheads. Although the average loading of the Poseidon C3 is ten warheads, it has been tested with as many as 14 warheads; this is relatively unimportant for START, however, because Poseidon missiles and submarines are being replaced by Tridents. The Trident D5 was designed to carry up to 15 warheads,[19] but it has been tested with only eight so far; it is unclear whether it will ever be tested or deployed with more than eight warheads. The status of the SS-N-23 is somewhat of a mystery: although early reports credited the missile with ten warheads,[20] it will be counted as having only four under START.

Assume, for the sake of argument, that the SS-N-23 could be equipped with ten warheads without further flight testing. How many OSIs would be needed to provide assurance that a militarily significant increase in SLBM warheads had not secretly occurred? If all the SS-N-23s were outfitted with ten instead of four warheads, the increase in the START-constrained SLBM force would be less than 70 percent.[21] Five random OSIs would give 90 percent confidence that the total increase in the SLBM force was no more than 25 percent, and 50 percent confidence that the increase was no more than 10 percent (see Figure 1d). If future SS-N-23 deployments are smaller, or if less than ten warheads can actually be placed on a SS-N-23, then fewer inspections would be necessary for the same degree of confidence.

If all Trident D5 missiles are secretly equipped with 15 warheads, the total increase in the SLBM force would be 50 to 90 percent.[22] If the United States deploys Trident D5 only on the next 9 to 10 submarines built, a 25 percent increase in the SLBM force could be ruled out with 90 percent confidence by three random on-site inspections; the same number of inspections would rule out a 10 percent increase with almost 50 percent confidence.

One should note that if missiles are not accurate enough to destroy hardened targets, the degree of fractionation is not militarily significant. No currently deployed SLBM has such accuracy; SLBMs are assigned to the destruction of soft targets, such as cities or bomber bases. The area that can be destroyed by a warhead is proportional to its equivalent megatonnage (the megatonnage raised to the two-thirds power). For a given throwweight, the equivalent megatonnage of a missile is roughly independent of fractionation. For example, the Trident D5 is said to be capable of carrying eight 475-kt warheads or fifteen 100-kt warheads. Although the total throwweight is approximately the same in both cases, the combined destructive potential of the fifteen smaller warheads is less than that of the eight larger warheads. The destructiveness of a missile can only be increased by increasing the throwweight, which decreases the range of the missile.

In the absence of accurate SLCMs, the verification of fractionation limits would probably be unnecessary. The next generation of SLBMs - the Trident D5 and possibly the SS-N-23 - are, however, attaining the accuracy needed for attacks on hardened targets. It is unfortunate that the missiles for which fractionation is important are precisely those for which there is uncertainty. Unless intelligence analysts can convince themselves that the Trident D5 and SS-N-23 cannot accommodate more warheads than the counting rules allow without additional testing, then some OSI is probably necessary, though certainly no more than three to five inspections (0.1 to 0.3 percent of the total SLBM force) per year.

Strategic Bombers

Like ICBM silos and SSBNs, strategic bombers are fairly easy to count with photoreconnaissance satellites; the problem is determining their capabilities. There are five main problems in bomber verification: (a) distinguishing between nuclear-capable and conventional bombers; (b) distinguishing between strategic and tactical nuclear-capable bombers; (c) distinguishing between strategic bombers equipped with air-launched cruise missiles (ALCMs) and those that are not; (d) counting the number of ALCMs on each ALCM-equipped bomber, and (e) distinguishing between nuclear and conventional ALCMs.

Nuclear vs. conventional

To comply with the START limits on strategic bombers, the United States would prefer to assign older strategic bombers to conventional roles rather than destroy them. The Soviet Union has proposed deploying such conventionally armed strategic bombers at certain airfields where nuclear weapon storage would be banned; all strategic bombers at other airfields would be considered nuclear-capable. If for some reason this proves unacceptable, perhaps random on-site inspections could confirm that conventional strategic bombers are not nuclear-capable (e.g., the fire-control system would be different in a nuclear-capable bomber). Without such OSIs, it might be feared that these bombers could be loaded with nuclear weapons during a crisis.

Strategic vs. tactical

The distinction between strategic and tactical is usually based on the range of the aircraft. Strategic bombers typically have an unrefueled combat radius of more than 7,000 km. With in-flight refueling, however, tactical bombers could be used for strategic attacks. In the SALT II talks, the United States claimed that the Soviet Backfire bomber, which has an unrefueled combat radius of 4,000 km, should be counted as a strategic system because it could reach the United States with in-flight refueling. The Soviet Union subsequently agreed not to deploy the bomber in a strategic mode and to limit its rate of production, but this did not satisfy critics in the U.S. Senate. Even without refueling, tactical bombers could be used for strategic attack if they were equipped with long-range ALCMs. The best solution to this problem is to ban the testing and deployment of ALCMs on all tactical aircraft.

ALCM-carrier vs. penetrating bomber

Under the START proposal, bombers equipped to carry ALCMs will be counted differently from those carrying only bombs and short-range attack missiles (SRAMs). But how does one distinguish between the bombers that carry ALCMs and those that do not? SALT II resolved this question by requiring ALCM-carriers to have functionally related observable differences from non-ALCM carriers. This worked well for the B-52 bombers, which were modified to carry ALCMs under their wings. It does not work, however, for bombers that carry ALCMs internally--there is no functionally related observable difference between a B-1B bomber carrying ALCMs internally and a B-1B carrying only bombs and SRAMs. In fact, the B-1B is equipped with a rotary launcher that can hold any combination of ALCMs, bombs, and SRAMs.

The most verifiable solution to this problem is simply to limit each type of bomber to an ALCM or non-ALCM role. The United States, for example, could use nuclear-capable B-52s only as ALCM carriers and B-1Bs (and later B-2s) only as penetrating bombers; the Soviet Union could use Bear-H as an ALCM carrier and Blackjack as a penetrating bomber. If this limits the flexibility of the strategic bomber forces too much, one could resort to random short-notice on-site inspections to verify that particular B-52 or Bear-H bombers are not equipped to carry ALCMs.

Number of ALCMs per bomber

Verification of the number of ALCMs on each bomber is best accomplished through counting rules, just as the fractionation of ballistic missiles is limited with counting rules. In the START talks, the United States has proposed counting each bomber as having ten ALCMs. The Soviet Union, on the other hand, would like to count each bomber as having the maximum number of ALCMs for which it is equipped (eight for Bear H, 12 for B-52, and 24 for B-1B).[23] Although the Soviet approach seems more logical, a B-1B is not 2.4 times more potent or threatening than a SS-18 or MX missile. Moreover, the average ALCM loadings would likely be substantially less than the maximum.

If a counting rule of less than the maximum number is unacceptable without verification, short-notice OSIs could be used to verify actual ALCM loadings.

Only a few inspections per year would be necessary. As with de-MIRVing, however, breakout from such constraints would be quick and simple. A limit on ALCMs that is substantially less than the maximum loading might be supplemented with production and inventory controls on the ALCMs themselves, but this is unlikely to be worth the trouble since the clandestine production, storage, and testing of ALCMs could be difficult to detect.

Nuclear vs. conventional ALCMs

There are now no ALCMs armed with conventional warheads. The United States wants to keep this possibility open, and does not want START to limit conventionally armed ALCMs. To solve the verification problems this would create, the United States and the Soviet Union have agreed that all currently deployed ALCMs would be considered nuclear, that any new conventionally armed ALCMs would be distinguishable from nuclear-armed ALCMs, and that all dual-capable ALCMs could be carried only by strategic nuclear bombers. If all of these conditions can be met (and it is not clear that they can be), then there should be few verification problems.

Sea-Launched Cruise Missiles

Long-range land-attack nuclear SLCMs have only been deployed since 1984. At that time, the United States introduced the Tomahawk, a subsonic missile less than 6 meters long and half a meter in diameter and weighing only about 1,500 kilograms. The Tomahawk can be configured as an anti-ship missile (TASM) or as a land-attack missile (TLAM). The land-attack missile is dual capable; that is, it can be armed with either a nuclear or a conventional warhead. The United States plans to deploy about 600 TASMs and 3,300 TLAMs by 1993; about 760 of the TLAMs will be armed with nuclear warheads.[24] In all, nearly 4,000 Tomahawks will be deployed on some 200 surface ships and attack submarines.

The Soviet Union deployed its first long-range land-attack nuclear SLCM, the SS-N-21, in 1988. The SS-N-21 is similar to the Tomahawk, although it is not believed to have a conventionally armed variant. It appears that the deployment of the SS-N-21 will be limited to attack submarines; only about 60 have been deployed so far. The Soviet Union has also tested a larger, supersonic SLCM, the SS-NX-24, but claims that it has no plans to deploy the missile.

There are numerous problems with SLCM verification: (a) the as-yet undetermined structure of an agreement limiting SLCMs; (b) distinguishing long-range from short-range missiles; (c) distinguishing nuclear from conventionally armed versions; (d) the difficulty of production controls and the problem of rapid breakout; and (e) the incompatibility of SLCM controls with the U.S. Navy's policy of neither confirming nor denying the presence of nuclear weapons on naval vessels.

What to limit?

Although the United States and the Soviet Union have agreed not to include SLCMs as strategic nuclear delivery vehicles in START, they have so far not agreed about how SLCMs should be limited, if at all. The United States has suggested that both sides simply make nonbinding declarations of their plans for the deployment of long-range nuclear SLCMs. The Soviet Union wants a formal limitation as part of a START treaty. The Soviet Union has suggested limits of 400 long-range nuclear SLCMs and 600 long-range conventional SLCMs; it has also indicated that an overall limit of 1,000 missiles with freedom to mix between nuclear and conventional versions would be acceptable. The United States has adamantly refused any restriction on conventionally armed SLCMs. The most likely compromise is a limit on long-range nuclear SLCMs only, with the limit set at 400 to 800 missiles. Perhaps 600 nuclear SLCMs--10 percent of the START warhead limit--would be a satisfactory compromise.

Long-range vs. short-range SLCMs

The distinction between long-range and short-range SLCMs is meant to distinguish land-attack missiles, which might be used in strategic attacks, from anti-ship missiles, which would not. Current anti-ship SLCMs have ranges of less than 600 kilometers; therefore, the Soviet Union has proposed limiting only those SLCMs with ranges greater than this. This presents problems, however, because the range of some anti-ship weapons could be increased substantially. Because nuclear warheads are lighter and smaller than conventional warheads, and because nuclear-armed versions require smaller and less-accurate guidance systems, more fuel can be carried on a nuclear SLCM. The nuclear TLAM, for example, has a range five times greater than that of the TASM, even though their airframes are identical. Moreover, the range of several Soviet SLCMs could be increased by 50 percent simply by using a more-efficient turbofan engine rather than the cheaper turbojet now in use.[25]

Since cruise missile tests are difficult to monitor using NTM, cooperative measures to enhance verification, such as the advance announcement of the time and place of all tests, should be included in an agreement. This would facilitate the verification of range limitations. Limits could be extended to include all nuclear SLCMs regardless of range, but this would only shift the difficulty from verifying range to distinguishing conventional SLCMs from nuclear SLCMs.

Nuclear vs. conventional SLCMs

As mentioned above, the U.S. land-attack SLCMs are dual capable. Observed from the outside, the conventional version is indistinguishable from the nuclear version. Although the Soviet SS-N-21 and SS-NX-24 are believed to carry only nuclear weapons, the medium-range anti-ship SLCMs mentioned above are dual-capable. If an agreement limits the total number of SLCMs, with freedom to mix between conventional and nuclear versions, then dual capability poses no verification problem. Such an agreement, to which the Soviet Union has indicated it would be amenable, could be verified by a combination of data exchanges, perimeter-portal monitoring of production and loading, tagging, and on-site inspection to verify that the total number of long-range SLCMs was within the limit.

If, as the Soviets prefer, there is a sublimit on the number of nuclear SLCMs, or if, as the Americans prefer, there is no limit on conventional SLCMs, then there will have to be some means of distinguishing nuclear from conventionally armed missiles. After final assembly, those SLCMs declared to be conventionally armed could be radiographed through the canister to ensure that they were not nuclear armed or nuclear capable. All canisters could be tagged before leaving the final assembly facility, and those containing conventionally armed SLCMs would be sealed with a tamper-revealing seal. The seal would not interfere with the operation of the missile in any way--it would only indicate that a conventional missile had not been swapped for or converted into a nuclear version.

A possible loophole in this scheme is that conventional SLCMs might be quickly converted into nuclear SLCMs. The U.S. Navy has stated that this is not possible with the Tomahawk - the missile must be returned to the factory for all maintenance. The Soviet Union may accept this at face value. The ease with which the Soviet dual-capable SLCMs can be converted is unknown. Unless major structural changes must be made, it is hard to see why conversion would be impossible at sea. It might be possible to satisfy the monitoring party that conversion is difficult by releasing certain design information. Alternatively, one could divide the warhead compartment of conventional SLCMs with baffles welded to the airframe, with the spacing between the baffles too small to accommodate a nuclear warhead but sufficient to contain conventional submunitions. Some missions may, however, require a unitary high explosive.

Rapid breakout

Even under the best controls, rapid breakout from treaty limitations would be possible. As mentioned above, secret cruise missile production facilities and secret tests would be difficult to detect. Cruise missiles are produced and assembled in rather undistinctive buildings. Covert storage and testing would be much easier for cruise than for ballistic missiles. Stockpiles of secretly produced nuclear SLCMs could be stockpiled for quick delivery to aircraft carriers, and helicopters could distribute the missiles to ships and submarines.

No-confirm-no-deny

SLCM verification would be greatly simplified if certain ships could be declared SLCM-free, or at least declared free of nuclear SLCMs or long-range nuclear SLCMs. But any revelation that nuclear SLCMs are or are not on certain ships, whether through declarations, data exchanges, or on-site inspections, would be incompatible with the neither-confirm-nor-deny (NCND) policy of the U.S. Navy. The NCND policy, which states that the United States will neither confirm nor deny the presence of nuclear weapons on U.S. ships, was promulgated to facilitate the use of ports in countries that would object to the presence of nuclear weapons. The Soviet Union does not have a comparable problem. This problem could be minimized by keeping the data exchanges and the results of OSIs confidential.

Possible solutions to the SLCM problem

There are several ways to frame the SLCM "problem." The most simplistic is to view it solely as an impediment to achieving a START agreement. To solve the SLCM problem in this narrowest sense--that is, to remove it as an obstacle to START--one must know why the Soviet Union wants restrictions on SLCMs. Alternatively, one can understand the SLCM problem from a more theoretical point of view: do SLCMs enhance or detract from crisis stability and arms race stability? What kind of SLCM arms control regime would improve stability?

The United States maintains that the characteristics of nuclear land-attack SLCMs make them ill-suited for preemptive attack. They have limited ranges (about 2,500 kilometers) and they are slow (about 850 kilometers per hour). Only those SLCM-equipped ships or submarines that were within 2,000 kilometers of Soviet borders could participate in an attack. This distance is greatly reduced for attacks on targets in the interior of the Soviet Union. Flying at top speed, SLCMs would take nearly three hours to reach their targets.

The planned number of U.S. nuclear SLCMs is not large (760), and would not represent a substantial increase in U.S. forces even after the START reductions. Moreover, the United States plans to distribute its nuclear SLCMs more-or-less uniformly among nearly 200 surface ships and attack submarines: an average of less than four SLCMs per platform. It would be extremely difficult to coordinate an attack using such a large number of dispersed platforms, half of which (the attack submarines) are difficult to communicate with. Thus, SLCMs appear to be ideally suited for tactical missions and retaliation, not preemptive strategic attack.

This is why many U.S. strategists view them as a stabilizing contribution to deterrence.[26]

Most Soviet analysts do not agree that SLCMs are stabilizing. While they acknowledge that current SLCMs are slow, dispersed, and not excessively numerous, future versions may travel at much higher speeds (the United States is developing a supersonic cruise missile) and, without a suitable arms control agreement, SLCMs may become much more numerous in the future. In addition, these analysts claim that the small size of SLCMs makes them ideal for sneak attacks. SLCM launches are very difficult to detect, as are SLCMs in flight. A small SLCM attack might occur without warning, disrupting command and control centers and delaying retaliation long enough to permit the near-complete destruction of ICBMs and bombers. This scenario is a bit far-fetched, since SSBNs at sea would survive and could retaliate. It is also risky, since detection of the slow-flying SLCM attack would disastrously upset the strategy. Still, the option might look more promising than the alternatives to a leader deep in crisis.

The primary purpose of arms control is to decrease the incentives of striking first, and thereby decrease the probability that a crisis would escalate into nuclear war. SLCMs make a first-strike both more and less attractive: more attractive because they could be used for a precision sneak attack; less attractive because they constitute a slow-flying, survivable nuclear deterrent. It would be nice if a SLCM force could be configured so that the latter capabilities could be attained without the former, but this is impossible, since a surprise attack would require only dozens of nuclear SLCMs. If we are worried about the possibility of a surprise attack, then a total ban on nuclear SLCMs is required. There are good reasons for the United States to favor a ban, since it has a much greater proportion of coastal targets that would be vulnerable to SLCM attack than the Soviet Union. Compared to the alternatives, a ban on nuclear SLCMs would be relatively easy to verify. Since the superpowers already have more than enough survivable retaliatory weapons, a ban probably enhances stability, and is the best solution to the SLCM problem in the broadest sense. But since the United States appears committed to deploy nuclear SLCMs, and since the Soviet Union has already indicated that a limit on nuclear SLCMs would be acceptable, it is not a solution to the SLCM problem in the narrow sense.

The most likely structure of a SLCM agreement is a limit of 400 to 800 nuclear SLCMs, with no limit on the number of conventional SLCMs. How would this be verified? As with ballistic missiles, all SLCM production, storage, maintenance, testing, and deployment areas would be declared in an initial data exchange. Baseline OSIs would establish the initial inventory, and perimeter-portal monitoring at assembly facilities would keep track of the production rate and tag missiles as they exit. A perimeter-portal system would also be installed at the facility where nuclear warheads are mated to the airframes and the completed, ready-to-fire missile is placed in a canister. As missiles exit the facility, canisters are tagged. All missiles declared to be non-nuclear are radiographed to ensure they do not contain nuclear weapons and that they are not nuclear capable, after which their canisters are sealed with a tamper-revealing seal. Loading SLCMs on ships could be confined to a limited number of declared ports; loading and unloading SLCMs anywhere else would be banned. A perimeter-portal system could then be installed at designated ports to ensure that only legal SLCMs are being loaded and unloaded. A few random on-board inspections each year could ensure that only legal SLCMs are deployed. The location and time of all cruise missile tests would be declared; on-site observers at a few randomly selected tests could verify that only legal missiles were being tested, and that range limitations on shorter-range missiles were being observed.

Although very extensive, these verification arrangements are not airtight. Cruise missiles could be produced secretly and flown out to ships during a crisis. Future long-range conventional cruise missiles could be designed to be easily converted at sea to carry nuclear warheads. At this juncture, however, these possibilities are remote. In the case of the Soviet Union, at least, it is simply not credible to assume that a country that has not produced more than a few SLCMs in the open could manufacture, test, and ready for deployment large numbers of these missiles in secret. Indeed, this possibility seems so remote that the verification scheme described above could be relaxed considerably without losing confidence in the ability of the U.S. to verify Soviet compliance.

Notes

1. For a review of START, see Robert Einhorn, "Strategic Arms Reduction Talks: The Emerging START Agreement," *Survival*, July/August 1988, pp. 387-401.

2. For a review of INF verification procedures and their relation to START verification, see Jeremy K. Leggett and Patricia M. Lewis, "Verifying a START Agreement: Impact of INF Precedents," *Survival*, July/August 1988, pp. 409-428.

3. For an in-depth discussion of tags, see Steve Fetter and Thomas Garwin, "Using Tags to Monitor Numerical Limits in Arms Control Agreements," in Barry M. Blechman, ed., *Technology and the Limitation of International Conflict* (Washington, DC: The Johns Hopkins Foreign Policy Institute, 1989), pp. 33-54.

4. Clandestine static firings are possible, and could be used to assess the reliability of aging stocks of clandestine missiles. Static firings alone would *not* be sufficient to assess the reliability of clandestinely produced missiles. Static firing would be useful only when full-scale testing of allowed stocks of the same missile is possible.

5. U.S. Congress. House Committee on Armed Services. *Breakout, Verification, and Force Structure: Dealing with the Full Implications of START*. 100th Congress, 2nd session, 24 May 1988, p. 36.

6. The number of spare missiles is already a source of contention. The U.S. Defense Intelligence Agency (DIA) believes that the Soviet Union under-reported the number of nondeployed SS-20s under the INF Treaty; the CIA disagrees. The Soviet Union reported 405 deployed and 245 nondeployed missiles; DIA believes that the numbers of nondeployed and deployed missiles were about equal. *Ibid.*, p. 3.

7. Agreement Between the United States of America and the Union of Soviet Socialist Republics on Notifications of Launches of Intercontinental Ballistic Missiles and Submarine-Launched Ballistic Missiles, reprinted in *Arms Control Today*, July/August 1988, pp. 20-21.

8. The probability of detecting at least one of n illegal tests is equal to one minus the probability of all n tests escaping detection. The probability of all n escaping detection is equal to $(1 - p)^n$, where p is the probability of detection per test. In the example given in the text, $1 - (1 - 0.2)^{10} = 0.89$.

9. The United States conducts about 30 to 40 test launches per year; the Soviet Union may test twice as many. Inspecting 4 of 80 tests (5 percent) would give a 40 percent chance of detecting at least one in a program of ten tests, a 23 percent chance of detecting at least one of five tests, and a 10 percent chance of detecting at least one of two tests.

10. The latter rule presented problems for the U.S. SALT II delegation, because Minuteman II missiles are deployed in silos that are identical to those in which the Minuteman III (and now, the MX) is deployed. In accepting the rule but agreeing not to apply it to the Minuteman II, the Soviets acknowledged the "informational asymmetry" between the United States and the Soviet Union. See Strobe Talbott, *Endgame: The Inside Story of SALT II* (New York: Harper and Row, 1979), pp. 114-115.

11. The SS-18 has been tested with a maximum of 10 warheads, but one test included the simulated release of two additional warheads. The geometry of the bus suggests 14 warhead positions, and tests already performed with various combinations of 10 or fewer warheads probably would be sufficiently to ensure reliability with a full load of 14 warheads.

12. Assuming the Soviet Union maintains 154 SS-18s and 3,000 to 3,300 ICBM warheads.

13. Article IV of the SALT II Treaty (Part 10, First Agreed Statement) states the Minuteman III was tested with a maximum of seven reentry vehicles, although in a following Common Understanding it is stated that the United States has never deployed Minuteman with more than three warheads. The tests occurred in 1975 under the Air Force "Pave Pepper" program.

14. This relationship can be represented by the equation $p = 1 - (1 - \beta\ f)^n$, where n is the number of inspections, p is the probability of detecting a violation, f is the fractional increase in warheads, and ß is the number of permitted warheads divided by the maximum number of extra warheads. For the SS-18 example in the text, $n = 3$, $f = 0.2$, and $\beta = 10/(14 - 10) = 2.5$, which gives $p = 0.88$.

15. See Steve Fetter, Robert Mozley, O.F. Prilutskii, S. Rodionov, R.Z. Sagdeev, and Marvin Miller, "Detecting Nuclear Warheads" *Science and Global Security*, Vol. 1, No. 3-4 (in press).

16. Richard Garwin, "Tags and Seals for Verification," *The Council for Arms Control Bulletin*, No. 40 (October 1988), p. 4.

17. Both the proposed rail-mobile MX and road-mobile SICBM systems would consist of 500 warheads. The latest U.S. Air Force proposal is to convert the 50 silo-based MX to rail-mobile mode and to build 300 road-mobile SICBM. George C. Wilson, "Air Force Acts to Break ICBM Impasse," *The Washington Post*, 24 March 1989, p. A1, A6.

18. Each Trident submarine carries 24 missiles, and each missile carries 8 warheads, for a total of 192 warheads per submarine. Thus, 17 Tridents would carry 3,264 warheads. When the Soviet Union proposed a sublimit of 3,300 SLBM warheads (to match the

corresponding limit on ICBMs), the United States objected, but claimed that it would in any case not deploy more than 3,300 SLBM warheads. Some analysts assume a force of 18 Tridents under START; indeed, the construction of the 18th Trident has already been authorized by Congress.

19. Richard Halloran, "Navy Trident 2 Missile Explodes In Its First Underwater Test Firing," *The New York Times*, 22 March 1989, p. 1.

20. *Soviet Military Power* (Washington, DC: Department of Defense, 1987), p. 33.

21. This assumes a total Soviet SLBM force of 1600 to 1900 warheads under START, and that the Soviet Union builds no more Typhoon submarines. The five Typhoons already built will count as 200 warheads each under START, leaving at most 600 to 900 warheads for 144 to 224 SS-N-23 SLBMs on 9 to 14 Delta IV submarines. Six extra warheads on each SS-N-23 would then amount to 864 to 1,344 extra warheads, or 54 to 71 percent of the total allowed force. The Soviet Union is unlikely to allocate more than 1900 warheads to their submarine force, since this would require even larger cuts in the ICBM force. If the Soviet Union builds more Typhoons, the SS-N-23 problem would become less significant.

22. The percentage depends on whether the eight existing Trident submarines equipped with Trident C4 missiles are backfitted with Trident D5 missiles.

23. *The Military Balance: 1988-1989* (London: International Institute for Strategic Studies, 1988), p. 211.

24. Valerie Thomas, "Verification of Limits on Long-range Nuclear SLCMs," *Science and Global Security*, Vol. 1, No. 1-2 (in press).

25. The Soviet Union has only 280 turbojet-powered SLCMs with ranges of 550 km (SS-N-12 and SS-N-19).

26. For examples of this view, see Linton Brooks, "Nuclear SLCMs Add to Deterrence and Security," and Henry C. Mustin, "The Sea-Launched Cruise Missile: More Than a Bargaining Chip," *International Security*, Vol. 13, No. 3 (Winter 1988/89), pp. 169-174, 184-190.

8

Verification and Chemical-Warfare Weapons

*Karlheinz Lohs (GDR), Julian P. Perry-Robinson (UK) &
Nikita P. Smidovich (USSR)*

Introduction

Resort to chemical warfare (CW) is contrary to international treaty and custom. Widespread belief that this ancient law needs strengthening is sustaining a multilateral negotiating effort to extend the prohibition into a verified total ban on the actual weapons of chemical warfare. Expressions of support for the enterprise have issued from the highest levels of government in all the major countries; and many ingenious people are working on the practical problems involved. Among today's international arms issues, it looks like the one that is nearest to resolution.

On closer inspection, however, the grounds for optimism about CW disarmament can appear rather less solid. Intergovernmental talks on the subject have been proceeding almost continuously since the 1960s. States joining the 1972 Biological Weapons Convention bound themselves, by Article IX of that treaty, to "continue negotiations in good faith" for counterpart agreement on CW weapons. In 1984, after more than a decade of exploratory discussion and preparatory study at what is now the 40-nation Conference on Disarmament in Geneva, that negotiation commenced. But not one iota of formal international constraint on CW armament has resulted from all those years of effort. In fact at least one and possibly several more of the negotiating, and therefore ostensibly supportive, governments are actively arming themselves with the weapons. And no possessor government has chosen to declare a unilateral renunciation of its existing CW weapons in order to promote the treaty (as the United States did for biological weapons). One message discernible in this state of affairs unfortunately is that the option of CW armament yields a better quality of security than could an international régime of CW disarmament.

Yet that is patently a false message. At the national if not the international level, the negotiations have in some countries induced constraint on CW armament. Moreover, if one stands back and takes a rather longer view of CW, the pessimistic appearances fade still further. One can see in the history of CW a pattern of action and reaction, of advance and constraint, from which, in the light of recent developments, it seems not at all improbable that strengthened international law will soon crystallize. If, however, the product is to comprise the global, comprehensive and properly verified Chemical Weapons Convention which the negotiators are currently seeking, not a little political capital must be invested by governments in building domestic consensus. It is in the field of verification, especially in the negotiation of measures for monitoring civil chemical industry, that the requisite political accommodations have been hard to achieve.

Some historical considerations

The international law on CW reflects a most ancient taboo against fighting with poison. Among the earlier of its latter-day codifications are the declarations which the major powers of the time adopted at Brussels in 1874 and The Hague in 1899. Most probably those codifications stemmed from a shared sense of what the newly emergent technology of industrial chemistry might bring to future battlefields if the taboo were not expressly reinforced. State papers from the early years of the present century can be found in national archives which demonstrate that the declarations were an active constraint upon toxic-weapons projects which were then starting to take shape.[1] Neither the declarations, however, nor the further codifications contained in the 1899 and 1907 Hague Conventions, proved to be sufficient once the Great War of 1914-18 had started its escalation. Industrial chemistry afforded the means for toxic warfare on a large scale; more important, through its provision in great quantity of the high-explosive and propellent chemicals that hugely increased the firepower of forces in the field, industrial chemistry induced precisely those battlefield conditions that favoured CW. For protection against high-explosive artillery and machine guns, vast trench systems spread across the combat zones; but troops immobilized within them were vulnerable to weapons that laid down airborne clouds of toxic vapor, aerosol or spray-- CW weapons of a type made feasible by the new technology. Many hundreds of thousands fell victim. Reaction against this form of killing was especially vigorous after the war, and in the Geneva Protocol of 1925 (as, too, in the peace treaties) governments negotiated a new reinforcement of the taboo.

That reaction at the international level coincided with certain technological changes which also operated to constrain CW armament. Protection good enough to negate the mass-destructiveness of CW weapons had been starting to appear even within days of the first chlorine clouds of the war; and the battlefield conditions which had so favored CW were becoming outmoded by the mechanization of forces now evident in the proliferation of tanks and combat aircraft. Such military usefulness as remained to CW weapons seemed likely to have value only against an enemy denied those particular benefits of technology. The subsequent history of CW has borne out that assessment, for recurrences of CW have been both rare and confined to the Third World.

At the time of World War II, technical changes within the field of CW itself, exemplified by the emergence of the nerve gases and powerful new herbicides, were beginning to promise increased military utility. But the requisite development work was too slow and generally too little encouraged for the changes to be assimilated into military forces and doctrine, and CW remained unused in the campaigns of the war. Some commentators today attribute the non-use to mutual like-with-like CW deterrence, pointing for their evidence to the stockpiles of CW weapons accumulated by many of the belligerents. But this is shallow commentary, for it is clear from the accessible state papers of the time that, at the uppermost levels of government, all belligerents were content to be bound by the international ban on use: on all recorded occasions when initiatory use came up for serious consideration, none of them judged the military benefit to be gained from CW to be worth resorting to it. The taboo survived, despite the increasing harshness of its environment.

That the taboo was nevertheless under serious threat is clear, now the state papers are open, from the reconsideration of executive policy on CW-weapons employment which a number of governments embarked upon during the decade after World War II. In particular, it cannot be said that the wartime policy of no-first-use continued to find universal advocacy within the secret counsels of state. In fact at least one government formally abandoned the policy for a while,[2] seeing that as the only way of loosening bureaucratic constraints on acquisition of the new nerve-gas weapons. Nor was technical change the only threat to the taboo. In the emerging, and practized, concepts of limited war and of counterinsurgency, new modes of warfare were coming into prominence which could conceivably confer new value, even in high-tech arsenals, on certain types of toxic chemical. Utility in Third-World conflicts remained, so the net effect was a new advance for CW armament. Once again, however, the advance induced its own constraint. Under the immediate stimulus, during the mid 1960s, of the use of chemicals in, especially, the Vietnam War, the UN General Assembly moved to revitalize the Geneva Protocol, and talk of further CW arms control began.

Down even to today, two or three hundred wars on from the Great War of 1914-18, CW remains a rare occurrence. It has been employed, indisputably, in less than a dozen of those conflicts. It appears still more rare if the use of chemical herbicides or chemical irritants in counterinsurgency weapons is not regarded as chemical warfare. We are now, however, in the immediate aftermath of a major episode of poison-gas warfare, in the Gulf War. Successive investigations by the UN Secretary-General during 1984-88 provided incontrovertible verification of repeated and large-scale use by Iraq of mustard gas and perhaps other CW agents too, even nerve gas, against Iran. It is an episode that is comparable in several hideous respects to the CW of the Great War. It suggests that other countries, especially ones in the same region, may have moved to arm themselves with CW weapons. And for both those reasons it raises the question of whether existing international law on CW has not now become substantially eroded.

Countervailing reaction, however, is once again setting in. The idea of instituting chemical-weapon-free zones, pending a global ban on the weapons, has been spreading.[3] The year in which Iraqi CW was first verified by the UN was also the year in which the talks on the global ban began to accelerate, starting at last to hold out real promise of success. It is true that, even though Iraq eventually admitted its resort to CW weapons, it has been protected by economic and special political factors from the outlawry of international trade sanctions or other such measures. That dereliction, however, promoted the process which culminated in the Declaration of Paris: a resounding reaffirmation of the Geneva Protocol and of commitment to the objective of a global ban which 149 states, including Iraq, adopted on 11 January 1989.

The Declaration of Paris has expressly strengthened the power of the UN Secretary-General to investigate any future allegations there may be of chemical (or biological) warfare. So the ban on resort to CW is becoming a verified ban. The limitations of CW weapons are thus further compounded, for the political liabilities of using them are now much heavier than at the time of the Gulf War. And with the technology of conventional weaponry continuing its rapid advance, little if anything remains to CW in terms of military utility unmatched by other weapons--only capacity to terrorize and to kill the defenceless. It is thus understandable why, in most peoples' eyes, CW weapons remain fit only to be outlawed.

So the taboo is still alive, and there is hope yet for its reinforcement by treaty. It has not become attenuated by technical change or by military cost-benefit calculation to the point where all that remains are empty forms of words - though the risk, quite clearly, is there.

The Projected Chemical Weapons Convention

Success in the CW negotiation at the Conference on Disarmament (the CD) will consist in consensus on the form of a new treaty régime which the negotiating partners believe they would rather be inside than outside: a new state of international cooperation preferable, in the judgement of the participating governments, to the status quo. Like-with-like CW deterrence, being the only justifiable feature of the status quo that would be abandoned, is to be traded for a régime of CW disarmament. That régime would bring other benefits, such as elimination of the hazards posed by toxic stockpiles to neighboring populations. There would, to be sure, be certain costs attaching to the treaty, most notably in the maintenance and the intrusiveness of its oversight machinery; but so too are there costs in the status quo--as, for example, in the continuing spread of CW-weapons to a growing number of countries. Through negotiations on what should go into the treaty and what should be left out of it, especially as regards verification, the perceived reliability of the régime is to be built up to the point at which the competing option of CW armament would seem to afford a lesser degree of security and at greater cost. The trade would be worthwhile: we would feel ourselves worse off if we did not have the treaty.

The actual negotiation at the CD has been advancing through the gradual elaboration of a single set of draft treaty articles and associated annexes which

Table 1.   Structure of the projected Chemical Weapons Convention

Preamble

Articles:
I	General provisions on scope
II	Definitions and criteria
III	Declarations
IV	Chemical weapons
V	Chemical weapons production facilities
VI	Activities not prohibited by the Convention
VII	National implementation measures
VIII	The Organization
IX	Consultations, co-operation and fact-finding
X	Assistance and protection against chemical weapons
XI	Economic and technological development
XII	Relation to other international agreements
XIII	Amendments
XIV	Duration, withdrawal
XV	Signature
XVI	Ratification
XVII	Accession
XVIII	Deposit of Instruments of Ratification or Accession
XIX	Entry into force
XX	Languages

Annexes

Other documents: Preparatory Commission

Source: CD/952 of 18 August 1989.

together will comprise the projected Chemical Weapons Convention. This 'rolling text' serves as a non-binding register of emergent consensus.[4] An interlocking structure of consultations and working groups under the auspices of the CD's Ad Hoc Committee on Chemical Weapons, whose chair changes each year in a rotation from Non-Aligned to East to West, provides the machinery of negotiation. The delegations of the Soviet Union and the United States maintain close bilateral contacts.

The basic structure of the rolling text was first agreed by the Ad Hoc Committee, under Swedish chairmanship, in 1984. The titles of its component articles are listed in Table 1; their chief provisions are outlined in Tables 2-5.

Table 2.   The primary commitments of each State Party to the projected Chemical Weapons Convention

Negative Obligations

Art I.1	Not to develop chemical weapons.
Art I.1	Not to produce chemical weapons.
Art I.1	Not otherwise to acquire chemical weapons {which means, in effect, not to buy them from a State Non-Party}.
Art I.1	Not to stockpile chemical weapons.
Art I.1	Not to retain chemical weapons.
Art I.1	Not to transfer chemical weapons directly to anyone.
Art I.1	Not to transfer chemical weapons indirectly to anyone.
Art I.2	Not to assist, encourage or induce, in any way, anyone to engage in activities prohibited to States Parties.
Art I.3	Not to use chemical weapons.
Art I.4	[Not to [conduct other activities in preparation for use of chemical weapons] [engage in any military preparations for use of chemical weapons].]

Positive Obligations

Art I.5	To destroy chemical weapons in its possession.
Art I.5	To destroy chemical weapons which are under its [jurisdiction or] control.
Art I.6	To destroy chemical weapons production facilities in its possession.
Art I.6	To destroy chemical weapons production facilities which are under its [jurisdiction or] control.

Source: CD/952 of 18 August 1989.

Scope

The primary obligations, both positive and negative, which States Parties are to accept under the treaty in the current version of the rolling text are set out in Article I. The positive obligations call for the destruction of stockpiled CW weapons ("chemical weapons") and of production facilities for them. A disarmament or *elimination régime* is thereby to be established. It is likely to affect only a minority of States Parties, however, because only a handful of states today possess the weapons or the factories. Alongside it there is to be the nonarmament or *preclusion régime* that flows from the negative obligations, which are summarized in Table 2. This second régime will affect all States Parties, or at least all of them that wish to continue benefitting from the security afforded by the treaty; for they will have to take positive steps to make sure that their potential adversaries or those of their allies can see that they are indeed refraining from developing, producing or stockpiling chemical weapons and everything else which Article I has enjoined them not to do. They will of course be looking to the treaty's verification system to assist them in this building of confidence and assurance.

Agreement has not yet been negotiated on what exactly is to be understood by the term "chemical weapon", so the full scope of the projected treaty is not yet clearly delimited. Such things as high explosives, rocket fuels, incendiaries and smoke agents are all chemicals but will need excluding, so eventually lines of definition will need to be drawn rather carefully around the term. Too broad a definition might bring so many chemicals and associated activities into the scope of the treaty that important sectors of support would be lost. Too narrow a definition might risk losing some of the taboo: legitimizing activities which at least some of the world regards as outrageous and impermissible. There is firm agreement, nevertheless, that, whatever the precise meaning that is to be given to "chemical weapons", it is to cover not only CW agents but also munitions and specialized delivery-systems for them.

Clearly the correct course is to be guided by the Geneva Protocol. This uses the words "asphyxiating, poisonous or other" to describe the weapons whose use it proscribes. In the equally authentic French text, the words are "asphyxiants, toxiques ou similaires". So by 'chemical weapon' we should understand weapons whose primary mode of action is *toxicity*: chemical interference with the biochemical processes of life and of living, an interference that may be immediate in its effects or delayed. A "toxic chemical" is defined in the Rolling Text thus: "any chemical, regardless of its origin or method of production, which through its chemical action on life processes can cause death, temporary incapacitation or permanent harm..."

For purposes of specifying control procedures, the treaty will also need subsidiary definitions, for under conducive circumstances any chemical can be toxic, including chemicals so devoid of military utility that their control would be pointless. The current approach rests upon a *general purpose criterion* whereby the treaty will outlaw possession of all chemicals except where they are intended for purposes not prohibited by the treaty, these purposes being listed in it. This would mean that, in cases of doubt, States Parties will in effect be obliged to prove that all their chemicals are justified for permitted purposes. The attractions of so Draconian an approach are that it is forward-looking and all-embracing, capable of capturing, therefore, chemical weapons as yet unknown. Quantitative-toxicity criteria are envisaged for part of the requisite subcategorization. Thus, super-stringent controls are to be applicable to "supertoxic" chemicals, these being defined as ones having a subcutaneous 7-day LD50 no greater than 0.5 mg/kg, or an inhalation LCt50 no greater than 2000 mg-min/m^3, in young adult male albino Wistar-strain rats. The rolling text also uses qualitative criteria, as in the concept of "key precursor" chemicals, to which controls of a special stringency are to be applied. Applicable qualitative criteria are ones reflecting the military significance of the chemicals concerned, for example their amenability to weapons-use or, as here, their applicability as production intermediates for military toxicants.

Qualitative criteria may perhaps also be necessitated by the many different ways in which toxicity can manifest itself. The acute toxicity of a nerve gas can be differentiated from the chronic or delayed toxicity of a carcinogen or of a poison like dioxin. Toxicity may threaten vital function, or its threat may be limited to cognitive or motor functions: it may, in other words, be a lethal or a nonlethal toxicity--that of a nerve gas contrasted with that of, say, a psychotropic incapacitant (such as agent BZ). Further, its effects may be transient or permanent, meaning that a tear gas is as much a toxic agent, qualitatively speaking, as is a nerve gas. And toxicity can afflict more forms of life than humankind alone, as the conferees in Geneva recognized in June 1925 when they took cognizance of chemical herbicides as well as poison gases during their drafting of the Geneva Protocol.

Is there any sound reason for not bringing herbicides, and tear gases too, within the scope of the treaty, where they would take their place alongside the many other varieties of "dual-purpose" chemical which the general purpose criterion can accommodate? In December 1969, the UN General Assembly, by resolution 2603A (XXIV), defined "chemical agents of warfare" as "chemical substances...which might be employed because of their direct toxic effects on man, animals or plants".

Verification system

The rolling text sets out a rather well-developed system for verifying compliance. There are aspects which have still to be worked out, but the present state of agreement, covering the basic structure of the system, how it is to work, and many of its particulars, is impressive. It is the outcome of an East-West convergence of view which seemed unattainable a short while ago. Its chief features are its intrusiveness and the degree of support which it has nonetheless secured from leading sectors of chemical industry in the industrialized countries. Now

Table 3.   Declarations to be required under the projected Chemical Weapons Convention, (a): Within 30 days of entry into force

Topic	Initial information to be declared by each State Party (SP)
Chemical weapons--by which is meant: • toxic chemicals and their precursors, save where intended for permitted purposes; or • munitions specifically for such chemicals; or • equipment specifically for such munitions.	Does the SP possess any? If yes, then: • particulars of types and quantities • locations; and • general plan for their destruction. Are any foreign-owned ones stored by the SP? If yes, then: • particulars. Have any been transferred/received by the SP since [1946][1975]? If yes: • particulars.
Storage facilities for chemical weapons	Locations. Detailed inventories.
Production facilities for chemical weapons	Does the SP possess any? Did the SP possess any since [1946]? If yes to either, then, for each factory: • location and type; • ownership; • products and dates of production; • capacity; and • detailed description. Are there, or have there been, foreign-owned ones on its soil? If yes, then: • particulars. Closure measures. General plan for their destruction.

Table 3a   (continued)

Topic	Initial information to be declared by each State Party (SP)
Production equipment for chemical weapons	Has any been transferred/received by the SP since [1946]? If yes, then: • particulars, including current disposition.
Development labs for chemical weapons	Does the SP have any? Has it since [1946]? If yes to either, then: • location; and • nature and general scope of activities.
Scheduled chemicals: specific chemicals or families of chemicals that warrant control in the civil chemical industry are being listed in four control schedules, as follows: • Schedule 1, comprising supertoxic chemicals and special key precursors without significant commercial use. • Schedule 2A, comprising key precursors. • Schedule 2B, comprising supertoxic chemicals not in Schedule 1 and other threatening chemicals (not precursors). • Schedule 3, comprising chemicals produced in large commercial quantities that could be used for chemical weapons purposes.	For each Schedule 1 chemical: • location of the plant that is to be designated as the permitted Single Small-Scale Production Facility; and • locations of all other facilities where production exceeding 0.1 kg/yr is permissible. For each Schedule 2A and 2B chemical: • aggregated national data on prior-year production, consumption, import and export, including the countries and purposes involved; and • location of each facility which produced/processed/consumed more than **** tonnes during the prior year. For each Schedule 3 chemical: • aggregated national data on prior-year production, consumption, import and export, indicating the final-product/end-use categories; • location of each facility which produced/processed/consumed or transferred more than **** tonnes during the prior year; and • location of any facility which has produced the chemical for CW purposes

Table 3a   **(continued)**

Topic	Initial information to be declared by each State Party (SP)
The Single Small Scale Facility (SSSF) authorized for Schedule 1 chemicals	Detailed technical description and inventory.
Other Schedule-1 chemical facilities of declared location	For each such facility: • detailed technical description.
Schedule-2A and -2B chemical facilities of declared location	For each such facility: • ownership, nature, convertibility, purpose and production capacity; • amount of each scheduled chemical produced, consumed, imported and exported during the previous year; and • category of site-activity associated with each scheduled chemical (production, processing &c), including any prior-year on-site storage exceeding **** tonnes.
Schedule-3 chemical facilities of declared location	For each such facility: • ownership, capacity and approximate amount of the chemical produced and consumed during the previous year.

Table 3.   **Declarations to be required under the projected Chemical Weapons Convention, (b): Annual reports**

Topic	Information to be declared annually by each State Party (SP)
Chemical weapons	Data on progress in implementing the declared plan for stockpile destruction.
Production facilities for chemical weapons	Data on progress in implementing the declared plan for destruction of chemical weapons production facilities

Table 3b (continued)

Topic	Information to be declared annually by each State Party (SP)
Schedule-1 chemicals	For each Schedule-1 chemical: • data on prior-year imports and exports, including quantities, recipients and purposes; • detailed prior-year production, consumption, storage and shipment data, including the identities and quantities of any other scheduled chemicals involved, the data to be submitted separately and individually for the SSSF and each facility of declared location where production exceeding 0.1 kg/yr is permissible; and • particulars of any other facilities in which Schedule-1 chemicals were synthesized during the prior year in quantities less than 0.1 kg/yr.
Schedule-2A and -2B chemicals	For each Schedule-2 chemical: • aggregated national data on prior-year production, consumption, import and export, including the countries and purposes involved; and • location of each facility where production/processing/consumption of more than **** is projected for the year ahead.
Schedule-3 chemicals	For each Schedule-3 chemical: • aggregated national data on prior-year production, consumption, import and export, indicating the final-product/end-use categories.

Table 3b   **(continued)**

Topic	Information to be declared annually by each State Party (SP)
The SSSF and other Schedule-1 chemical facilities declared for production exceeding 0.1 kg/yr	For each such facility: • particulars of any alterations during the previous year; and • particulars of activities projected for the coming year, including anticipated production quantities.
Schedule-2A, -2B and -3 chemical facilities of declared location	As for the initial declarations outlined in Table 3a.

Table 3.   **Declarations to be required under the projected Chemical Weapons Convention, (c): Ad hoc notifications**

Topic	Information to be provided by the State Party (SP)
Chemical weapons	Detailed plans for destruction of chemical weapons to be submitted at least 6 months prior to each destruction period. Certification of destruction within 30 days of its completion.
Chemical-weapons production facilities	Detailed plans for the destruction of each such facility to be submitted at least *** months prior to commencement.

Table 3c   continued

Topic	Information to be provided by the State Party (SP)
Schedule-1 chemicals	Notification of any inter-state transfer at least 30 days beforehand.
	Information on new SSSF to be provided 6 months prior to startup.
	Advance notification of any changes to be made to the SSSF or to facilities declared for production exceeding 0.1 kg/yr planned since the initial declaration.
Schedule-2A and -2B chemicals	At least one-month advance notification of startup of any production/processing/consumption planned after submission of last annual declaration.
Schedule-3 chemicals	Location of any facility intended, during the year following submission of the last annual declaration, for industrial-scale production, processing or consumption.

Source: CD/952 of 18 August 1989.

emerging is comparable support from the developing countries.

The system is founded on the use of international on-site inspections. It has a layered structure of overlapping components in recognition that some shortfall from complete certainty of compliance is inevitable, at least when the system is applied to large industrial economies.

The foundation is to be a data-base that is regularly updated. This is to be compiled from information which, under Articles III, IV, V and VI, each state party to the treaty will be obliged to declare: information about its CW capabilities and about other capabilities that could be diverted for CW purposes--information of kinds that would allow other states parties to gain confidence that the capabilities were indeed diminishing, or coming under international control, in accordance with the requirements of the treaty. Table 3 summarizes the current

Table 4.   The elimination régime of the projected Chemical Weapons Convention: Routine measures for verifying destruction of stockpiles and factories

Subject	Verification task	Verification method*
Chemical weapons	Validating the declarations of possessed stocks (i.e. confirming the identities and quantities of weapons declared)	**D**
	Confirming that declared stocks have been destroyed	**B+C**
Storage facilities for chemical weapons	Ensuring that no undetected removal of chemical weapons occurs from declared facilities	**A + B** or **C**
Production facilities for chemical weapons	Validating the declarations of facilities	**D**
	Ensuring that declared facilities are properly closed	**A**
	Ensuring that declared facilities remain closed and that no resumption of production or removal of declared items would remain undetected	**A + B** or **C**
	Confirming that declared facilities have been eliminated as such	**A/C**

Source: CD/952 of 18 August 1989.

* **A** - Systematic verification by on-site inspection.

   B - Continuous monitoring by on-site instruments.

   C - Continuous presence of international inspectors.

   D - Site visit by international inspectors

state of consensus in the rolling text on the types of information that are to be declared.

The declared information is to support both the elimination régime and the preclusion régime. For the purposes of the former, it is to include details of any stockpiles of CW weapons or production facilities for them possessed by a state party; and it is to include information about the applicable destruction procedures and their scheduling, regularly updated so as to record the progress of destruction. For the preclusion régime, the declared information is to include data on elements of civil chemical industry which could in principle support a CW arsenal. Such elements include production capacity for a variety of "dual purpose" chemicals--such as industrial intermediates like phosgene and hydrogen cyanide which have in the past been used as military toxicants, or like trimethyl phosphite which can be used as a production intermediate ("precursor") for nerve gas. Those abusable elements of civil industry also include dual-purpose production facilities, ones having design or structural characteristics which make them readily convertible

Table 5.   The preclusion régime of the projected Chemical Weapons Convention: Routine measures for verifying nonproduction of chemical weapons

Subject	Verification task	Verification method*
SSSF for Schedule 1 chemicals	Validating the information declared about the facility, including verificationthat production can occur only in small reactors unsuited to continuous operation	**D**
	Validating the declarations of quantities of Schedule 1 chemicals produced, and ensuring that their aggregate amount does not exceed 1000 kg	**A + B**
Other facilities of declared location for Schedule-1 chemicals	Validating the information declared about the facilities, including verification that only very small-scale production beyond 0.1 kg/yr will be possible	**D**

TABLE 5   (continued)

Subject	Verification task	Verification method*
	Ensuring that the quantities produced, processed or consumed are correctly declared and consistent with the stated purposes; that they are not diverted to prohibited purposes; and that undeclared Schedule-1 chemicals are not being produced	**A + B**
Schedule-2A and -2B chemicals	Ensuring that the quantities produced, processed or consumed are consistent with needs not prohibited by the CWC, and that they are not diverted to prohibited purposes	**E** + facility control (see below)
Schedule-3 chemicals	Ditto	**E**, perhaps with "spot-check" inspections of facilities as well
Facilities for Schedule-2A/B chemicals	Ditto. And ensuring that declared facilities of this type are not used to produce any Schedule-1 chemicals	**E + A + B**

Source: CD/952 of 18 August 1989.

* **A** - Systematic verification by on-site inspection.

  B - Continuous monitoring by on-site instruments.

  C - Continuous presence of International Inspectors.

  D - Site visit by international inspectors

  E - Monitoring of reported data.

to illicit production. Negotiation continues, in consultation with chemical industry, on the precise types of civil information to be declared, its level of detail, and its timing. Particular attention is being paid in this negotiation to the problems presented by the confidentiality of some of the requisite commercial and industrial data. Remedies are at hand. Strong expressions of support from representatives of chemical industry worldwide, and expressions, too, of their willingness to cooperate in the design and inplementation of the requisite control régimes, resulted from the Government-Industry Conference Against Chemical Weapons held in Canberra, Australia, during 18-22 September 1989.

The second component of the verification system is provision in the treaty for procedures whereby States Parties may challenge one another in the event of suspicions of incomplete or false declarations arising, and whereby fact-finding investigations involving international on-site inspections may thereupon be set in motion as necessary. The key feature here is the element of obligation. There is now East-West agreement that a challenged State Party should not have the right to refuse a proper request for challenge inspection: acceptance is to be mandatory. The practical details are still being worked out at the time of writing. In contrast to the challenge inspections of, for example, the INF Treaty, those under the Chemical Weapons Convention are not to be limited to declared facilities only: "anytime, anywhere" is the proposal that was put forward by the United States[5] and subsequently accepted by the Soviet Union.[6]

The third component fits between the first and the second. It comprises provision for systematic international inspection procedures that allow information declared for the data-base to be validated. Originally the idea had been that such validation could be left to the cross-checks that would be possible with a sufficient profusion and variety of declared information and to national intelligence machinery--satellite surveillance and the like. The view subsequently took hold, for various reasons, that more was needed, and the idea of validation inspections then came to be accepted for an increasing range of targets, starting with the facilities to be used for destroying CW weapons and now extending to various types of civil and other chemical plant as well. The full range is still being negotiated. These inspections would be labelled "routine" to differentiate them from the "challenge" inspections described above. They might be continuous in their application or intermittent, or performed in part, or even wholly, through the use of emplaced instruments and automated data-links. Table 4 summarizes the routine inspection measures which the current rolling text envisages for the elimination régime; Table 5, those of the preclusion régime.

To oversee the implementation of the treaty and its three-layered verification system, the rolling text envisages the creation of an "Organization for the Prohibition of Chemical Weapons". This would have a staff of international civil servants and would be responsible, through an Executive Council whose composition and procedures have yet to be agreed, to a "Conference of States Parties". No one can yet estimate how big this new international organization will have to be. Its size will largely be governed by the number of inspectors needed, but this cannot be determined until the data-base is fuller. The multilateral data-sharing scheme initiated in the CD in 1988 has now attracted voluntary disclosures of pertinent data from eleven countries, with more expected, the most recent of them being the USSR. Ballpark estimates put the size of the Organization on the same scale as the Safeguards Division of the International Atomic Energy Agency.[7]

Special problems

It is in the nature of any process that is still advancing towards completion that resolution of outstanding problems reveals others yet to be overcome. What had once seemed relatively trivial impediments thus become rate-determining obstacles, even though their magnitude remains unchanged. Or they may indeed have grown in size, inflated by changes in the broad political context. These are phenomena which the CW treaty negotiation continues to display.

With East-West disagreement on the broad structure of the treaty verification system now past, other issues have come into prominence. The picture will be different later on, but a snapshot view during the 1989 CD session-- shows three problems as most obstructive in the sense that, for as long as decisions on how to resolve one or another of them remain untaken in the key capitals, progress in other areas as well is liable to be delayed, and suspicions about true negotiating intentions inflamed. Two have to do with verification, and have been mentioned here already: the modalities of challenge inspection, and the controls needed in the civil chemical industry to cope with potentially dual-purpose facilities. The third is the seemingly petty question of the order in which stockpiles and production facilities should be destroyed under the elimination régime.

An explanation of why issues such as these, and those that will succeed them, become rate-determining in the negotiation is that they have an especially strong political bearing on that fundamental calculation which potential States Parties must make about the projected treaty: given the degree of assurance likely to be available about compliance, will we be better off in than out? And if, at the national level, an issue touches areas additional to that of security policy, as it does in the case of industry controls, the requisite decisions, properly reflective of the additional political accommodations necessary, are going to become more difficult still.

The transitional period--that interval between the entry of the CWC into force and the end of the 10-year period to be allowed for destruction of stockpiles and production facilities--has a special salience. CW capability has never been an element of military strength on which any country has rested its national security at all heavily. CW weapons are not in practice part of the NATO deterrent structure, for example. But the transition will nevertheless be one in which military means give way to political means in a particular area of security (at a pace conditioned by the order of destruction). It will thus be a shift away from traditional ways of responding to external threats; a transition from the known to the unknown. It is a setting in which at least some people, understandably enough, will regard the possibility of hidden CW stockpiles, or other devices whereby an enemy might break rapidly out of the constraints of the treaty, as especially menacing. Not until a good way into the transitional period will States Parties have gained sufficient experience to place a proper degree of confidence in the treaty; and, even then, break-out fears may still persist.

Success in finding ways for allaying or diminishing such fears could thus substantially promote the treaty. Three areas that seem promising in this regard are as follows.

"Routine challenge" inspection. Within the more developed industrial economies of East and West, market forces are shifting an increasing proportion of chemical production out of dedicated facilities into multipurpose ones. The design requirements that are specified for new multipurpose plant are liable to make it as readily convertible for manufacture of military toxicants or their key precursors as for manufacture of new commercial products. So those people who fear break-out are finding their fears exacerbated.

Under the present rolling text, civil chemical production facilities become liable to international inspection under two types of circumstance. One is if the facilities are actually used, or have been so used, to manufacture particular chemicals listed in the Schedules of Article VI. But for facilities that only *could* be so used, no provision is made for any such routine systematic inspection. The other circumstance is their becoming the subject of a challenge. But the way the modalities of challenge inspection are being developed, such challenges could become highly confrontational, even, therefore, self-deterring, except perhaps in cases where violation was virtually certain. Such procedures might, in other words, provide no remedy for genuine doubts.

The routine inspection procedures of the rolling text are designed to avoid that shortcoming of challenge inspection, this being achieved by resting the initiative for conducting the inspections with the international inspectorate, not with governments. So one solution would be to expand their scope so that they would embrace a better range of dual-purpose facilities. A proper form of wording to make such provision in the treaty would not be easy to develop. A much more serious difficulty is that, for the provision to be effective, it would have to increase very greatly the number of facilities liable to inspection. This would magnify the tasks of the inspectorate; and it could jeopardize the support of the chemical industry, which at the corporation level is nervous of outside intrusion, particularly if systematic, in regard not least to the security of unpatentable know-how in which R & D resources have been heavily invested. Alleviation of these difficulties would require some way of restricting the facilities liable to inspection. To this end the FRG has proposed an industry-register scheme alongside its CD/ 791 proposal for *ad hoc checks*, a proposal aimed in part at the dual-purpose facility problem.[8] But much consultation with industry will be required to ascertain whether such a scheme can be both adequate and feasible.

An alternative approach, exemplified in the British proposal for *ad hoc inspections* (not limited to civil chemical facilities),[9] is to introduce a third mode of inspection, intermediate between the challenge and the routine modes, that would lack the systematic character of routine inspections and the confrontational character of challenge inspections, but which would retain something of the 'anytime, anywhere' aspect of the latter as well as its mandatory nature, but without implying any presupposition of noncompliance. In the British proposal, the initiative for third-mode inspections is left with States Parties, subject, however, to a strict quota system. Experience of the Stockholm-Document inspections on which the proposal is modelled is said by the British CD delegation to suggest that the confrontational character of challenge inspections can be avoided in this way, even when the inspections are directed against economically important civil facilities. Here again, much consultation on the proposal with the civil chemical industry of different countries would seem to be prudent before going ahead.

It is not obvious, however, that either approach can be effective in addressing the basic problem without the International Organization being given much more power of initiative--whether in selecting targets for inspection from the German-type register or in triggering British-type third-mode inspections--than potential states parties yet seem willing to contemplate.

R & D controls. Break-out fears are also associated with the possibility of novel CW-weapons technologies, ones which escape the controls of the treaty's preclusion régime and which also have a security-threatening significance. The remedies thus far envisaged in the rolling text lie in the still-preliminary work on Schedule 2b of Article VI, in the proposed modalities for amending the Article-VI schedules, and in the Scientific Advisory Board mentioned in a footnote to Article VIII.

A prohibition of the development of CW weapons appears in Article I, but measures for verifying compliance with this obligation are not yet explicit in the rolling text except insofar as the provisions just mentioned might, once they are fully elaborated, provide sufficient assurance. Supplementary measures can be envisaged, for example the scheme proposed at one of the early Pugwash CW workshops for information-exchanges between national CW-defence laboratories that would gradually build up towards complete openness.[10] Other such confidence-building measures could include recurrent technical exchange visits between those same laboratories, perhaps also involving staff of the International Organization.

This is an area of the treaty negotiation to which the scientific community at large could contribute constructively. It is also an area which, if treated clumsily, could do that community much harm.

Capability preclusion. CW weapons on their own do not constitute a capability for chemical warfare. Users have to be taught the special skills needed to use the weapons; they must be exercised, equipped and supplied; and the weapons may need continuing specialized maintenance. So a variety of CW-specific activities must be undertaken and specialized organizational structures created in order for hidden stockpiles of CW weapons, or suddenly produced supplies of them, to become threatening. Constraining those broader aspects of CW capability would be a way of diminishing break-out dangers.

Potentially important, therefore, is the skeleton language, currently square-bracketted, in Article I para 4 of the rolling text. It would place an obligation on States Parties not to engage in preparations to use chemical weapons. Compliance with such a ban might be monitored in several ways. For example, some have suggested a role for observers at military exercises and manoeuvres.[11]

Wider Lessons from the CW Negotiation

The Geneva talks have now built up a large body of experience in the arts and skills of arms-control negotiation on chemical weapons. It seems to us that, from those 20 and more years of effort, a number of lessons can be drawn which have a wider application--which may benefit negotiation in other areas. They are these.

Simple solutions are best

"Chemical and bacteriological warfare", conjunct as in the Geneva Protocol, was the item that formally entered the agenda of the Geneva talks on 15 August 1968.[12] But because of US employment of chemical herbicides and irritants in Vietnam at that time, no real progress was possible until chemical warfare had been separated out and the item disaggregated. The 1972 Biological Weapons Convention was agreed soon afterwards. Its Article IX obliged States Parties to continue negotiations on chemical weapons "in good faith". So CW remained on the Geneva agenda, but headway against the obstacles was slow. Remedies were again sought in disaggregations.

Thus it was that, in August 1973, Japan proposed a treaty banning all CW weapons save for those defined in a supplementary document on which agreement (regarding verification) had not yet been reached but which would continue to be sought.[13] Likewise, the bilateral US-Soviet summit communiqué of 3 July 1974 envisaged a "first step...dealing with the most dangerous, lethal means of chemical warfare". In these and other such graduated expedients of the time, quantitative toxicity criteria were proposed for the demarcation of successive stages--thereby at once opening up all sorts of technical questions about how exactly the criteria were to be specified, and exciting suspicions that actually the real purpose of the disaggregation was to legitimize some forms of CW weapon (such as binary munitions) while appearing to do exactly the opposite. Ultimately the simplicity of the comprehensive approach prevailed, embodied in the general purpose criterion.

Other forms of demarcation in support of interim measures have been proposed at moments when the CW negotiation has seemed to be going badly, again countenancing the complexity of clustered partial bans in place of a simple complete ban. Recurrent in varied forms over the years has been the idea first proposed by Canada in 1974 in which development and production of CW weapons would be banned but not, until some later stage, the retention of stockpiles.[14] The now-abandoned "security stock" idea of France is a more recent embodiment. While alleviating one set of difficulties, such schemes have invariably aggravated or created others, such as the reaction of nonpossessors against discrimination and the incentives to which they might then be subject, as agreement approaches, rapidly to acquire stocks of their own. Regional demarcations, too, have been opposed because they may create more problems than they solve, as in the special monitoring arrangements needed for assurance that chemical-weapon-free zones really are free of CW weapons. Quantitative demarcations, as in the level-of-stocks or ceiling agreements that have occasionally been mooted, would present even greater verification complexities.

In short, the CW talks are replete with instances of "simple is best": destruction, not conversion, of proscribed items; global arrangements in preference to a succession of regional ones; the comprehensive in preference to the partial.

Disaggregation can be essential

CBW arms control proved unnegotiable, whereas BW followed by CW did not. Disaggregation may run counter to simple-is-best, but can bring results. The CW talks have shown that disaggregation of the *scope* of the projected treaty--whether by weapon-type, activity, region or quantity--is liable soon to run into difficulties, perhaps because it diminishes too severely the options for constructive ambiguity in the presentation of intentions. When applied to *verification*, on the other hand, disaggregation has brought continuous progress.

In the CW area, in contrast to other fields of arms control, verification needs have consumed a disproportionately large share of the negotiating effort. This is not because CW presents an abnormally grave security problem; it is because the industrial, military and societal background against which any CW-treaty-noncompliant events might be occurring is especially broad and obscuring. The world chemical industry--huge, multifarious and employing millions of people--is only a part of that background. So breaking-down the verification task into manageable portions is essential.

An important principle that the CW talks are establishing in this regard is that the scope of the verification system can, without detriment to the overall treaty régime, be narrower than the scope of the treaty itself. It may not be essential, in other words, for the treaty to provide its own arrangements for verifying compliance with each and every one of its obligations. Use of the general purpose criterion in fact makes this unavoidable.

Several other lines of demarcation--such as single-purpose vs dual-purpose, and CW-specific vs CW-nonspecific--have proved valuable. Most important of all has been the idea of differentiating the CW-weapons-related activities or facilities which a State Party would be willing to declare under the treaty from those which would not be so declared. The overall verification problem is thereby fractionated into two self-contained categories. For one, the verification task is straightforward though laborious, namely that of validating declared information under circumstances in which the declarers have every incentive to assist the process. Elaboration of the requisite systematic and routine procedures requires technical more than political decision-making. The other category is more problematic if the verification task is seen to be ascertaining the absence of hidden stockpiles, factories. But it is at the same time less problematic in that the likelihood must be small of a state joining the treaty without expectation of complying with it. The verification task here is accordingly one of establishing a modest degree of deterrence against subsequent backsliding. That is the function of the challenge-inspection procedures envisaged for the treaty.

The challenge procedures now contemplated are unprecedented: the intrusiveness of their 'anytime, anywhere' character, and the derogation of national sovereignty implicit in their mandatory character, are not even approached in other treaties. Cannot the disaggregation which inspired them be taken a stage further? Why not establish the obligations and machinery for verification-by-challenge under a separate treaty, one that would be applicable not only to CW arms control?

Be realistic

For a decade and more, the CW talks were afflicted by a reluctance on the part of all those participants which possessed CW weapons, except the United States, to acknowledge their possessor status. This meant that any collective deliberation of such matters as the number of CW-weapon-destruction facilities which the projected treaty would call into being, the magnitude of the verification task which they would impose, as well as a whole host of other practical matters, remained uninformed with reliable data. Such talk therefore had to take place at a largely abstract level, and looked like remaining there even after questions of general principle had been resolved to the point where negotiation of concrete particulars could begin.

Responsible, for the most part, were the secretive attitudes which security practices and extreme mistrust had generated. Nor was the view confined to the possessor states that, from the standpoint of the national security, it would be imprudent to disclose any significant information about CW preparedness before the projected treaty had entered into force. When Britain proposed, in its draft CW convention of 1976,[15] that states should declare information for the basic verification data-bank ahead of entry-into-force, legal arguments could be heard from several quarters to show why this could not be done.

Reticent states eventually came to recognize that it was simply unrealistic to expect their negotiating partners to enter into the bargain or deal which the treaty would represent without knowing what was being given up and gained in return- -even if some way could be found for establishing the international oversight machinery without knowing in advance how big it would need to be. There might be risks to security in disclosure, and it was proper to be concerned about them. But there could also be risks in non-disclosure, from the inadequacies or deficiencies in the verification régimes that might thereby be caused.

Reciprocation, and how to promote it safely, was the key. The discussions of the modalities of pre-treaty information sharing which began to get under way, first bilaterally between the USA and the USSR and then multilaterally, during 1985 onwards thus represented a most important change of attitude. It is this new realistic approach, evident also in the learn-by-experiment notion imbuing the 1988-89 National Trial Inspections, which has finally brought the CW treaty within reach. As these words are written, events appear particularly promising, for the US Secretary of State and the Soviet Foreign Minister have just signed, in Wyoming on 23 September 1989, a "Memorandum of Understanding...Regarding a Bilateral Verification Experiment and Data Exchange Related to Prohibition of Chemical Weapons".

Orientation towards problem-solving

That same new sense of realism signified recognition that the CW negotiations were no longer ones in which the participants sought relative advantage over one another, but were instead an alliance of effort to overcome shared problems. This is perhaps the most important lesson of all from the CW talks: that unless arms-control negotiating strategies change, reorientating themselves towards mutual problem solving and away from nationalistic pursuit of asymmetrical benefit, they will always fail in their avowed objective.

A corollary is that the negotiators should not be hesitant about soliciting outside help. Many of the problems they must address involve specialist matters- -ones which only the most arrogant of officials could reasonably consider themselves competent to handle unaided. Not least within the scientific community, there is on hand a large body of knowledge, experience and goodwill.

Notes

1. See, for example, Stephen G Hewitt, "Aspects of the social history of chemical warfare in World War One", M Sc dissertation, University of Sussex, England, August 1972.

2. William C Fredericks, 'The evolution of post-World War II United States chemical warfare policy', M Litt dissertation, University of Oxford, England, January 1988.

3. Ralf Trapp (editor), *Chemical Weapon Free Zones?* (Oxford University Press, 1987, no 7 in the series *SIPRI CBW Studies*).

4. At the time of writing, the latest version of the rolling text is to be found in CD/952 of 18 August 1989.

5. US Vice-President G Bush, statement at the CD in plenary session, 18 April 1984, CD/PV.260 at pp 8-15; USA, "Draft convention on the prohibition of chemical weapons", CD/500 of 18 April 1984, at Article X.

6. USSR Foreign Minister E Shevardnadze, statement at the CD in plenary session, 6 August 1987, PD/PV.428 at p 11; USSR Ambassador Y Nazarkin, statement at the CD in plenary session, 11 August 1987, CD/PV.429 at pp 2-7.

7. See, for example, R Trapp and W Rehak, "Principal objectives of verification methods and results" in S J Lundin (editor), *Non-Production by Industry of Chemical-Warfare Agents: Technical Verification under a Chemical Weapons Convention* (Oxford University Press, 1988; no 9 in the series *SIPRI Chemical & Biological Warfare Studies*), pp 14-30.

8. Federal Republic of Germany, "Verification of non-production of chemical weapons: ad hoc checks", CD/869 of 6 September 1988.

9. United Kingdom, "Chemical Weapons Convention: ad hoc inspections", CD/909 of 30 March 1989.

10. J P Perry Robinson, "Controls on chemical-warfare research and development", a paper presented at the 2nd Pugwash CW Workshop, Stockholm, 22-23 April 1975.

11. Sweden. "Working paper: Prohibition of retention or acquisition of a chemical warfare capability enabling use of chemical weapons", CD/142 of 10 February 1981.

12. ENDC/236 of 28 August 1968.

13. Japan, CCD/413 of 21 April 1973.

14. Canada in CCD/PV.643, 16 July 1974.

15. United Kingdom, "Draft convention on the prohibition of the development, production and stockpiling of chemical weapons and on their destruction", CD/512 of 6 August 1976.

9

Verification of Biological and Toxin Weapons Disarmament

Matthew Meselson (USA), Martin M. Kaplan (Switzerland/USA) &
Mark A. Mokulsky (USSR)

Introduction

The development, production, stockpiling, acquisition, and transfer of biological and toxin weapons are prohibited by the Biological Weapons Convention of 1972 (the BWC), to which more than 100 states are party. Unlike the Geneva Protocol of 1925, that prohibits the use but not the possession of biological and chemical weapons, the BWC is a true disarmament treaty, in that it seeks the actual elimination of a class of weapons. Since the BWC entered into force, in 1975, its very limited confidence-building and verification provisions have been significantly augmented. This has been accomplished not by amending the Convention itself but rather through agreements among its States Parties, reached at its First and Second Review Conferences, and also through actions taken at the United Nations. Additional strengthening of the regime for verifying biological and toxin weapons disarmament is expected to result from the Third BWC Review Conference in 1991.

In this article, we summarize the characteristics of biological and toxin weapons; the nature, capabilities, and limitations of protective measures; and the existing provisions and agreements for confidence-building and international verification of compliance with the BWC. We also present some proposals to enhance the effectiveness of the BWC.

Characteristics of Biological and Toxin Weapons[1,2]

Infectious agents

Biological weapons employing infectious agents pathogenic to man have the potential to kill or incapacitate populations over large areas. This potential derives from the extreme smallness of the amount of agent sufficient to initiate infection. Delivered by aircraft, missile, or other means and dispersed near the ground as wind-borne aerosols to be inhaled by a target population, certain infectious agents could in theory approach the anti-personnel effectiveness of thermonuclear warheads, in terms of the weight of the agent and associated dissemination devices required to attack a given area. Moreover, infectious agents could lend themselves to modest, perhaps even rather inconspicuous means of delivery.

Today, no nation is known to possess biological weapons. During World War II, however, Great Britain, Japan, and the United States developed biological weapons based on explosive and insect dissemination of the agents of anthrax, plague, and other diseases. The infectious anti-personnel agents stockpiled for use in weapons by the United States before its unilateral renunciation of biological weapons in 1969 included *Francisella tularensis*, the bacterium responsible for tularemia, *Coxiella burnetii*, the rickettsial organism responsible for Q fever, and VEE, the virus that causes Venezuelan equine encephalomyelitis. In addition, there were stocks of biological agents intended for use against food crops: *Pyricularia oryzae* and *Puccinia graminis*, the fungi responsible for rice blast and wheat rust, respectively. Examples of other infectious anti-personnel agents that have been studied for use in weapons or have been actually stockpiled are the viruses that cause Chikungunya fever, eastern equine encephalomyelitis, and yellow fever; the bacteria that cause brucellosis, cholera, and glanders; and the rickettsiae responsible for Rocky Mountain spotted fever and epidemic typhus. In addition, many other naturally-occurring infectious agents may have the stability, infectivity, virulence, and other characteristics suited to use in weapons for use against people, animals, or plants.

Contrary to a prevalent misconception, the development and production of reliable weapons based on infectious agents would be a major undertaking. Large technical resources and expenditures would be required for initial study, development, testing, and production of the biological agent itself, the devices for its dissemination, the means for their delivery, and the fully integrated biological weapon system. Even then, serious uncertainties in performance would remain. Nevertheless, such weapons could be simpler and less expensive to produce than nuclear weapons. Moreover, rudimentary but highly dangerous biological weapons of lower reliability could be produced with much less effort and expense, using widely available technology. Crude biological weapons are within the reach of many nations and even dissident groups and terrorists.

New infectious agents

The view is sometimes expressed that new methods in biotechnology, especially genetic engineering, could yield infectious biological warfare agents with military properties fundamentally different from those of infectious agents that are already known. It is undoubtedly true that additional agents could be developed by genetic engineering and also by more classical techniques. But no one has even proposed a realistic set of biological, physical, or other properties of a hypothetical novel agent that would endow it with military characteristics fundamentally different from those of known agents. One source of confusion in this regard is the widespread belief that previously developed agents were likely to cause widespread contagion beyond the immediately exposed target population and that more controllable effects would require the development of novel agents. This is not correct. For example, the agents of tularemia and Venezuelan equine encephalomyelitis, formerly stockpiled as biological warfare agents, can initiate infection if artificially disseminated as aerosols, but neither disease is effectively transmitted from person to person.

Toxins

Toxins are poisonous substances made by living things. The term is also applied to the synthetically produced analogues of such substances. Unlike infectious agents, toxins cannot reproduce. While infectious agents generally require incubation periods of a few days following exposure before illness develops, some toxins can cause incapacitation or death within minutes or hours. Examples of toxins that have been studied for use in weapons are the botulinal toxins, produced by the soil bacterium *Clostridium botulinum*, the enterotoxins produced by the bacterium *Staphylococcus aureus*, and ricin, present in castor beans, the seeds of *Ricinus communis*. Even humans produce substances that could in theory be used to cause poisoning leading to incapacitation or death. The neuropeptides known as tachykinins are an example.

Some toxins, for example tetrodotoxin, made by the globefish, have been chemically synthesized. The BWC states that its prohibitions apply to toxins regardless of their means of production. This point was emphasized in the Final Declaration of the Second BWC Review Conference, which states:

> "The Conference reaffirms that the Convention unequivocally applies to all natural or artificially created microbial or other biological agents or toxins whatever their origin or method of production. Consequently, toxins (both proteinaceous and non-proteinaceous) of a microbial, animal or vegetable nature and their synthetically produced analogues are covered."

It is for tactical battlefield use, where rapid action is an important factor, that toxins have been principally considered. For this purpose, however, the utility of toxins, including those that might be developed by genetic engineering or other new technologies, must be judged in comparison with that of already developed, weaponized, tested, and stockpiled chemical warfare agents, such as the highly lethal and rapidly-acting organophosphorus nerve agents and the blister and blinding agent, mustard. Unlike these well-known chemical warfare agents, which are highly stable liquids of simple chemical structure, toxins are generally complex organic substances. Accordingly, they are solids and often have lower stability to heat, surface forces, and oxidation. Not unexpectedly, attempts to weaponize toxins encountered serious difficulties in maintaining agent stability during and after release and in achieving efficient aerosolization. Other factors, including the difficulty of formulating toxin agents able to penetrate the skin and the expense and difficulty of manufacture also mitigated against successful development of toxin weapons.

Although considerable efforts were made to weaponize certain toxins during World War II and afterwards, no nation is known to possess toxin weapons or to have developed a battlefield weapon based on toxins that would be competitive with chemical weapons already stockpiled.

Table 1.   Estimated Weight Requirements For Various Weapon Types

Weapon Type	Illustrative Agent	Approximate Weight to Attack 100 km^2 Target (tons)
Thermonuclear		0.5 (warhead weight)
Biological	*F. tularensis*	5*
Toxin	botulinal toxin	300* (assumes toxin can be stabilized)
Chemical	nerve agent (sarin)	800*

* Based on estimates in *Health Aspects of Chemical and Biological Weapons*, World Health Organization, Geneva, 1970. The estimates depend on a number of uncertain variables and should be regarded as only illustrative. The weight of devices for disseminating the agent payload is assumed to be 3 times that of the agent for sarin, 10 times for botulinal toxin, and 25 times for dry *F. tularensis*.

Weight requirements

For purposes of comparison, the approximate weights of representative bacterial, toxin, and chemical weapons estimated to be sufficient to kill or incapacitate a high proportion of an unprotected population within a 100 square kilometer target under atmospheric conditions favorable for efficient dispersal are listed in Table 1. In addition, the table gives the approximate weight of a 200 kiloton thermonuclear warhead, for which the area of high casualty production for air burst is also about 100 square kilometers.

Protection against anti-personnel biological and toxin weapons

Under certain conditions, medical procedures such as immunization or administration of antibiotics or other drugs can offer protection against some biological agents and toxins. For immunization, adequate supplies of vaccine or anti-serum against the specific threat agent must be on hand in advance and sufficient time must be available for administration to the population at risk. In addition, for vaccines, a period of days to weeks must be allowed for immunity to develop. For many infectious agents and toxins no effective vaccines or anti-sera have been developed and, in some cases, even persistent development efforts have been unsuccessful. For certain infectious agents, but excluding most viruses, antibiotics can be effective, either as prophylaxis or as therapy. Such protection may be circumvented, however, by the use of strains resistant to antibiotics. Moreover, no cure is known for any of the numerous systemic virus diseases of man. These severe limitations on medical means of protection against infectious agents and toxins make such protection ineffective or impractical except under certain quite restrictive conditions.

The only generally effective protection against all airborne biological agents and toxins is not medical but mechanical, namely the provision of filtered or otherwise purified air. A well-fitted military gas mask provides a high degree of protection against inhalation of infectious agents and toxins. Collective shelters and vehicles with filtered air serve the same purpose. Such equipment is already widely deployed with modern armed forces for protection against chemical warfare agents and radioactive fallout. There is as yet, however, no completely reliable equipment for rapid detection of airborne biological and toxin agents. Of course, if a sufficient degree of threat is thought to exist during a particular mission, military units could be placed in protective posture for the duration of the mission. Moreover, if chemical or biological weapons have once been used in a particular conflict, military forces are likely to be ordered into an advanced state of protection when under any form of surface or air attack.

The protection of large civilian populations would be much more difficult than the protection of military units. It would require the development and provision of reliable alarm systems, the issuance of gas masks, the construction of neighborhood and workplace shelters, the conduct of regular education and drill for the entire population, and massive preparations for medical diagnosis and care. Such a defense would be immensely expensive and stressful to create and maintain.

Of course, there is clearly merit in having fast-response epidemiological teams and limited emergency supplies of certain vaccines, antibiotics and other supplies in order to cope with natural threats to public health. Such preparations may also be able to mitigate the effects of limited acts of sabotage, depending on the agent employed. Nevertheless, protection of the civil population against a determined large-scale biological attack would be a very large undertaking.

Clearly, the proliferation of biological weapons would constitute a grave threat to the civilian populations and economies of all states, including those of the nuclear powers. Once started, the proliferation of biological weapons could be much more difficult to arrest than that of nuclear weapons, owing to the relative simplicity and wide availability of the underlying technology. These considerations were central to the decision of the United States to renounce biological and toxin weapons unilaterally and to the achievement of the BWC.

The Biological Weapons and Toxin Disarmament Regime[3,4]

The Biological Weapons Convention of 1972

Biological weapons provide a case in which the usual approach to arms limitation was reversed. Instead of first negotiating a treaty and then implementing its provisions, an entire class of weapons was renounced by a major possessor without any prior international agreement. This was in November 1969, when President Nixon, after extensive review, declared that the United States would unconditionally renounce the development, procurement, and stockpiling of biological weapons, would destroy all stocks of agents and weapons, and would convert facilities for their development and production to peaceful purposes. In announcing these decisions, he also declared support for the principles and objectives of a draft convention prohibiting biological weapons that had been proposed by the Great Britain. Three months later, the United States unconditionally renounced toxin weapons. These events were soon followed by international agreement at the Conference of the Committee on Disarmament in Geneva on a treaty banning biological and toxin weapons--the BWC. After gathering the required ratifications, the BWC entered into force in March 1975 and now has more than 100 parties, including all members of the NATO and Warsaw Treaty alliances, Japan, and the People's Republic of China.

Article I of the BWC prohibits the development, production, stockpiling, acquisition, or transfer of (1) "Microbial or other biological agents, or toxins whatever their origin or method of production, of types and in quantities that have no justification for prophylactic, protective or other peaceful purposes" and of (2) "Weapons, equipment or means of delivery designed to use such agents or toxins for hostile purposes or in armed conflict." In order to avoid any suggestion of superseding the authority of the 1925 Geneva Protocol, the BWC makes no explicit reference to the actual use of biological or toxin weapons. Nevertheless, the provisions of the BWC clearly have the effect of proscribing any such use.

Verification provisions of the BWC

The verification provisions contained in the BWC are limited to:

1. An obligation of States Parties to consult and cooperate with one another in solving problems (Article V) and
2. An agreement to cooperate with any investigation the UN Security Council may undertake in response to a complaint submitted to it by a party (Article VI).

Any investigation sought under the latter procedure, however, would be subject to the veto power of the permanent members of the Security Council. Beyond the provisions of Articles V and VI, assurance of compliance with the BWC was left to national means of verification.

The United States had already decided, in 1969-70, that its own interests were best served by unilateral renunciation of biological and toxin weapons and was aware of the difficulties and delays that would be entailed in negotiating treaty provisions for more extensive international verification. It did not, therefor, seek such provisions in the BWC. Neither were they sought by the Soviet Union, which at that time generally favored national rather than international means of verifying compliance with arms control agreements. Other nations, particularly Sweden, sought to include additional measures of verification, but such proposals were not adopted.

Progress in procedures to verify compliance with the BWC

Notwithstanding the shortcomings of its verification provisions, the Convention has been strengthened to a limited although significant degree by a series of agreements reached by its parties at the First and Second BWC Review Conferences, held in Geneva in 1980 and in 1986, respectively. The BWC Review Conferences have not sought to amend the Convention, a time-consuming process that, unless essentially unanimous, could threaten the authority and near universality of the Convention. Instead, the Review Conferences have arrived at political agreements among the States Parties on certain clarifications of the Convention and have instituted a number of reporting procedures to enhance confidence in the operation of the Convention.

At the First BWC Review Conference, the practical operation of Article V was clarified by an agreement that any State Party may request a consultative meeting of experts to deal with problems that may arise. Such consultations could provide an opportunity to discuss and resolve issues at a technical level when exchanges at a political level might lead to premature conclusions difficult to retract if later found to be unsubstantiated.

More recently, at the Second Review Conference, in September, 1986 and at the following *ad hoc* Meeting of Scientific and Technical Experts in April, 1987, there was instituted a potentially far-reaching system of regular annual reporting of data on research centers and laboratories and on unusual outbreaks of infectious or toxin-related disease. Detailed information is required for all research centers and laboratories, whatever their purpose, having a "maximum containment laboratory" as specified by the World Health Organization (corresponding to Biological Safety Level 4 or BL4). In addition, such information is also required for all research centers and laboratories which specialize in biological defense work and which have a "containment laboratory", corresponding to the next-lower safety level (BL3 or P3)[5]. The required information includes the name, location, source of financing, size of containment units, and scope of activities including types of microorganisms and/or toxins involved. Nations not possessing such containment facilities and having no unusual disease outbreaks are not explicitly required to file declarations. In accord with this agreement, nearly 30 nations have deposited declarations with the United Nations Department for Disarmament Affairs.

The United States has declared one laboratory with BL3 containment facilities under contract to the Army (the Salk Institute vaccine unit at Swiftwater, Pennsylvania) and 5 research centers with facilities at or near BL4, one of them military (at Fort Detrick, Maryland). The Soviet Union declared 4 military research centers or laboratories with BL3 facilities and 8 research centers or laboratories with BL4 facilities, none of them military. Although not required to do so, the Soviet Union also listed a military establishment without containment facilities (the Division of Military Epidemiology in the city of Sverdlovsk) and gave references to papers published by staff members of the Scientific Research Institutes of Military Medicine and of Microbiology of the Ministry of Defense for the period 1968-88. Altogether, 11 parties to the Convention (Bulgaria, Canada, Czechoslovakia, the Federal Republic of Germany, France, Norway, the Peoples Republic of China, Sweden, the UK, the US, and the USSR) have declared military facilities with BL4 or BL3 containment units engaged in activities permitted by the BWC.

A development independent of the BWC that has also strengthened the prohibition of biological and toxin weapons is the mandate given to the UN

Secretary General by the General Assembly in 1987 and unanimously reaffirmed in 1988, requesting him to investigate reports of the use of chemical, biological, or toxin weapons brought to his attention by any Member State. Under this authority, the Secretary General may send expert investigators to sites of alleged chemical or biological attack. The role of the UN Secretary General in investigating alleged violations of the Geneva Protocol was also endorsed unanimously by the 149 nations represented at the 1989 Paris Conference on the Prohibition of Chemical Weapons.

It is interesting to compare the verification regime created by the BWC and enhanced by the agreements achieved at the Review Conferences and at the UN with the verification provisions of the first draft treaty for biological weapons disarmament, that proposed by Great Britain in July 1969. The British proposal would have given the UN Secretary General authority to investigate allegations of the use of biological weapons, an authority he now indeed possesses, not from the BWC itself, but rather from the more recent actions of the General Assembly. In the 1969 proposal, as now, UN investigations of other allegations of non-compliance, such as production or stockpiling of biological weapons, cannot be undertaken solely on the authority of the Secretary General, but require a request from the Security Council. The annual data-exchanges agreed to by the Second BWC Review Conference, however, go well beyond the provisions of the original British proposal, which had no such reporting provisions. Thus, although the verification of biological and toxin weapons disarmament can certainly be strengthened further, as will be discussed below, there has been considerable progress beyond the British draft treaty of 1969 and beyond the BWC itself.

Allegations of non-compliance

Regardless of the progress that has been made and is expected to continue in strengthening the international regime for verifying compliance with the BWC, no treaty provision or political agreement can provide confidence in the functioning of the Convention unless its parties make proper use of its provisions and behave responsibly when suspicions arise. Unfortunately, the performance of both the United States and the Soviet Union in dealing with compliance issues has fallen short of this standard.

Two major allegations of non-compliance with the BWC have been made, both of them by the United States against the Soviet Union. Both allegations continue to be made at the highest political level, as recently as February, 1990.[6] In the first, an outbreak of anthrax in the Soviet city of Sverdlovsk in April and May 1979 is claimed by the United States to have been caused by an airborne release of anthrax spores from an alleged biological weapons factory.[7] The Soviet Union maintains that the outbreak resulted from handling and consumption of meat from cattle and sheep that had contracted anthrax from contaminated animal feed. Since 1986, Soviet physicians who dealt with the outbreak have provided a considerable amount of detailed information.[8] The U.S government has welcomed the provision of new information and, according to recent Congressional testimony, has begun publicly to recognize that it may not be able to determine the true explanation of the outbreak.[9]

Nevertheless, neither government has undertaken the full and frank exchange of evidence and views that will be required to resolve the dispute. On the Soviet side there needs to be a political decision to allow qualified US officials freely to examine what remains of the relevant evidence and to meet with surviving patients and local medical, public health, and veterinary personnel in Sverdlovsk. In addition, US experts should be invited to visit, on a suitable reciprocal basis, the facility described in its allegations. This apparently corresponds to the Sverdlovsk military epidemiology center declared by the Soviet Union pursuant to the agreement reached at the Second BWC Review Conference. On the US side there needs to be a political decision to conduct a full and objective review of its earlier conclusions. This should be structured so as to be unprejudiced by the understandable reluctance of intelligence and political authorities to revise a highly publicized previous conclusion.

The second compliance issue that continues to undermine confidence in the BWC concerns the allegation by the United States that the Soviet Union was involved in the production, transfer, and use of trichothecene mycotoxins in Southeast Asia and Afghanistan, in violation of the BWC and the Geneva Protocol.[10,11] The scientific and other evidence presented by the United States to support its allegation of toxin warfare has been discredited, in large part by unpublished studies conducted by the US government itself.[12] Nevertheless, the charge continues to be made, with no serious attempt to take account of the new information. Such lack of accountability in making allegations of non-compliance with the BWC and the Geneva Protocol is a threat to the effectiveness of both treaties and to the achievement of stronger constraints against chemical and biological weapons. The common interest of the United States and the Soviet Union in eliminating biological and toxin weapons requires resolution of these disputes.

Measures to Strengthen the Prohibition of Biological and Toxin Weapons

Further strengthening of the international biological disarmament regime can be accomplished in a number of ways, most of them requiring increased openness.

Today there is much greater acceptance of openness in verifying arms-control agreements than there was when the BWC was negotiated. Examples of this include the stationing of American and Soviet inspectors on each others' territory under the Intermediate Nuclear Forces Agreement; the routine and challenge inspections of NATO and Warsaw Treaty Alliance military exercises under the

Stockholm Agreement on Confidence and Security Building Measures in Europe; and the wide acceptance of the concept of mandatory challenge inspection for the Chemical Weapons Convention now in an advanced phase of negotiation at the Conference on Disarmament in Geneva.

The growing realization of the value of openness as a factor for stability in international relations and the long-standing tradition of free communication and international cooperation in biology, medicine, and public health create an outstanding opportunity to strengthen the verification of biological and toxin weapons disarmament and to reinforce the international consensus against such weapons.

Multilateral political impetus and machinery for improving the verification of biological and toxin disarmament and otherwise strengthening the Convention will be provided by the Third BWC Review Conference. A number of States Parties to the Convention are seeking practical ideas for discussion at the Preparatory Conference scheduled for the Fall of 1990 and for possible agreement at the Review Conference, including ideas from independent scientists and others outside government. The measures we outline in what follows represent our view of what may be particularly useful and achievable.

Universal adherence

A serious threat to the BWC exists in certain areas of the world where nations involved in bitter regional conflicts have refrained from joining the Convention. In the Middle East, for example, Jordan, Lebanon, and Saudi Arabia are parties to the BWC while Egypt, Iraq, and Syria have signed but not ratified, and Israel has done neither. The U.S., the Soviet Union, and other parties to the Convention have made little diplomatic effort to encourage non-parties to join the treaty. The need is now urgent to remedy the situation, through bilateral diplomatic representations and also in the context of multilateral regional peace efforts. Parties to the BWC should make every effort to draw the attention of non-parties to the desirability of joining in time to attend the Third BWC Review Conference as full members of the Convention. Although even non-signatories may attend as observers, only full members of the Convention may take part in decisions of the BWC Review Conferences. Consideration might also be given to elevating diplomatic representation at the Third Review Conference to the Ministerial level, as a means of increasing the priority given to the matter by national governments and motivating those that have not yet seriously reviewed the case for becoming parties to do so.

Declarations of research centers and laboratories

The system of data-reporting agreed upon at the Second BWC Review

Conference has now passed through three annual cycles. At this stage it would be useful to have informal consultations among the parties regarding the functioning of the reporting system and its possible improvement. Subjects for discussion include completeness and ambiguities of the information provided in the declarations, additional information the inclusion of which would effectively advance the objectives of the BWC, and procedures for States Parties having nothing to declare to give explicit annual notice to that effect.

In the category of additional information, it would be a useful confidence-building measure to list all publications in the open literature authored or co-authored by staff members of each declared research center or laboratory. While the Second BWC Review Conference agreed that "results of biological research directly related to the Convention" should be published in generally available scientific journals, there is no requirement to list such publications in the annual exchanges of information. By giving a concrete picture of work being done at each declared establishment, the provision of such reference lists could enhance confidence in the operation of the Convention.

Another important area for consideration at the Third BWC Review Conference is the further specification of research centers and laboratories to be declared. At present, declarations are required only for those with BL4 containment facilities or with BL3 facilities if they also specialize in biological defense work. This fails to include certain sites that are unquestionably of interest in connection with the BWC. Examples are the US Army Dugway Proving Ground in Utah and the Division of Military Epidemiology in Sverdlovsk. Although permitted work on biological defense or military epidemiology is said to be done at these sites, they apparently have no BL4 containment units nor do they have BL3 units and specialize in BW defense work. The later installation is included in the annual Soviet declarations even though, according to its description, it need not be. Nevertheless, a less restrictive definition of installations to be declared is clearly desirable. Such a broadened definition might include: (1) all research centers and laboratories that specialize in biological defense work, whether or not they have containment units, and (2) all research centers and laboratories that have containment units and conduct biological defense work, whether or not they "specialize" in it.

Verification at declared sites

Following the precedent established by recent conventional and nuclear arms-control agreements and the draft Chemical Weapons Convention, agreement might be reached on a system for on-site verification at declared research centers and laboratories conducting work relevant to the BWC. This could be done in a number of ways, ranging from bilateral and multilateral inspection tours to working visits and exchanges of individual scientists and others.

Particularly valuable and also consistent with the generally open practice in biological and medical science would be longer-term exchanges of working scientists, accompanied by their families when appropriate. Such exchanges could enhance confidence in the openness of the participating facilities and could also lead to scientifically beneficial collaboration and joint efforts in medicine and public health.

A type of exchange not previously considered would be that of scientific administrators and biological safety officers. If genuinely integrated into the operation of a research center or laboratory, individuals with such duties would acquire a particularly broad understanding of its activities and might also make useful contributions both at the host institution and, upon return, at their home establishments.

Challenge inspections

The Chemical Weapons Convention being negotiated in Geneva is expected to provide for a special system of inspections that could be conducted anywhere at any time on short notice by a team of inspectors designated by the Technical Secretariat of the Convention. Such inspections on challenge could be requested by any party to the Convention, with no right of refusal by the requested party. Since toxin weapons will be covered by the chemical treaty, its provisions for challenge inspection will automatically extend into an area also covered by the BWC. A system of challenge inspection could also be considered for verification of those prohibitions of the BWC that are not included in the chemical treaty. It would probably be impractical and distracting, however, to seek additional agreements on challenge inspection for biological disarmament until the challenge provisions of the Chemical Weapons Convention are agreed.

Non-secrecy of work at declared facilities

Verification of compliance with the BWC can be simplified if it is accepted as a basic principle that there should be no secret work at declared installations. This simplification results from two factors. First, if there is no secret work, the practical impediments to verification activities on-site are greatly reduced, both for the inspectors and for the managers of an installation. Second, non-secrecy is in itself an indicator of compliance, and the task of defining and verifying it may often be simpler than that of defining and verifying more technical indicators of compliance. To take an example, the presence of unrestricted international researchers or safety officers at an installation, by demonstrating non-secrecy, may by itself provide adequate confidence in its compliance with the BWC, without the need for formal inspections.

Acceptance of the principle of non-secrecy at declared facilities hinges on the proposition that any benefit of secrecy in permitted biological defense programs is outweighed over time by the effectiveness of openness in reducing the biological threat and enhancing confidence in the Convention.

Non-secrecy at declared facilities could be embodied as a basic principle in the international political agreement expected to emerge from the Third BWC Review Conference, or in a more formal protocol or treaty dealing with BW verification. If that cannot be accomplished at this time, individual states wishing to do so might declare non-secrecy unilaterally in their annual declarations.

The specific scope to be encompassed in affirmations of non-secrecy deserves careful consideration. For example, while secret laboratory research in BW defense should be renounced, the commitment to non-secrecy should not be so broad as to preclude confidentiality in legitimate national means for verification of the BWC.

Dealing with compliance issues

With general improvement in international relations, we may hope that hasty or mischievous allegations by governments of non-compliance with the BWC will not occur. Nevertheless, reliable procedures are needed to deal with honest suspicions that might arise and to curb any temptation to make political capital of ill-founded allegations. The system of declarations established by the Second BWC Review Conference and the new authority of the UN Secretary General to investigate allegations of use are important steps in this direction. In addition, it would be useful to consider institutionalized mechanisms that could address BWC compliance issues at a technical rather than a political level. In some cases, this could be accomplished pursuant to a request by a State Party for a consultative meeting of experts, as agreed at the First BWC Review Conference. In order to facilitate the procedure, the Third Review Conference might consider establishing a standing panel of experts, along with suitable mechanisms for its activation and financial support.

If compliance questions that may arise in the future are to be addressed responsibly, it is important that the US and the Soviet Union make every effort to resolve the outstanding compliance issues between them before the Third BWC Review Conference takes place. Failure to make sincere efforts in this direction sets a poor example for other States Parties and imperils the successful operation of the Convention.

Summary

All nations have a profound interest in ensuring the success of the BWC. This derives from the potential of biological weapons for indiscriminate mass destruction and from the ease with which such weapons could proliferate. The unilateral renunciation of biological and toxin weapons by the United States in 1969-70, followed by the BWC in 1972, and subsequent agreements at the BWC Review Conferences and at the United Nations constitute a sound framework for biological disarmament. Especially noteworthy is the system of data reporting agreed at the Second Review Conference and the authority unanimously given by the General Assembly to the Secretary General to conduct on-site investigations of allegations of chemical or biological attack. Additional progress is expected to result from the Third BWC Review Conference in 1991. Measures for further strengthening the biological disarmament regime, outlined above, include: (1) efforts to achieve universal membership in the BWC; (2) improvements in the system of data reporting; (3) procedures for on-site verification of compliance, including challenge inspection; (4) agreement on non-secrecy of work at declared facilities; and (5) resolution of past compliance disputes and provision for technical consultations to avert or resolve possible future disputes.

Notes

1. United Nations, *Chemical and Bacteriological (Biological) Weapons and the Effects of Their Possible Use*, (New York: United Nations, 1969).

2. World Health Organization, *Health Aspects of Chemical and Biological Weapons*, (Geneva: World Health Organization, 1970).

3. Nicholas A. Sims, *The Diplomacy of Biological Disarmament*, (New York: St. Martin's Press, 1988).

4. Erhard Geissler, ed., *Strengthening the Biological Weapons Convention by Confidence-Building Measures*, (New York: Oxford University Press, 1990).

5. The terms "maximum containment laboratory" and "containment laboratory" are defined in: World Health Organization, *Laboratory Biosafety Manual*, (Geneva: World Health Organization, 1983).

6. The White House, *Report to the Congress on Soviet Noncompliance with Arms Control Agreements*, (Washington: The White House, February 23, 1990).

7. Department of Defense, *Soviet Military Power*, 6th edition, (Washington: Department of Defense, March 1988).

8. Matthew S. Meselson, "The Biological Weapons Convention and the Sverdlovsk Anthrax Outbreak of 1979", Federation of American Scientists *Public Interest Report*, volume 41, No. 7, (September 1988).

9. "Global Spread of Chemical and Biological Weapons", *Hearing Before the Committee on Governmental Affairs and the Permanent Sub-committee on Investigations*, United States Senate, 101st Congress, 1st Session, (May 17, 1988).

10. Alexander M. Haig, Jr., "Chemical Warfare in Southeast Asia and Afghanistan", *Special Report* No. 98, U.S. Department of State, Washington, (March 22, 1982).

11. George P. Shultz, "Chemical Warfare in Southeast Asia and Afghanistan: An Update", *Special Report No. 104*, U.S. Department of State, Washington, November 11, 1982.

12. Julian Robinson, Jeanne Guillemin, and Matthew Meselson, "Yellow Rain: The Story Collapses", *Foreign Policy*, Number 68, Fall 1987, pp. 100-117. Reprinted with additions in Susan Wright, ed., *Preventing a Biological Arms Race*, (Cambridge: Massachusetts Institute of Technology Press, 1990).

10

Verification and Conventional Arms Reductions *

Jürgen Altmann (FRG), Peter Deak (Hungary),
Catherine McArdle Kelleher (USA) & Vadim I. Makarevsky (USSR)

Introduction

There is no question that verification will be one of the most complicated yet critical components in conventional arms reductions. The problem of definitions is itself more difficult than that faced in past arms control agreements. Difficulties stem from the number of weapons and sites to be reduced and controlled; under discussion, for example, in the present Conventional Forces in Europe (CFE) negotiations are more than 300,000 weapons.[1] The sheer number of different ways to offset limitations in forces and weapons systems presents its own problems. In addition, there is an unprecedented geographic scope to be monitored, as in the Atlantic to the Urals (ATTU) approach. Conventional weapons are also becoming more complicated and more lethal; recent advances in accuracy and range mean increases in battlefield depth and intensity at least 10 times of those experienced in World War II.

Moreover, verification of a conventional arms control agreement will involve unprecedented amounts of multilateral cooperation and unilateral constraint. This will be true throughout the process--from the structuring of the negotiations themselves to the operational implementation of reduction regimes for forces and/ or equipment and the execution of information checks and monitoring, on-site and off. This will have to be founded on new political agreements, and significant rethinking of past arms control positions.

A conventional verification regime in Europe now appears certain. Even

* The authors wish to acknowledge the helpful comments of Steve Fetter, the assistance of Peter Petrihos in the preparation of this essay, and the help of Itshak Lederman, Lisa McAnany, James Meen, Marie McPherson, and Michael Shirer.

before the revolutionary political changes in Eastern Europe in 1989, there had
already been major new thinking in both East and West on verification principles,
which, especially on the Soviet side, had led to fundamental shifts regarding
intrusive inspection measures. The Stockholm Conference on Disarmament in
Europe (CDE) Accords of 1986 not only marked new levels of East-West
agreement on the principles and methods of monitoring but also has met general
satisfaction with the operation of the exercise inspection regime.[2] Permanent
monitoring of standing force levels will certainly require more intensive verification
measures than was necessary for the CDE maneuver limits. The verification
precedents set by the Intermediate Nuclear Forces (INF) Treaty are path breaking:
the initial establishment and revision of the data base, the short-notice inspections,
and the procedures for weapons destruction. In the conventional arena, verification
measures will have to deal with ceilings for various weapons rather than the zero
limits of INF. Nonetheless, the experience of inspections under both Stockholm
and INF has revealed much about the problems of on-site inspection (OSI) and has
led to new levels of confidence on both sides. Finally, preliminary agreements on
a future Strategic Arms Reduction Talks (START) verification regime have also
put aside one of the more troublesome verification requirements: namely, the
"anytime, anywhere" inspection requirement that was part of the initial Reagan
START proposals.

What follows is a discussion of the many different forms that conventional
arms control verification may assume and the technologies that will make this
possible. What we are describing is not the scheme that we expect will most
probably be adopted in CFE-I, for that appropriately will rely largely on OSI and
aerial surveillance of declared facilities to monitor both the presence and the
destruction of restricted weapons. Moreover specific details will depend on final
political agreements set in the context of a reunifying Germany and a still fast-
changing Eastern Europe. Our goal in this chapter is rather to examine the
universe of available options for conventional verification in order to assess their
feasibility, their relative strengths, and their probable costs. We hope that this
"maximum approach" will allow greater relevance for all future conventional
force reductions schemes, in Europe and elsewhere.[3]

Basic Issues

Verification of conventional disarmament and confidence-building agreements
is now in its most formative and influential period. Despite the volume of new
attention to the subject and the rapid pace of specific negotiations, several basic
aims and functions are common to verification in the conventional arena.

One fundamental aim is geographic integrity, that is, confidence that any
future surreptitious entry of forces into strategic areas is logistically difficult, will
be incapable of achieving broad military objectives, and--above all--will be

highly visible. A second aim can only be described as verification confidence at the margins--reasonable certainty that an agreement is being carried out in good faith. The military indecisiveness of any single weapon, coupled with dispersal over large geographic areas, makes achieving absolute confidence in the location and disposition of all treaty-limited equipment impossible. Confidence at some less-than-perfect level must serve as a proxy for total certainty. As a result, conventional verification regimes must place great emphasis on confidence-building and cooperative measures as a means to augment the limitations of verification proper. The drive for meaningful confidence-building measures is a key element of current conventional arms control efforts and promises to test limits of cooperative measures between adversaries.

The functional requirements of verification have grown as probable agreements appear to be increasingly complex and wide-ranging. The basic function of any verification regime is information collection. A steady stream of data, ideally provided by each participant to the agreement, is necessary as evidence of good behavior and future good intent. A second function of verification is the ability to provide timely warning should war preparations occur. Warning requirements are the bedrock of compliance monitoring. Relative certainty about one's own ability to mobilize against an attacker serves as an important way of gauging the level of verification needed. A third function is transparency. Information about the disposition and location of forces, along with the right to observe exercises, is vitally important to maintaining stability.

At present, conventional verification must serve both the expected CFE Treaty and the Confidence and Security Building Measures (CSBM) negotiations. Throughout this chapter, we use the first phase of CFE as a way of exploring the limitations and possibilities inherent in all future European arms control verification schemes. But the coincidence of these negotiations with those on CSBM illustrates an important general point about the need for flexibility in verifying agreements. Reduced force levels are a necessary, but in no way a sufficient, source of stability writ large; the way in which an agreement is verified is fundamental to achieving stability. This was recognized in the context of the Conference on Security and Cooperation in Europe (CSCE), which culminated, first, in the Helsinki Final Act in 1975 and, most recently, in the CFE and CSBM mandates.

The CSCE process symbolizes the broader security needs of the whole of Europe.[4] It speaks to a range of verification requirements--political more than technical--that will, at times, serve as both disarmament and confidence-building measures. Thus, our discussion of CFE-I will represent a *tour d'horizon* of verification issues and methods but will assume parallel progress in CSBM.

For the CFE-I regime that is presently under negotiation, early efforts are likely to focus on the verification of baseline data, that is, the data exchanged by alliances on forces at the signing of a treaty.[5] This validation of data, itself a confidence-building measure, will give way to a reduction/destruction phase that could last up to three years. Over the duration of the treaty there will be a mix of verification measures, such as site inspection, inspection aids, overflights, and national technical means. The mix of measures at each stage will be greatly affected by the specific limits imposed and the ways in which the Atlantic-to-the-Urals (ATTU) area is to be divided into zones.

Proposals for Conventional Arms Control in Europe

The mandate for the CFE negotiations was signed and appended to the CSCE Concluding Document by the representatives of all 23 states in Vienna on 10 January 1989. Calls for a disarmament forum under the CSCE umbrella followed successful review conferences in Belgrade, Madrid, and Stockholm.

Formal reduction postures under consideration in CFE grew out of a larger body of arms control proposals that emerged over the last several years from the academic, political, and scientific communities, many of which would go further than those currently discussed at CFE.

For example, Ambassador Jonathan Dean proposed reductions to equal ceilings, with the North Atlantic Treaty Organization and Warsaw Treaty Organization cutting to 90 percent of NATO's present levels in a first phase in Central Europe. Over the following 10 years there were to be reductions in the whole of Europe to 50 percent of the present NATO levels.[6] A more balanced, although asymmetric, proposal was presented by Vadim Makarevsky in a 1988 Washington, D.C., debate.[7] Makarevsky's proposal required NATO to cut back six divisions while the WTO was to cut back sixteen divisions (23 percent to 31 percent of current levels). This would have limited both parties to twenty divisions in a first zone (with an equivalency ratio of 1:1.3). These forces would have allowed for a defense of the 780-kilometer front (from the Baltic to the Alps) but would not have been sufficient for large-scale offensive actions.[8] A third proposal, presented in the *Disarmament and Security Yearbook 1987*, called for the reduction of equivalent armed forces by an average of 40 percent within the so-called "Jaruzelski" zone, comprised of five NATO and four WTO member states (the Federal Republic of Germany, the Netherlands, Belgium, Luxembourg, Denmark, the German Democratic Republic, Czechoslovakia, Poland, and Hungary).[9] The goal was to achieve a general level of 25 equivalent divisions in each zone. *Yearbook* data indicated that this would have required the WTO to cut thirty-one equivalent divisions; NATO would cut sixteen divisions.[10]

In March of 1989, the Soviet Union announced a plan put forward by Foreign Minister Edward Shevardnadze for phased treaty implementation. During the first phase (two to three years), East-West asymmetries in basic weapons (fighter aircraft, combat helicopters, tanks, artillery, troop carriers, etc.) were to be reduced to "equal collective ceilings which would be 10-15 percent lower than the lowest level possessed by either of the politico-military alliances."[11] In stage two,

(two to three years), both sides were to reduce troops by another 25 percent (approximately 500,000 men, including their weaponry). In stage three, armed forces were to be reconfigured into purely defensive units, with lowest possible limits on weaponry. This early Soviet proposal was significant for two reasons; 1) its phased timing was a recognition of the problems of implementing a far reaching agreement, and 2) it placed emphasis on ceilings at substantially lower levels--both important considerations where verification is concerned.[12]

NATO's proposal was presented in detail on 6 March 1989 at the opening of the CFE talks in Vienna.[13] Essentially, it foresaw reductions of 5 to 10 percent below the lowest current levels in main battle tanks, artillery, and armored troop carriers. The reductions would have resulted in a remaining force of 20,000 tanks, 16,500 artillery pieces, and 28,000 troop transporters on each side.[14] The proposal also suggested two new limits; 1) sufficiency, or limiting a single country's holdings to 30 percent of the total alliance entitlement, and 2) stationing or limiting the number of weapons located outside national territory to 3,200 tanks, 1,700 artillery, and 6,000 troop carriers.

Verification arrangements outlined in the proposal were to include "the exchange of detailed data about forces and deployments, with the right to conduct on-site inspection, as well as other measures designed to provide assurance of compliance with the agreed provisions."[15]

In addition, the NATO proposal identified the need for deeper cuts and force restructuring so as to limit capabilities for surprise attack and large scale offensive action. Subsequently, complete measures for notification of the call-up of reservists and limits on the number and size of military exercises were added to meet these needs.

The scope and complexity of the verification task were recognized early on. At the end of the first round of talks, on 23 March 1989, at Hungary's instigation, a working group on verification and information exchange was formed.[16] NATO organized its own group, dubbed Green Team, to discuss verification under the banner of the NATO High Level Task Force for CFE.

On 11 May 1989, President Gorbachev announced that the Warsaw Pact would reduce tank strength by 40,000, cannons and mortars by 46,000 and armored troop carriers by 42,000--as part of a CFE cut. Reductions by both sides, he proposed, should result in equal levels of armaments, namely 1,350,000 men, 20,000 tanks, 1,500 tactical strike aircraft, and 1,700 helicopters.[17] On 18 May Soviet Ambassador Grinevsky tabled Mr. Gorbachev's proposal on behalf of the Warsaw Pact. The Pact itself appended stationing and sufficiency limits, including additional systems, at substantially different levels.[18]

NATO's March 1989 proposal was expanded significantly on 29 May when U.S. President George Bush proposed additional cuts of 15 percent below current levels in land based combat aircraft, and attack helicopters.[19] The move brought both sides closer to agreement in that Mr. Shevardnadze indicated that aircraft reductions by the United States were a prerequisite for Soviet tank cuts.

In the early winter of 1990, both the Soviet Union and the United States proposed major cuts in military manpower to be accomplished in CFE-I. At American instigation, both sides agreed to hold no more than 195,000 ground and air personnel in the central zone of the ATTU area, with the United States allowed an additional 30,000 forces stationed elsewhere in Europe.[20] The Soviet Union also suggested an overall manpower (indigenous and stationed) limit of 700-750,000 in Central Europe, instead of what Soviet CFE negotiator Grinevsky said was the now-obsolete 1,350,000 proposal for the ATTU zone.[21]

These proposals deal only with quantitative issues. In a comprehensive conventional arms reduction agreement in Europe, however, qualitative aspects would also be key. For example, artillery could be limited to 30 km range, and rockets and missiles limited to 50 km range. Another important challenge would be to devise a mechanism to limit the development of new weapons technologies which might otherwise endanger the future of an agreement.

The Importance of Zones

Methods and intrusiveness of inspection will differ with the depth of the reduction zone, whatever the size and character of the cuts agreed upon. Both the reduction of forces and verification will most likely be performed by zone. Various zonal proposals have been emphasized in the policy community and in scholarly discussions over the past five years. They range from the three zone proposal of Andreas von Bülow of the Federal Republic of Germany to the six zone formula of the IMEMO *Yearbook* proposal.[22] In the official CFE forum, both East and West have tabled proposals for subzones within the ATTU. NATO's zonal approach uses four concentric zones and sets ceilings within each zone in addition to a single ATTU wide limit. The four zones and the maxima for each are:

Zone One
NATO: Belgium, FRG, the Netherlands, and Luxembourg;
WTO: Czechoslovakia, GDR and Poland;
Maxima: 8,000 main battle tanks, 4,500 artillery, and 11,000 armored troop carriers.[23]

Zone Two
NATO: Zone 1 and France, Italy, U.K., and Denmark;
WTO: Zone 1 and Hungary, and the USSR Military Districts of Baltic, Belorussia, and Carpathia;
Maxima: 10,300 main battle tanks, 7,600 artillery, 18,000 armored troop carriers.

Zone Three
NATO: Zone 2 and Spain, Portugal;
WTO: Zone 2 and the USSR Military Districts of Moscow, Ural, and Volga;
Maxima: 11,300 main battle tanks, 9,000 artillery, and 20,000 armored troop carriers.

Zone Four
NATO: Zone 3 and Norway, Iceland, Greece and Turkey;
WTO: Zone 3 and Rumania, Bulgaria and the USSR Military Districts of Leningrad, Kiev, Odessa, North Caucasus and Transcaucasus;
Maxima: 20,000 main battle tanks, and 16,500 artillery pieces, and 28,000 armored troop carriers.

The East has tabled two zonal formulae. On 25 May, a detailed Eastern zone proposal included the following three zones and corresponding maxima for active and stored items:

Central Europe
NATO: Belgium, Denmark, FRG, the Netherlands, and Luxembourg;
WTO: Czechoslovakia, GDR, Hungary, and Poland;
Maxima: 8,700 main battle tanks, 7,600 artillery pieces, 14,500 armored personnel carriers, 420 strike aircraft, 800 assault helicopters, and 570,000 personnel.

Line of Contact
NATO: Central Zone and Greece, Italy, Norway, and Turkey;
WTO: Central Zone and Bulgaria, Rumania, and the USSR Military Districts of Baltic, Leningrad, North Caucasus, Transcaucasus, and Odessa;
Maxima: 16,000 main battle tanks, 16,500 artillery pieces, 20,000 armored personnel carriers, 1,100 strike aircraft, 1,300 assault helicopters, and 1,000,000 personnel.

Rear Zone
NATO: France, Iceland, Portugal, Spain, and the U.K.;
WTO: USSR Military Districts of Belorussia, Carpathia, Kiev, Moscow, Volga, and Ural;
Maxima: 4,000 main battle tanks, 7,500 artillery pieces, 7,500 armored personnel carriers, 400 strike aircraft, 400 assault helicopters, and 350,000 personnel.

On 27 June 1989, the East tabled a second zonal approach that included the following nonconcentric zones and maxima again for active and stored items:

Center of Europe
NATO: Belgium, Denmark, FRG, France, Luxembourg, the Netherlands, and U.K.;
WTO: Czechoslovakia, GDR, Hungary, Poland, and the USSR Military Districts of Baltic, Belorussia, Carpathia, and Kiev;
Maxima: 13,300 main battle tanks, 11,500 artillery pieces, 20,750 armored personnel carriers, 1,120 strike aircraft, 1,250 assault helicopters, and 910,000 personnel.

North of Europe
NATO: Norway;
WTO: Northern part of the Leningrad USSR Military District;
Maxima: 200 main battle tanks, 1,000 artillery pieces, 150 armored personnel carriers, 30 strike aircraft, 30 assault helicopters, and 20,000 personnel.

South of Europe
NATO: Greece, Italy, and Turkey;
WTO: Bulgaria, Rumania, and the USSR Military Districts of Odessa, North Caucasus, and Transcaucasus;
Maxima: 5,200 main battle tanks, 8,500 artillery pieces, 5,750 armored personnel carriers, 290 strike aircraft, 360 assault helicopters, and 270,000 personnel.

Rear Area
NATO: Iceland, Portugal, and Spain;
WTO: Southern part of the Leningrad Military District and the USSR Military Districts of Moscow, Ural and Volga;
Maxima: 1,300 main battle tanks, 3,000 artillery pieces, 1,350 armored personnel carriers, 60 strike aircraft, 60 assault helicopters, and 150,000 personnel.

In spring 1990, few significant East-West differences still remain. The flexibility shown on both sides suggests that a final agreement is near.

Basic Principles

What basic principles apply not only to the present CFE and CSBM but to all foreseeable agreements on conventional weapons reductions in Europe? Four basic features seem clear:

A. One hundred percent verifiability is not achievable within a conventional arms control regime.

One hundred percent verifiability has certainly never been the true standard met by existing arms control regimes, whatever the promises given during congressional hearings or election campaigns. Nonetheless, the "completely verifiable" demand has been given new credence by the steady improvement in monitoring capabilities and by the seeming exhaustiveness of the INF regime.

Conventional arms control involves a number of critical constraints and problems, however, that complicate any public claim to one hundred percent verifiability. Even with the strictest of definitions, a number of conventional weapons and support elements resemble the normal products of advanced industrialized states, whereas a nuclear missile would not be mistaken for a benign civilian item. A prime example is the inherent difficulty in differentiating civilian aircraft and trucks from military transport vehicles. In the present CFE process, the primary focus is on a limited number of equipment items, with only secondary emphasis on associated manpower. There will be the clear parallel link to the Conference on Security and Cooperation in Europe and follow-on confidence-building measures--which themselves constitute another form of verification.

Although now overtaken by events and the magnitude of Soviet unilateral reductions, the initial goals of the CFE talks suggested two different sets of requirements. Minimizing the risk of surprise attack emphasized the need for a verification regime that approached those of START and INF in rigor, timing, comprehensiveness, and complexity. Yet limitations aimed at preventing the capture of decisive advantage in a protracted conventional conflict suggested a regime crafted not only to increase transparency but also to ensure slow action and reaction.

B. Verification regimes must be as simple and as transparent as possible, and must be designed within feasible limits of political and economic costs.

Perhaps the greatest difficulty in designing a conventional verification regime will be the temptation to strive for technical elegance without regard for the political and economic costs involved. The latest technical wrinkle--as in perimeter/portal monitoring of the movement of troops, equipment, or support goods--may involve costs high enough to limit its scope unnecessarily. A perimeter/portal system is estimated to cost 1 million U.S. dollars per kilometer.[24] These expenditures will undoubtedly decrease given the benefits of scale and the serious consideration of satisfactory alternatives over time. Nonetheless, the crucial cost questions will come in the initial stages of the verification regime, when reduction opponents may well claim the cost not only is prohibitive but still does not provide for complete verifiability. Small states will be most affected by these high outlays.

The more important political costs will involve trade-offs between the levels of intrusiveness that may be thought necessary for broad foreign policy goals and those that will be acceptable to the territories and the populations most directly affected. The experience of the INF inspections, which so far has been very positive, involves a limited number of sites and a fairly exclusive set of manufacturing facilities. The intrusiveness of a wide ranging CFE regime will be significantly greater, and far more care will have to be given to the definition of the requirements of "normal" life on the territory of allies, adversaries, and even "associated" states.

The political costs of gaining acceptance for the intrusiveness required will be mitigated if the standards of simplicity and transparency of verification, at least for key areas of reduction, can be met from the outset. Simple measures, which involve less continuously intrusive measures, will always appear more attractive and will also contribute to the political credibility of the reduction agreement itself. One example is separating turrets at some significant distance from demobilized tanks for secured storage. Mobilization of these tanks will be a decision taken with deliberation and at a slow pace. Requiring munitions to be stored at a distance from weapons may be an easier initial step. A verification scheme that involves frequent or continuous monitoring (manned or unmanned) will appear that much more logical and will ultimately perhaps inspire confidence in other reduction measures.

Transparency of the outcomes from verification regimes will help offset claims of industrial, if not military, espionage that have always plagued discussions of on-site monitoring in Europe. However, some confidentiality in the diplomatic/ military process will help to eliminate highly publicized accusations of non-compliance and may make the correction of questioned behavior easier. Confidentiality may reduce, but not eradicate, concerns about political equity among the Central European states, which will almost certainly be subject to the most intensive and comprehensive set of verification measures. It will certainly make it easier to move toward the sharing of both information and evaluations of effectiveness that the multilateral nature of the reduction process will require. But once the 23 CFE states agree upon a reduction regime, this will imply a far wider involvement of all 35 CSCE states in evaluating the output of NTM; in addition, it may provide new incentives for additional transparency with third-party satellite monitoring as an independent check.

C. Verification is a multilateral enterprise.

A conventional arms control agreement will be multilateral in almost every phase. For the first time, an arms control agreement will involve both the territory and the forces of the allies of the Soviet Union and the United States. Every indication now is that the success of the CFE-I agreement will depend on the participation of the 23 at every step. This will change every aspect of verification, even those aspects that are tied to unilateral measures. And there will have to be a significant amount of sharing: in terms of information, the intrusiveness of verification, and the costs--political, military, and economic--that will be involved.

Initially, the most critical aspects will be those that involve considerations of equity. The provisions of the INF Treaty regarding the frequency of inspection and the percentage of inspections confined to particular national territories represent a promising start. But there will have to be far more consideration and far more balancing of burden and risk with allied partners than has ever been the case before for both the U.S. and the Soviet Union. This applies as much to the drawing of limitation zones and the types of equipment that are limited as it does to specific verification measures. It is clear, however, that any "overtly discriminatory regime"--specifically one that touches political sensitivities in the two Germanys unduly--will prove counterproductive to agreement to, or implementation of, a first stage in what is hoped to be an evolutionary process.

A less important but still interested political constituency will be those states that are indirectly associated with the CFE-I debate--the neutrals and the nonaligned European states. They see the CFE process as one in which they have critical stakes and a right to oversight, given the structure of the group of 35. Their inclusion in verification measures at some level will add complexity, but it may as well broaden political support and provide further for reliability and equity. They too will be concerned with the procedures for the timely, equitable sharing of information on both long-term trends and shorter term developments.

D. Verification of conventional arms control will involve reliance on a mixture of cooperative and unilateral measures, including reliance on American and Soviet national technical means.

Traditionally, NTM have been the principal instrument for verification. They include satellites that take photographs, detect infrared emissions, listen to radio communications, and measure radar signals. In the European context, military reconnaissance on both sides includes high-altitude flights along inter-alliance borders with cameras and electronic intelligence equipment, as well as listening posts and radar stations on high ground. Such autonomous measures will certainly continue to be used by both sides to assess the military situation in the other's territory and to detect possible treaty violations.

NTM alone will not be sufficient for conventional arms control. Perhaps their principal value will be as deterrents against clandestine treaty circumventions, given uncertainties about their real capabilities. They suffer from several specific drawbacks:

- The most effective systems are in the exclusive possession of the United States and the USSR. Even both countries' allies have come to realize that information exchange is not always satisfactory. It is improbable that equal access to these means can be negotiated;
- National technical means are normal parts of military intelligence operations, the results of which are regularly used for targeting and attack planning. In a conventional stability context, it will be important to limit the new information gained in an attempt to ensure that verification procedures do not lead to possibly destabilizing advantages in information collection;
- Conventional equipment is more easily concealable and mobile than all but a few strategic systems.

As under the INF treaty provisions, a mixture of measures is needed to increase reliability, especially during the crucial initial phases. The specific increase may involve only modest technical gains given the expense and effort involved, but the side benefits in terms of the testing of political intentions and the parallel ratification of NTM results will prove significant. Too, the actual components and their mix are crucial for success, as are the inclusion of manned and some unmanned measures--some of which are continuous and others of which involve short-notice, cooperative efforts. These will help develop public confidence and sustain joint and unilateral efforts in the absence of precedent or a base of previous cooperation beyond the limited Stockholm/INF experience.

Measures often talked about include:

- Inspection teams and observation posts, either permanent or temporary, (near major equipment depots, barracks, exercise grounds, air and sea ports, railway lines and roads crossing zone boundaries (the latter are sometimes called exit/entry points, or EEPs)) could be used in combination with sensor systems or bases for the dispatch of inspectors or for short-notice inspections;
- Overlapping sensor systems of various types that are both mutually reinforcing in their output and differentially vulnerable to mechanical failure and interference, or "spoofing";
- Systems of reliable identification--as in electronic tags or accurate navigational transponders capable of reporting location - that can be attached to the most important equipment units (such as aircraft, helicopters, tanks, and rocket launchers) and made virtually tamper-proof;
- Aerial surveillance systems, including overflights (according to specific

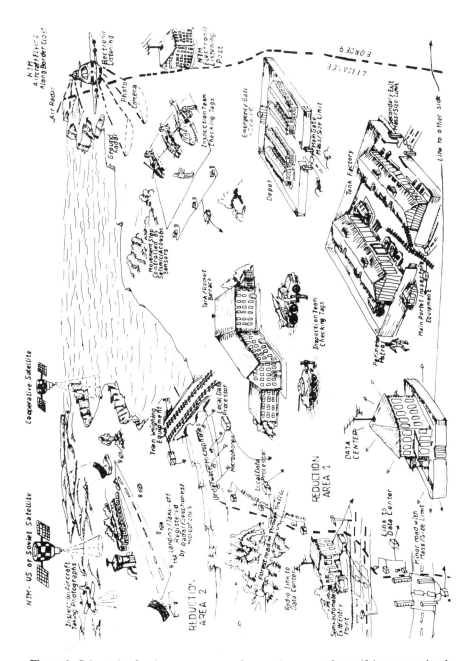

Figure 1. Schematic of various components of a complex system for verifying conventional arms reductions.

quotas, regions, and depth), aerial photography, highly capable ground-linked or airborne radar, and perhaps third-party monitoring;
- Space-based monitoring systems.

Elements of a Comprehensive Verification System for Conventional Arms Reductions in Europe

Designing an adequate, mixed, cooperative verification system for conventional arms reductions in Europe is a major task. Any negotiable regime will have to include a number of different elements and inspection techniques. Challenge inspections and NTM will probably be included under all circumstances. The practicality of including other elements remains subject to considerations of reliability, confidence levels, and, above all, cost. Our discussion here will be a comprehensive review of the methods and technologies now available or foreseeable for inclusion in any conventional verification regime.

What Is to Be Limited?

In the unsuccessful Mutual and Balanced Force Reduction (MBFR) negotiations,

Table 1.   Types of Equipment Eligible for Limitation by Treaty

On Land :
Tanks
Rocket artillery, --by caliber
Self-propelled artillery, --by caliber
Armored vehicles, --armored troop carriers (ATCs)
Other tracked vehicles (e.g., bridge-building tanks, pioneer tanks)
Missile launch vehicles
Heavy military trucks
Bridge-building equipment

In the Air :
Attack aircraft (including helicopters)
Surface-to-surface missiles
Air-to-surface missiles
Air defence missiles
Antitactical missile defence missiles
Bombers

Table 2.   Military Installations at which Limitations May Apply.

Barracks
Training/Exercise Areas
Air Bases
Storage Sites for:
  weapons
  weapons parts
  other equipment
  ammunition
  fuel

---

the focus was on numbers of personnel, which are inherently difficult to verify.[25] The CFE talks will mainly deal with major military equipment; limits on personnel will probably involve withdrawal of units or individual soldiers (thinning). Personnel may also be limited for maneuvers. As discussed, different limits will probably be devised for different geographical subzones within the total ATTU reduction area. One could also envisage local movement limits: for example, tanks to be confined to the vicinity of their barracks. The verification tasks will thus probably comprise at least the following:

- Checking that the specific military equipment (sometimes called TLE, for treaty-limited equipment) in a certain region is below the agreed limit;
- Checking that specific units have left a certain region or location;
- Checking that certain declared military installations are out of service;
- Checking that the equipment stored at certain depots is not moved away.

A more comprehensive verification regime would entail controlling the flow of treaty-limited equipment into and out of a certain region. This can mean installation of exit/entry points at major roads, railway lines, ports, and airports. An all-encompassing system would require controls at production and destruction facilities and the prevention of clandestine transport cross-country or along minor roads. Alternatively, a scheme of random inspections and counting can provide a strong incentive to keep the agreed limits. (Counting actually can be avoided with the help of reliable tags, see below.)

Data Exchange

Official exchanges about the numbers and properties of equipment will serve different verification purposes at different phases of the reduction process. Baseline data will allow the certification of the point of departure as well as the correction of errant estimates collected through NTM. As reductions proceed, frequent exchanges on equipment withdrawn, destroyed, or eliminated will permit updating. Finally, when agreed limits are reached, data exchanges will support compliance monitoring. Signatories will probably also want continuing information on equipment moved in or out for repair, decommissioning of declared military sites, or replacement of personnel.

On-Site Inspection

On-Site Inspection. A central verification element in a conventional arms control regime in Europe will be on-site inspection. The reasons relate to both the political and military requirements in the West and East and the precedential impact of both the Stockholm Accords and the INF Treaty. OSI takes different forms that can be used in combination for discrete purposes:

- Permanent stationing of inspectors at declared exit/entry points of reduction areas. As in INF, inspectors may also be needed at the portals of production or destruction facilities with the additional right of random checks of the perimeter. A different scheme would see liaison officers permanently attached to larger military units of the other side, perhaps at the division level.
- Systematic inspections to monitor locations of a specific type according to a planned schedule. This procedure can be used for an initial inventory of delimited items or for the validation of the exchanged data. This method of inspection is currently used for the observation of large-scale maneuvers. Even automated sensors require periodic servicing by inspectors. In order to verify agreed limits on testing of new weapons types, the presence of inspectors may be required at respective testing grounds.
- Random inspections defined a priori in general terms, as by total number per year, type of installation, and region. The exact location to be visited and the exact date when a visit will occur are not disclosed in advance. These decisions are made at will by the inspecting side, after which the inspected side is then obliged to transport inspectors to the location within a definite time span, say between six to nine hours. The INF and Stockholm regimes dealt with agreed-upon entry and exit points, timetables for reports, and composition of inspection teams; the regimes, however, did not include random inspections.
- Challenge inspections for the purpose of analyzing suspicious events or locations. The suspicion may be true or false; they will often be based on information gained from NTM, other national intelligence sources, or

other verification systems, as in the Stockholm Accords. Within the cooperative verification system, information gained by automated sensors or during an overflight may trigger a request to inspect a site at which illegal activity may be present. This inspection type will only be defined in very general terms: for example, a maximum number per year and the handling of restricted areas. To make the inspection effective, a stringent time schedule is required. States will probably be obligated to accept only a certain number of such inspections per year.

One interesting proposal for a specific inspection regime is the envelope scheme, designed by a Western European Union working group. It allows for reliable verification of total holdings of treaty-limited equipment without revealing the structure and organization of the force as a whole.[26] Under this system, both alliances exchange a list of declared locations of treaty limited equipment. (A stringent challenge inspection scheme has to ensure that no items are kept at undeclared, illegal locations). A second list contains the number of items at various locations but identifies those locations only by code number. Sealed envelopes containing location numbers and descriptions of treaty-limited equipment and their locations are put in a dual-key safe. During the year, a specified number of envelopes are randomly drawn. The locations drawn from the safe are then inspected and checked against the envelope contents and also against the second list. Unopened envelopes are destroyed annually. Inspection of 5 to 10 percent of sites annually would provide a high degree of verification certainty and give a strong incentive to supply accurate information.

The random nature of this scheme may allow for a violation to go undetected for several years, but a buildup of military significance will certainly not evade timely detection. The current spirit of inspection openness and the lessening fears of disclosing military structure may make this practice unnecessary.

Procedures. A precondition for OSI or cooperative verification of any other type will be an agreement on a comprehensive set of procedures that meet a number of requirements. First, there is the goal of adequate verification. Second, there should be an attempt to minimize the risk that treaty information will be used for improved targeting and attack planning. Third, legitimate concerns for privacy have to be respected. Fourth, there should be means of communication and methods of solving ambiguities and compliance disputes that work even in situations of political tension and crisis.

Specific aspects to be agreed on would include, at least, the following elements:

- Rights of inspectors (e.g., movement, equipment, transport, transport vehicles);
- Process of inspections (e.g., escorts, minimum/maximum times, halting movements of troops and military equipment at an inspected site between

the inspection request and actual arrival of the inspectors);
- Modes of communication between sides (for data exchange, inspection requests, and inspection results);
- Support and integration of monitoring equipment: regular maintenance, access in case of failures, inspection in case of suspicious activity, rules preventing or banning saturation (e.g., forbid earth-moving work in the vicinity of ground vibration sensors), facilitate observation (e.g., forbid covered transport of treaty-limited items through exit/entry points);
- Specific informational obligations designed to aid in the identification of legal and illegal objects;
- Process for organized learning from past experience and for regular review, to allow for modification of verification schemes (specifically, this would include incorporating adequate regulations for new technologies that are militarily significant).

For the handling of short-notice inspections, it may be advisable to establish small task forces in all 23 CFE countries and perhaps in all 35 CSCE states as well. A smaller first step in this direction could be a working center of the 35 CSCE states that could be created in a neutral state with appropriate communications. The second step of system building could be the establishment of so-called crisis management centers with central databanks, where precision, correction, and explanations concerning the faults of limitation systems are judged. It may also be useful to create special information centers that would handle all communication and information gained by sensors. Computerized data bases and communication links would facilitate the verification task. Devising an appropriate structure-- probably to be extended in phases--requires a significant amount of scientific and engineering work.

Sensors

After an initial balance is reached in a reduction zone, sensors can be used to detect movement of limited equipment. Movement can occur through import or export--across borders, at ports or airports, or by production/destruction (see Figure 2). Legal movement, possibly prenotified, would take place at declared exit/entry points and at production/destruction facilities. Inspection teams could supplement sensors in these locations. At the lines between exit/entry points, sensors would serve to detect any clandestine movement or transport of treaty-limited items. Higher sensor sensitivity requirements would apply near intersystem borders.

Automated Sensors. Placing automated sensors permanently on the territory of the inspected side can provide several advantages over manned inspection schemes. Sensors can provide a more intensive coverage in space and time at

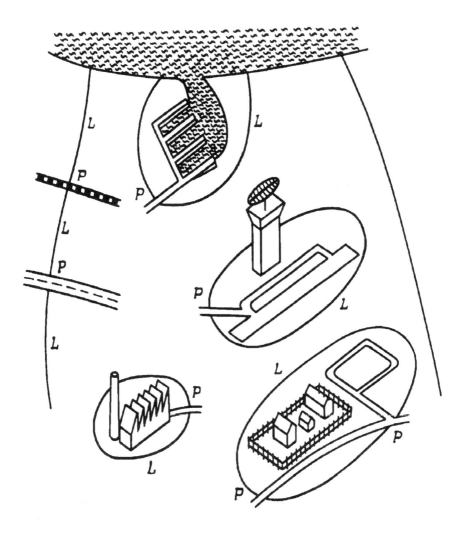

Figure 2. The number of treaty limited items within a reduction zone can change by import/export or production/destruction. A comprehensive sensor system can be established using point controls (P) at traffic routes and portals and line controls (L) at the sectors in between, and at places augmented by physical barriers. Sensors along coastlines are not essential since surface ship transport is easily identified by NTM. Similarly, NTM would be efficient in detecting illegal production facilities and unreported airstrips. Sensors can monitor compliance with movement limits within zones; this could be applied to tanks restricted to areas surrounding barracks or training grounds.

Table 3.   Sensors for the Immediate Vicinity (0 to 20 meters)

Infrared intrusion detector
Ultrasound intrusion detector
Microphone
Array of light beam interruption lines
Induction loop
Television camera
Large vehicle weighbridge

These could be used at points where treaty-limited equipment could enter or leave a reduction area. For automated use, a computer with appropriate hardware and software would have to do the data processing.

lower cost than could be provided by inspectors. Continuous functioning is normal with machinery, while inspection teams have to be relieved after days or hours; in addition, as opposed to machines, inspectors vary in alertness, arousal and attentiveness. Sensor monitoring systems can be tailored exactly to the specific measurement purpose; this can be completely transparent to the inspected side and therefore allay suspicions of spying. With inspectors, there will always be the temptation--as well as the suspicion--that they are used to collect more information than has been agreed upon in the negotiations. Inspectors will continue to perform tasks of highest importance, such as visiting a site where sensors detect suspicious activity. For the foreseeable future, human intervention will also be necessary to repair and maintain failed equipment or to ensure maintenance. More importantly, the human element will help discourage attempts to fool automated sensors, for example, by random inspections of sensor sites.

The task of a sensor system is to detect treaty-limited equipment as well as to potentially discriminate between different classes of objects. They could be deployed along the border of a reduction area, and additional sensors would be required at points where treaty-limited equipment could enter or leave, such as production and destruction facilities and airports. Within a reduction area, sensors could be deployed around local zones of restricted mobility, for example, in order to verify that tanks do not leave the regions around their barracks and the neighboring maneuver area. The sensors provide an actual count of exits and entries, and allow a real-time balance of the numbers of objects; while violations would potentially show up much later in a tagging, random-inspection scheme, they instead produce an immediate alarm. In a certain sense, the remotely readable electronic tag with the interrogating transmitter (described below) acts like an interactive sensor.

Sensors for the Immediate Vicinity (0 to 20 meters). Such sensor systems can be used at portals (of a factory, depot, barracks, maneuver area, port, or airport);

and at a road or railroad crossing a zonal border. These point observation stations have to be augmented by controls along the perimeter of the installation or along the remaining border between the traffic routes.

Physical properties of objects passing through the portal or exit/entry points that could be measured include length, height, form, mass, type of propulsion (i.e., tracked or wheeled, number of axles), sound and infrared emission. Table 3 lists several sensor types which could be used for such purposes.

A simple system could monitor a minor exit of a tank factory where only persons and small cars were allowed to pass. An induction loop and a linear array of light beams will suffice to make sure that no tanks, or trucks carrying tanks, exit. With appropriate data processing equipment such a system will cost no more than $100,000 (including cost of installation).

At the main portal of such a factory, it may be necessary to discriminate between different types of heavy vehicles. Here a sophisticated television camera system might be required along with a weighbridge for large vehicles. With other devices like induction loops, such a system will cost roughly $1 million (including installation costs). These figures compare favorably with the cost of a truck (on the order of $100,000) and a tank (about $2 million).[27]

All the sensors mentioned here are available commercially, and they are used regularly at present in the fields of security and traffic control technology. Similar techniques--and a few others--are being applied at the Votkinsk and Magna missile plants under the INF Treaty. Open questions include: What sensors should be deployed at a given point? What is the appropriate mix of automated sensor techniques and human observation and control?

Sensors for Greater Distances (20 meters to 2 kilometers). Sensor systems for greater distances can be used to monitor both the perimeter of an installation between the normal exits or the border separating different reduction zones between the established exit/entry points (cross-country or at minor roads). The

Table 4.   Possible Sensors for Greater Distances (20 meters to 2 kilometers)

Sensor Types:
  Seismic sensor for ground vibration
  Microphone
  Television camera
  Infrared camera
  Magnetic field sensor

These can be used at the border of a reduction area between normal traffic lines. Underwater microphones might be used where major rivers act as area borders. Redundancy can be achieved by using several techniques in parallel. Signals from an area (say, 2 to 5 kilometers) are concentrated and processed at local data collection centers.

task is to detect any attempt to move treaty-limited objects across the perimeter or border. Repeated checks of the integrity of a fenced perimeter, together with seals at possible unused exits, may suffice; but where there is no fence, there will have to be special provisions to detect cross-border penetrations by treaty-limited vehicles. In principle, threatening concentrations of vehicles in forward areas could be produced by cautious crossing of the line cross-country or at minor roads, one by one over months; sensors thus should be able to detect a single vehicle at its slowest practical speed.

Physical properties to be measured include the following: form, ground vibration, sound (including infrasound and underwater sound if rivers are used as borders), infrared emission, and magnetic field disturbance. Form can be measured by cameras using visible or infrared light; visible light is limited by situations of low light and weather conditions--at night or in fog although infrared can be used at night and in haze. The other signatures are more or less independent of the weather and daylight.

Several sensor types are listed in Table 4 that could be used for medium distances. While such sensors are available commercially (of course, some modification for the verification purposes would be necessary), not much is known on an unclassified level about either the signatures that different military and civilian vehicles produce, or the environmental noise from which these signatures have to be distinguished. A significant amount of research and development is needed to establish the maximum detection distances for the different sensor types, objects, and environmental conditions. Theoretical considerations and early experiments suggest that 1) magnetic field disturbance measurements by existing high-sensitivity equipment will provide detection in the range of tens of meters; and 2) with ground vibration, hundreds of meters may be possible, and a range of hundreds of meters also seems possible for underwater sound in rivers.[28]

Combinations of microphones and seismic detectors can detect land vehicles, low flying planes, and helicopters. Thus, movements of aircraft across a zonal border can be detected with the same equipment as employed for land vehicles. Of particular importance is the registration of aircraft movements on air bases (see Figure 3). Take-offs and landings can be detected by both ground vibration and engine noise. Additionally, upwardly directed short-range radars can be installed at the ends of runways to provide a greater number of signatures, thus improving the redundancy of the system. In this way, a limit on the number of simultaneously present aircraft can be verified. It is also possible to monitor limitation on movement between an inspection request and the actual arrival of inspectors.

Beside the basic questions of detection and discrimination, other problems must be solved. What is the optimal way of communicating sensor measurements? What level of de-centralized data pre-processing should be chosen? How much redundancy and synergism is needed? What technical measures must be taken to prevent cheating? How are encryption techniques to be incorporated into sensor

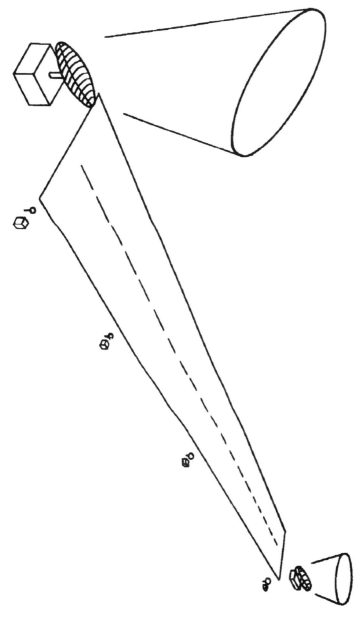

Figure 3. Take-off and landing of aircraft can be monitored by a combination of microphones, geophones, and upward-looking radars. Thus, a computer can have an actual count of the number of aircraft present and can continuously check this number against an agreed upper limit. By storing the movements for one-half day or so, movement restrictions between an inspection request and arrival of inspectors can be verified.

system design and to be reconciled with the requirements of transparency?

Tags & Seals

Tags. As we have argued before, we do not expect that most categories of conventional armaments and equipment in Europe will be banned in the near future. Numeric limits in CFE-I will be quite high and the zones quite large: for example, 5,000 to 20,000 tanks in Western and Eastern Europe, dispersed over millions of square kilometers. Too, in CFE-I the concern will not be with monitoring individual equipment items but rather with equipment concentrations.

Tagging each legitimate object is one way to avoid searching for all treaty-limited equipment in the total area of a conventional arms agreement. This approach requires that there be:

- an identical number of tags and permitted items;
- a method to permanently affix each tag to one item;
- an opportunity to check the authenticity and intactness of each tag.[29]

If these requirements are fulfilled, any illegal items in excess of the agreed limit can be immediately recognized as not having a valid tag. It will then be enough to perform a certain number of random inspections, say, at 10 percent of the installations where such objects are deployed per year. For higher effectiveness, there might also be additional challenge inspections at sites of suspected violations. Tagging could also be used for designating objects as belonging to a certain area.

Thus, tagging schemes would generally not associate treaty-limited equipment with a specific location. Rather, more global numeric thresholds would be employed, allowing greater freedom of movement in an extensive geographic zone. Random and, of course, challenge inspections would ensure that all items detected are legal. The randomness of inspections, while creating strong compliance incentives, also holds open the possibility of small undetected violations. Large violations, however, would certainly be detected promptly.

A tagging scheme that is reliable for arms control verification purposes must meet the following requirements:

- it must be impossible to duplicate a tag;
- it must be impossible to remove it from treaty-limited equipment;
- it must be impossible to deceive the equipment that checks the authenticity of a tag;
- the tag has to function reliably over long periods (say, 10 years);
- the tag has to remain functional under all environmental conditions to which the treaty item may be exposed in the area (e.g., extreme temperatures and other weather influences, low or high pressures, dust and dirt).

Military, practical, and strategic stability considerations dictate a few more demands:

- the tag must not hamper the normal functioning of the military object;

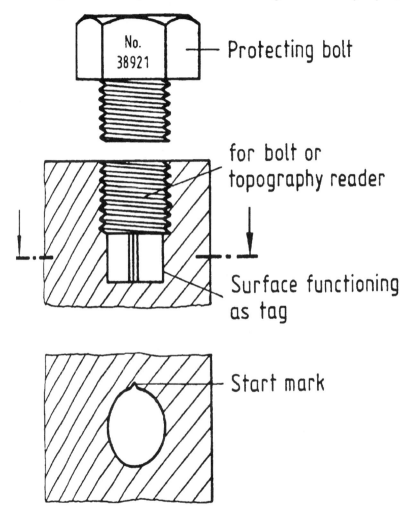

Figure 4. Surface roughness tag. Tanks or armored vehicles get a cylindrical borehole about 1 centimeter in diameter and 1 centimeter deep that is normally covered by a bolt carrying an identifying number. The bolt is removed and a cylindrical roughness profile is taken. A track record for the first time can be relocated using a reference hole or groove. If the measured profile is identical to the one that belongs to the bolt number, the object is legal.

- the tag must be cost-effective (i.e., generally less than 1 percent of the item cost);[30]
- the tag must not contain systems collecting non-sanctioned information (e.g., vibration sensors measuring motor/gun characteristics, eavesdropping devices on crew communication);
- the tagging system must not provide the real-time location of many objects, as this could confer potential military advantage to an attacker.

Tags could be handed over from the inspecting side; in this case a mechanism is needed to assure that tags are affixed within a certain time. Another option

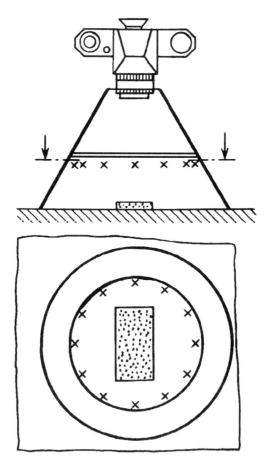

Figure 5. Reflecting particle tag. Randomly distributed reflecting particles are photographed when illuminated from many different directions. The resulting set of patterns is compared with the patterns recorded initially.

would be to have the inspecting side affix the tags within the host's territory. This would require visits to all installations during a short time period, being very intrusive or massing of forces in central locations which is very cumbersome. These difficulties could be avoided if a nonreproducible property of the treaty-limited item could be measured by the inspected side and reliably remeasured at each inspection (see the surface roughness tag in Figure 4).

Thus far, not many tagging schemes have been thoroughly tested for arms control verification purposes; none have been agreed upon in negotiations. The most promising concepts tested and considered include the following.

a. The surface roughness tag has been developed for control of fissile material flow.[31] This tag can be used on a number of land vehicles, including armor. A fine diamond tip is moved across a metal surface, measuring its structure with micrometer resolution, just as a stylus senses the groove of a gramophone disk. The inspected side would measure the roughness profiles of a special borehole in all its tanks and would give these data to the other side. Reproducing a surface pattern with such high resolution is beyond the limits of the most advanced machinery. In an inspection, a portable apparatus would measure a surface roughness profile. An identical profile means positive confirmation of the identity and legality of the item. This scheme motivates the inspected side to make exact measurements and to transfer correct data. In addition, this procedure is simple and robust. Large-scale tests and final development of this technology can begin immediately. Tag production and profile measurements should be possible at under $50.

b. The reflecting particle tag is being developed for verification of mobile strategic missiles.[32] It can be used on any mobile object. A transparent epoxy resin is mixed with light-reflecting particles and applied to an area of the treaty limited item of about 10x20 square centimeters. After hardening, this area is sequentially illuminated from 10 to 20 directions, and the resulting patterns of luminous points are recorded with a camera and stored in digital form for later comparison. These patterns follow from the random position of the particles in three dimensions; thus, they could only be duplicated with extreme effort and cost. Production of new tags costs no more than a few dollars, reading them constitutes the major portion of the costs involved. The technique is immediately available, large-scale tests and final development can begin immediately.

c. The electronic tag can be used with any mobile object. In its simpler form, using readout by immediate contact, it consists of an electronic circuit, perhaps in the form of a semiconductor chip, with long-life battery, appropriate read-only program memory, and some read-write data memory. An inspector would plug a portable computer with an appropriate verification program into the tag socket. Contact-less communication through infrared or inductive coupling will increase reliability. Once a start code is received, the chip would respond with an identity message, an indication that it has been functioning normally since the last readout,

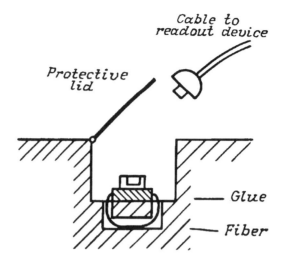

Figure 6. Electronic tag: The tag is located under a protective lid. Readout is taken by direct contact, e.g. a plug put into a socket on the tag, or by light emitters and receivers. The fact that the tag has not been removed can be established by special glue or by light pulses sent through an optical fiber threaded into a hole in the vehicle body.

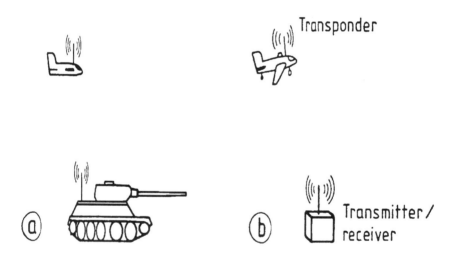

Figure 7. A remotely readable electronic tag readout is initiated by a transmitter; a transponder on board the treaty limited equipment then answers with a message; its coded contents reliably confirm the identity and intactness of the tag. This can be used to interrogate land vehicles from aircraft in a large area (a). A second application (b) is at air bases, where landing and take-off aircraft are interrogated by a fixed short-range transmitter.

and possibly the fact that it has not been separated from the treaty-limited item. This system requires a certain amount of secrecy and complexity to ensure that this information cannot simply be read out and reproduced.

The electronic tag is more delicate than the mechanical optical schemes discussed above. Problems of robustness under field conditions and of battery life are imaginable. The electronic tag's main advantage is that it can more easily be tailored to meet different needs should there be large numbers of objects to be identified or the need for a greater degree of security through encryption. It provides the possibility for some built-in secret pattern that can serve as an additional unilateral authenticity check. (Arguments about assumed cheating may be difficult to resolve in the agreed cooperative verification system, however.) Adapting the upcoming "smart" cards of the commercial field to the required robustness will need a few years of development and testing. With mass production, costs of a few hundred dollars per unit are plausible.

d. The remotely readable electronic tag, also available for use on mobile objects, is more complex. Here the identity and validity of the tag would have to be established purely by electromagnetic transmissions; signs of tampering would not be subject to regular inspection--random units could be removed, of course. Thus, more ingenious coding schemes and more secrecy are required. One use of remotely readable tags could be on mobile land vehicles that would be interrogated by overflight. In principle, then, thousands of TLE in an area spanning hundreds of kilometers could be verified in one day as opposed to the many weeks involved in comparable on-site inspection or other tagging schemes. The second possible use is for military aircraft, with an on-site fixed transmitter deployed at each air base. If an aircraft were detected (e.g., by short-distance radar, acoustic noise, or ground vibration near the airstrip), the electronic tag transponder on board each aircraft would be interrogated in order to establish its identity and legitimacy. Thus, control could be exercised not only over the total number of aircraft on air bases within a reduction zone but also the use of specified air bases by assigned aircraft. The problems and complexities of this tag, as opposed to the simple electronic tag, mean its application lies more in the future. Given the need for a transponder, its costs would also be markedly higher.

Seals. The presence of seals allows the determination that objects have not been tampered with and that doors have not been opened. A large body of knowledge and experience exists from the nuclear safeguards work of the International Atomic Energy Agency (IAEA).[33] A few of the existing methods include:

1. *The cup and wire seal,* in which two ends of a wire are knotted and enclosed by two metal cups. Each seal is marked individually, and it has to be removed and returned to a central office for analysis.
2. *The fiber-optic random pattern seal,* in which two ends of a bundle of glass

fibers are joined in a plastic housing and photographed. The unique random fiber pattern provides the signature for the seal, which can be measured and compared on site.

3. *The fiber-optic electronic seal,* consisting of a light emitter, one optical fiber, and a light detector. The integrity of the seal is monitored by the continuous arrival of light pulses transmitted through the fiber. The integrity of this seal can be verified on site. It is conceivable that one optical fiber could be "knit" to form a "bag," which could be unremovable and contain one big treaty-limited item. A missile, for example, could thus be connected to a launch vehicle while allowing access for smaller parts for maintenance, etc.[34]

4. *The adhesive label random pattern seal,* which consists of a special adhesive that would disintegrate if tampered with. Individual patterns are formed by small particles, like those of the reflecting particle tag. Validation can likewise be done on site.

The cost of these seals is only a few dollars, with the exception of the fiber optic electronic seal, which, by virtue of its complexity and need for energy supply, can cost up to $1,000.

Aerial and Space-Based Surveillance

Satellite Surveillance. Over the past several years there have been a number of proposals for international satellite monitoring of arms control treaties. On a French initiative, the United Nations performed a study of an international satellite monitoring agency.[35] Scientists have proposed a regional satellite-monitoring agency for Europe, which might be organized by the neutral and nonaligned countries.[36] Canada is investigating photographic and radar surveillance in this regard.[37]

Nearly three decades of experience with military and civilian remote-sensing satellites outline the technical properties of possible international surveillance satellites and their prospective costs. A ground resolution of some 10 meters can be achieved at a cost of about $200 million; resolution approaching the atmospheric limit (about 10 centimeters) will drive the satellite cost to at least $500 million.[38] A large ground operation is also necessary for processing the image data and, above all, for accurate interpretation.[39] While the technical and cost profiles of this technology are known, the most important questions remain unanswered. Who will bear the costs? Which data are to be collected, when, about whom? Which data are disseminated when, in which form, and to whom? A small agency focusing on Europe and managed by non-aligned states would represent a first step. In the future, its scope and participation could be expanded and organized under the aegis of the United Nations.

Table 5. **Typical Properties of Satellite and Aerial Photography.**[40]

| | Satellite | | Aircraft | |
	Civilian	Military*	High-Altitude	Low-Altitude
Altitude (km)	700-900	200-500	20-30	1-3
Ground resolution (m)	5-10	0.1-0.3	0.1-1	0.01-0.5
Swath width (km)	25-60	0.5-3	5-100	0.5-5
Cross-path range (km)	500-1500	100-500	100-200	10-20
Mostly below clouds	no	no	no	yes
Unit cost($ millions)	200	500	20-50	2-10

*high-resolution

Depending on the area overflown and the quality of the optical equipment, aerial photography can be very intrusive. Relaxation on the legal limits of aerial photography may be required in many countries; the verification system in Europe will have to include explicit rules to deal with these problems.

Given the high cost and the complexities of the problems to be overcome, however, it is doubtful that there will be an international satellite agency of any type in the near future. There is also the problem of limitations on satellite surveillance schemes. Satellites move periodically along fixed orbits; continuous coverage of one region requires many satellites. How many depends on a number of factors. Roughly, daily coverage needs two satellites; four or more are required for revisits every few hours. Moreover, photographic satellites cannot function with cloud cover or at night except those using infrared which can see at night and at least through haze. Radar satellites, while having the capability to penetrate cloud cover and to see at night, require large amounts of electrical power, and they have less resolution.

For monitoring relatively small, mobile conventional weapons systems, satellites would be very costly and impractical. They could, however, play a useful role in detecting and identifying military installations and possibly also in assessing the size of maneuvers. Fortunately, aerial photography--and potentially airborne radar--provide a much cheaper, and more practical, alternative.

Aerial Photography. One verification component discussed with increasing frequency both within CFE-I and outside it, is "open skies." As in the original Eisenhower proposal of 1955, the aim of the open skies approach is to have an extensive system of overflights over various national territories on either a regular--or limited--notice basis, and with coverage of both civilian and military infrastructure. There are now on-going discussions on a global or general system (as at Ottawa and Budapest in the spring of 1990) as well as consideration within

Figure 8. Magnification of an aerial photo of a town in the Federal Republic of Germany, with a barracks in the center. Buildings as well as military and civilian vehicles can be recognized. The aircraft altitude was 2.2 kilometer, the scale is approximately 1:5,000. Since the photo was taken for normal mapping purposes, the ground resolution of approximately 0.5 meters is not at its technological limits. Reproduced by permission of Hessisches Landesvermessungsamt, Reproduction no. 17/89. Passed by Regierungspräsident in Darmstadt by HLVA, 6/84-4-8783.

the Vienna talks on CFE-I. Obviously there would be differences in the requirements for each system. For the general system, for example, the present talks foresee capabilities for high altitude flights, long loiter time, and wide area coverage; while for CFE, there is emphasis on specific flight paths, pre-notification of observation targets, and no additional loiter time allowed.

Systematic, random and challenge inspections could be performed relatively easily by overflight. The main objects to be verified would be fixed installations (hardened aircraft shelters, tank garages) and troop movements. Overflights would also provide information on the interval between an announced inspection and the arrival of inspection personnel to insure that there is no movement of treaty-limited equipment.

Aircraft have several advantages over satellites. They are much less expensive; they return to their base regularly, so repair is much easier; they can be flown along arbitrary paths at any time; if clouds are present, they can in many cases fly below them. It was to avoid intrusion into national airspace that satellite surveillance was used for verification of the strategic arms control treaties. With the greater acceptance of cooperative verification schemes, and with the overflight precedent of the CDE Accord, aircraft surveillance may prove more practical for European verification tasks; it will also ensure equal treatment of large and small countries. A comparison of satellite and aerial photography is provided in Table 5, and Figure 8 gives an example of an aerial photograph.

Airborne Radar. Unlike satellites, power levels for radar equipment are readily available on board larger aircraft. Radar waves (in the appropriate frequency bands) are capable of penetrating clouds and rain. Since radar systems provide their own source of illumination, they can work day and night. Airborne radar, until recently, has been used only for airspace surveillance. Airborne synthetic aperture radar is now being developed to assess the state of the ground battle and to target long-range weapons (the planned U.S. JSTARS program is an example). Because such systems provide real-time location information of mobile equipment in a large area, it is not clear whether verification information can be separated reliably from other more destabilizing uses. If this problem is solved, airborne radar will be a quick and valuable tool to estimate the number of vehicles in the open.

General Cost Considerations

At present, the cost of a conventional verification scheme is impossible to determine. Costs will depend principally on the terms of the treaty, the mix of possible verification elements, and the level of confidence stipulated by verification guidelines. All indications are that in CFE-I, cost will be a significant consideration. The verification regime is to be specifically designed to be as inexpensive as possible but will surely cost more than the $100 million or so that each side has paid annually for INF verification. The following estimates are hazarded for the major components that might be chosen for future regimes. Securing a facility (barracks, depot, exit/entry point, factory) by a combination of sensors may cost a few hundred thousand dollars to a few million dollars. A treaty calling for 500 to 1,000 controlled installations, each costing on average one million dollars to verify, would place a one billion dollar price tag on the entire system.[41]

Installing a 1,000 kilometer line equipped with sensors and data processing/communication devices may cost as much as $100 million; in the extreme, $1 billion. A second 2,000 kilometer line installed farther back raises the cost from $300 million to $2 billion. Total system cost for a sensor scheme could exceed $1 billion or in the extreme case $3 billion to $4 billion.[42]

A fleet of 10 to 20 monitoring aircraft, at $10 to $20 million each, figures to a few hundred million dollars cost per side. Satellites and their ground systems start at a few hundred million dollars each. Total costs could reach the billion dollar mark if more than two satellites are needed.

The cost of tags and seals will probably be much lower. If all of the more than 300,000 existing weapons systems in the ATTU area are tagged, at an average cost of $100 dollars each, the total bilateral system cost would be in the $30 million to $40 million dollar range. It may well turn out that inspection costs--even with a random inspection scheme--will be higher than the original cost of producing and affixing all the tags.

All the installation costs mentioned could be distributed over a few years. After an initial installation period, annual expenditures would be for maintenance, travel, personnel, and equipment. If periodic maintenance expenses are estimated at 10 percent of installation costs, figures range from $100 million to $500 million per year if satellites are included. Other costs can be estimated from similar tasks performed by organizations like the IAEA. The IAEA's nuclear safeguards operation--including travel, equipment, and laboratory work--is approximately $300,000 annually per inspector. With a few thousand inspectors, total annual costs of a verification system may then be in the $1 billion range per side. Including installation, costs could be $2 billion to $3 billion per year in the start-up period.

Installation and maintenance costs must be compared with the annual expenditures for forces in Europe, which are on the order of $400 billion dollars annually for both alliances. Force reductions would lower these costs significantly (easily within a few years amounting to 10 percent or more of present expenditures), and verification costs could be as little as 1 percent of the present total.

These are, of course, rough estimates. Detailed study of verification costs and arms control savings are still needed. They will take shape when a draft treaty, including verification provisions, is tabled.

A considerable amount of uncertainty surrounds the performance of various verification schemes. Interdisciplinary and international cooperation is needed to develop maturing technologies and to test stable ones. Common experiments across bloc boundaries can begin now, to be followed by formally agreed tests between alliances.

Conclusion

Our concluding remarks turn back from the technical questions of conventional verification to a discussion of the broad principles that characterize the linkage of a verification regime to the limitations contained in an arms control agreement. If one adopts a cybernetic perspective, verification is at the same time the output and the regulating element of the whole reduction system. It signals, registers the results of, and confirms the completion of the disarmament process. Yet it simultaneously controls the process through feedback (error messages) and thus allows for continuous regulation and self-correction.

But, operationally, verification in this sense can never achieve 100 percent accuracy. Part of the reason lies in the difficulties inherent in any sophisticated conventional reduction scheme stretching over a broad geographic area and involving the interaction of complex military hierarchies with large numbers of subordinate commands and large numbers of sites and systems to be controlled. Part, too, is attributable to human error. However committed the political leadership is to maintaining the reduction system, it is always subject to human and technical faults - from erroneous navigation to mechanical failures. There are also subjective or perceptual limits. For example, rigorous intrusive inspections may affront the national patriotic dignity of the soldiers examined.

The advantage of systematic verification regimes now under discussion for CFE-I and for potential follow-on regimes is that opposing forces and the political leaderships are made equally aware of these errors and their causes. Thus, verification becomes its own major confidence-building measure. And the training of inspection teams, their common activities, and their need to cooperate may mitigate the effects of intrusive measures on national military traditions.

In this chapter, we have been relatively imprecise in our discussion of the specific forms verification will assume under a CFE agreement--as it is presently being negotiated or as it may evolve. We have indeed left out several possible areas of future interest, if not of potential CFE agreement: naval forces and limits on conventional arms production and export. This reflects our fundamental argument that each verification regime must be tailored to the agreement it serves. It is the harmony between limitation and verification that is critical--whatever the final list of reductions, areas covered, or phases of implementation.

The proposals we have reviewed emphasize the systemic character of verification and the fact that seamless conventional verification is not possible given the complexity of data collection, integration, and analysis. The possibility of useful error-reducing or error-offsetting overlap between verification systems does exist--as between, say, a CFE accord and those under a CSCE agreement. In the future, we expect there will be a need for an integrated and uniform system of verification for different areas and levels of control. This may be less expensive than separate institutions and procedures. Smaller steps, as we have indicated, might be the establishment of a CSCE communication/monitoring center or a system of crisis management centers to track and correct supposed violations, perhaps under international or United Nations auspices.

In sum, we argue that verification of conventional forces and weaponry is now an accepted part of the diplomatic and military approach to arms control. It has evolved from being an obstacle to agreement to one of the important, integrating elements in the process of agreement. The creation of a comprehensive verification system for conventional reductions not only reflects but also builds confidence in compliance. Its existence is a symbol of the willingness of both sides to agree and to change one another's image of the enemy. Its impact may indeed culminate as the process itself suggests new steps toward arms limitation. Its strict enforcement will eliminate the risks of violation, dampen or deter aggressive impulses, and direct the settlement of conflicts into political channels. From this will evolve a fundamental verification framework, by which both sides act on the basis of confidence, presuming compliance, not violation. Together with the additional assurance of national technical means, a cooperative verification system will offset "suspicion" with the obligation to reply to questions and to permit challenge inspections whenever needed. At the beginning of the 1990s, this seems not only possible but achievable.

Notes

1. According to the statement of the defense ministers of the WTO, the common holdings of both alliances are: combat planes and helicopters, 23,000; tanks, more than 90,000; armored combat vehicles, more than 117,000; artillery systems, more than 128,000; tactical rocket launchers, 1,500. See *Pravda*, 30 January 1989. According to NATO, the common holdings of both alliances are: helicopters and combat aircraft, more than 26,000; main battle tanks, more than 80,000; armored infantry fighting vehicles and other armored vehicles, more than 144,000; artillery, over 64,000. These figures include weapons held in storage. See NATO, *Conventional Forces in Europe: The Facts* (Brussels: NATO Press Service, 1988).

2. Detailed information on the CDE monitoring experience can be found in the *SIPRI Yearbook on Armaments and Disarmament*, for 1987, 1988, and 1989. (Oxford: Oxford University Press). In 1987, see chapter 11, by Jozef Goldblat; in 1988 and 1989, see chapter 11, by Jane Sharp.

3. Our discussion reflects our understanding of materials publicly available and our analysis as of spring 1990.

4. The "whole of Europe" represents the broad security concerns of NATO, the Warsaw Pact and the neutral and nonaligned states, 35 in all, participating in the CSBM talks. Only the 23 NATO and Warsaw Pact members are represented in CFE.

5. By late fall 1989, both West and East had tabled formal verification proposals that were largely convergent. For details, see *The Arms Control Reporter*, 407.D.37 (Western Position Paper of 21 September 1989) and 407.43 (summary of WTO Working Paper of 19 October 1989).

6. At this point, holdings in central Europe would be 10,000 tanks, 3,500 artillery pieces, 15,000 armored troop carriers, 2,000 helicopters, and 1,400 ground attack aircraft each, for NATO and WTO. See Jonathan Dean, "The NATO-Warsaw Pact Confrontation in the Twenty-First Century: Rough Model for an Optimal Force Posture" (Paper for the American Committee for US-Soviet Relations, Washington, D.C., 23 May 1988).

7. Vadim Makarevsky, speech at Conference on Alternative Defense Postures, American Committee for US-Soviet Relations, Washington, D.C., 19 May 1988.

8. Both this and an earlier proposal by Senator Sam Nunn would have reduced US forces in West Germany by 2.5 to 3 divisions and Soviet forces in East Germany by 13 divisions. (For the Nunn proposal, see *Washington Post*, 17 April 1987.)

Note that these proposals predated the decision of the Soviet Union and the WTO to reduce unilaterally by 1991 combined conventional forces by 300,000 servicemen, 12,000 tanks, 9,100 artillery pieces, and 930 aircraft--and to reduce military expenditures by 15 percent. (See *Pravda*, 8 December 1988.) This amounts to the unilateral withdrawal of six Soviet divisions from Central Europe. If the Makarevsky or the Nunn proposal were to be implemented now without adjustments, the net force reductions on the Soviet side would be greater than intended.

9. Oleg Amirov, Nikolai Kishilov, Vadim Makarevsky, and Yuri Usachev, "Problems of Reducing Military Confrontation," in USSR Academy of Sciences, Institute of World Economy and International Relations (IMEMO) *Disarmament and Security 1987 Yearbook* (Moscow: Novosti Press Agency Publishing House, 1988).

10. The breadth of the IMEMO proposal is matched by the 1989 Atlantic Council paper by retired SACEUR, General Andrew J. Goodpaster, who suggests eventual reductions down to at least 50 percent of current NATO strength by the mid-1990s and at least a 50 percent withdrawal of American and Soviet forces from central Europe. Andrew J. Goodpaster, *Gorbachev and the Future of East-West Security. A Response for the Mid Term* (Washington, D.C.: Atlantic Council, April 1989).

11. Michael Gordon, *New York Times*, 9 March 1989.

12. This proposal was preceded by the decision of the Soviet Union and the Warsaw Pact to unilaterally reduce, by 1991, combined conventional forces by 300,000 servicemen, 12,000 tanks, 9,100 artillery pieces and 930 aircraft, as well as a pledge to reduce military expenditures by 15 percent. See *Pravda*, 8 December 1988.

13. *New York Times*, 9 March 1989.

14. "Breaking With Convention," *Arms Control Today* (April 1989):3-9.

15. CFE: Western Position Paper, in *The Arms Control Reporter* (6 March 1989):407.D.27.

16. Arms Control Reporter discussions with Canadian and Hungarian delegates in *The Arms Control Reporter* (22 and 24 March 1989): 407.B.143.

17. *Pravda*, 12 May 1989.

18. Warsaw Pact sufficiency: no more than 14,000 tanks, 18,000 armored personnel carriers, 17,000 artillery, 1,200 strike aircraft, 1,200 helicopters, and 920,000 troops by any single country in the ATTU. Warsaw Pact stationing: no more than 4,500 tanks, 7,500 armored personnel carriers, 4,000 artillery, 350 strike aircraft, 600 helicopters, and 350,000 troops deployed outside national territory.

19. *New York Times*, 30 May 1989.

20. See *Arms Control Reporter*, January 31-February 15, 1990 for details of Soviet and American bargaining on this figure.

21. See *ibid.*, February 22-March 6, 1990 for details of the Soviet proposal and the reception by both the Soviet allies and the NATO states. The new Soviet proposal presumably takes into account the various withdrawals of Soviet forces under expected bilateral agreements with Eastern European states, and the recalculation of the military forces to be allowed a reunified Germany.

22. See the discussion of zones in Jane Sharp, "Conventional Arms Control in Europe: Problems and Prospects," in *SIPRI Yearbook 1988 World Armaments and Disarmament*, (Oxford: Oxford University Press, 1988): 315-337.

23. Soviet Foreign Minister Eduard Shevardnadze's speech of 8 March 1989 also suggested that part of this area, 50 to 100 kilometers in width, would exclude forces capable of sudden attack or offensive action. In this zone, airborne monitoring through national technical means would be used up to a range of 300-400 kilometers.

24. All cost estimates in this paper are based upon 1989 U.S. dollars.

25. The MBFR talks, now completed, took place in Vienna for some 15 years between the NATO and WTO states regarding reductions in a Central European Zone including the two Germanies, Belgium, Czechoslovakia, Holland and Poland.

26. A. Meerburg, "The Verification of Conventional Arms Control Measures in Europe." Presentation at the Fifth Annual Symposium on Arms Control and Verification, Carleton University, Ottawa, Canada, March 23-26, 1988 (Paris: Western European Union, 1988); K. Jacob, "Aspects of the Verification of Conventional Arms Control Measures in Europe" in Jürgen Altmann and Joseph Rotblat, eds., *Verification of Arms Reductions: Nuclear, Conventional and Chemical* (Berlin: Springer, 1989).

27. For these comparative cost estimates, see *The Military Cost Handbook*, 7th ed., (Fountain Valley, California: Data Search Associates, 1986).

28. See also: D.A. Boutacoff, "Remote Sensors Extend Surveillance Capabilities," *Defense Electronics* (August 1984): 89-95; Ivan Oelrich and Victor Utgoff "Confidence Building with Unmanned Sensors in Central Europe," in *Technology and the Limitation of International Conflict* ed., Barry M. Blechman (Lanham Md.: University Press of America, 1989).

29. For a more extensive discussion of tagging schemes, see Steve Fetter and Tom Garwin, "Using Tags to Monitor Numerical Limits on Weapons in Arms Control Agreements," in *Technology and the Limitation of International Conflict*, ed., Barry. M. Blechman (Lanham MD: University Press of America, 1989). See also Western European Union, *Requirements for a Tag for Conventional Arms Control* (Paris: WEU, 1988), AG I (88) D/10.

30. In practice many tags will cost markedly less than 0.1 percent of the item cost.

31. WEU, *Requirements for a Tag*. op. cit.

32. *Ibid.*

33. An overview of IAEA safeguards and various seal techniques are described in C. Auerbach, *Safeguards Instrumentation - A Computer-Based Catalogue*, 2nd ed., BNL-51540, (Upton NY: Brookhaven National Laboratory, April 1985).

34. See Richard L. Garwin, "Tags and Seals for Verification," *The Council for Arms Control Bulletin* no. 40 (October 1988): 3-4.

35. "The Implications of Establishing an International Satellite Monitoring Agency,"

Disarmament Study Series, no. 9, A/AC.206/14 (New York: United Nations, 1983).

36. See, for example, Bhupendra Jasani, and T. Sakata, eds., *Satellites for Arms Control and Crisis Monitoring* (Oxford: Oxford University Press, 1987).

37. Canada, Department of External Affairs, "PaxSat Concept - The Application of Space-Based Remote Sensing for Arms Control Verification,"*Verification Brochure* no. 2 (Ottawa: Department of External Affairs, 1987).

38. These estimates come from the research of Jürgen Altmann. See U.S. Congress, Office of Technology Assessment, *Commercial Newsgathering From Space - A Technical Memorandum* (Washington, D.C.: U.S. Government Printing Office, May 1987), OTA-TM-ISC-40. See also William E. Burrows, *Deep Black: Space Espionage and National Security* (New York: Random House, 1986); and John Pike, "Eyes in the Sky - Satellite Reconnaissance," *Harvard International Review* 10, n. 6 (August-September 1988): 21-26.

39. Jeffrey T. Richelson, *The U.S. Intelligence Community*, (Cambridge Ma.: Ballinger, 1986), 29. Richelson notes that the U.S. National Photographic Interpretation Center, under the aegis of the CIA, employs more than 1,000 photo interpreters.

40. Bhupendra Jasani, ed., *Outer Space - A New Dimension of the Arms Race* (London: Taylor and Francis, 1982); SPOT Brochure, Satimage, Kiruna, Sweden; R.N. Colwell, ed., *Manual of Remote Sensing*, (Falls Church, Va.: American Society of Photogrammetry, 1983); Pike, "Eyes in the Sky", op. cit.; Burrows, *Deep Black,* op. cit.; calculations and estimates by Jürgen Altmann.

41. For a more detailed preliminary estimate on sensor systems see Jürgen Altmann, "Verification Techniques for Heavy Land Vehicles Using Short Range Sensors," in: Jürgen Altmann and Joseph Rotblat, eds.,*Verification of Arms Reduction: Nuclear, Conventional and Chemical*, (Berlin: Springer, 1989).

42. *Ibid.*

11

The Elimination of Nuclear Arsenals: Is It Desirable? Is It Feasible?

Joseph Rotblat (UK) & Vitali I. Goldanskii (USSR)

Introduction

The very first resolution of the United Nations, unanimously adopted by the General Assembly in January 1946--less than six months after the bombs on Japan--pledged "the elimination from national armaments of atomic weapons and of all other major weapons adaptable to mass destruction".[1] During the four decades since then, nuclear disarmament has been the recurrent theme in many UN fora, expressing the strongly held feelings of people in many countries. The huge nuclear arsenals accumulated during that period--in pursuit of greater security--have actually increased the probability of a nuclear war. At the same time, the growing knowledge of the awesome consequences of such a war, even if it could be limited in the number of weapons and type of target, made the avoidance of nuclear war the most vital issue.

The call for the removal of nuclear weapons has been echoed by the leaders of the superpowers. Creating a nuclear-weapon-free world is the declared goal of Mikhail Gorbachev, as part of his new way of thinking about common security. In his speech of January 15, 1986 he proposed a time-table for the complete elimination of nuclear weapons by the year 2000.[2] At the Reykjavik summit of October 1986, he and President Reagan discussed an even shorter period, ten years, to achieve the goal of a nuclear-weapon-free world. This discussion ended in failure, but nuclear disarmament, down to a zero value, has been placed firmly on the agenda of peace negotiations. China and India are also committed to the creation of a nuclear-weapon-free world, the latter giving the year 2010 as the target date.[3]

At the same time, the opposite view, that nuclear weapons must be permanently retained, has also been forcefully expressed. Originally, nuclear weapons were deployed for economic reasons. In 1954 NATO decided to deploy tactical nuclear weapons in order to compensate for its weakness vis-a-vis the Soviet bloc in conventional arms; to overcome this inferiority 96 divisions of conventional forces were thought to be required, and this would have been far too costly.[4] But later nuclear weapons became the cornerstone of NATO's strategy, the guarantor of peace. Having given credit to the deterrent action of nuclear weapons for the absence of war in Europe since 1945, the possession of these weapons became essential for the maintenance of peace. Various doctrines of that strategy, from mutual assured destruction to flexible response, were evolved, and a variety of ways of employing the nuclear deterrent were analyzed, but in all of them the detention of nuclear weapons was a *sine qua non*.

However, even the advocates of the doctrine of extended nuclear deterrence recognized the necessity of reducing the enormous nuclear arsenals and halting the arms race, either because of the fear of a pre-emptive first strike, or of accidental or inadvertent employment of nuclear weapons. Cuts in nuclear arms have been suggested down to a value that would be needed to prevent any type of war, by the threat of retaliation with nuclear weapons. For proponents of the "no-first-use" policy, a minimum deterrent is needed to guard against nuclear blackmail, to ensure against possible cheating. For them the value of the minimum deterrent is largely determined by the effectiveness of verification measures, and could be made vanishingly small if the verification regimes, discussed in the earlier chapters of this book, could be made sufficiently tight.

This paper looks at the longer perspective, after the implementation of the verification systems proposed in the earlier chapters. It argues that the permanent retention of nuclear weapons, even at a low level, is not acceptable for moral, political and strategic reasons. It then goes on to analyze ways to approach the goal of a nuclear-weapon-free world.

Nuclear Weapons and World Security

It is almost universally accepted that nuclear weapons are of no military value as an instrument for waging war. This is enshrined in the dictum: "A nuclear war cannot be won and must never be fought" agreed to by Presidents Gorbachev and Reagan during their first summit in November 1985. Nevertheless, these weapons are endowed with an important political and military role: they deter an adversary from using his nuclear weapons (simple deterrence) or indeed from using weapons of any kind (extended deterrence).

There is a vast literature on this subject and different approaches to it, but basically the arguments in favor of nuclear deterrence are predicated on the fact that there has been no war in Europe since 1945. It is alleged that this is due entirely to the existence of nuclear weapons and the threat of their use against an aggressor. Nuclear weapons are seen as a stabilizing factor, as "peacekeepers" (the name given to the U.S. MX missile). The invention of nuclear weapons was even described as the most beneficial of all discoveries in the 20th century.[5] Furthermore, it is stated that since they cannot be disinvented, and the knowledge of how to make them will always be with us, there is no alternative but to retain them.

That peace has been preserved thanks to the nuclear deterrent is an unproven supposition. But continuous assertion in dogmatic terms (for example "Nuclear deterrence has certainly prevented world war--that world war which would otherwise have inevitably broken out sometime, somewhere, after 1945 between America and her allies and Russia and hers"[6]), repeated by others in parrot-like fashion, has given it the aura of unshaken credibility and acceptance as the gospel truth. Actually, it can be challenged on several grounds.

There is a moral argument against nuclear deterrence. Considering the enormous destructive power of nuclear weapons, exceeding by orders of magnitude any other type of weapon, the very concept of nuclear deterrence runs into moral difficulties. If the purpose of nuclear weapons is to deter their use, or the use of other weapons, by your adversary , the latter will take the threat seriously only if you are prepared to use nuclear weapons in retaliation, whatever the consequences. You must show by your posture that you are prepared to do this; otherwise your adversary will conclude that you are bluffing. There cannot be half-hearted deterrence. But does any cause exist that would morally justify the killing of tens or hundreds of millions of innocent people? How can one reconcile the natural repulsion of committing genocide with the potential undertaking to carry out such a deed? The moral argument is usually dismissed by the proponents of deterrence as being of no significance in military considerations. "How many divisions does the Pope have?" But this ignores the fact that the whole fabric of civilized society is based on moral values. If these are violated in one important area, how can they be defended in others? Security achieved by a balance of terror is bound--in the long run--to erode the ethical basis of our civilization.

There is also a political argument. The assertion that absence of war in Europe since World War II is due to the nuclear deterrent ignores two facts: one, the many bloody wars outside Europe, in which some 22 million people perished and in some of which nuclear-weapon states were directly involved; and two, the completely changed political configuration in Europe since that time. There is no evidence based on history that war in Europe would have occurred without nuclear weapons, or that war is bound to occur as soon as these weapons are removed. One can argue to the contrary, that the existence of nuclear weapons is responsible for the state of tension and mistrust that existed between Est and West, and that this tension, and--in consequence--the probability of a non-nuclear war, would have been reduced if these weapons were removed. In any case, the concept of extended deterrence, that it prevents acts of aggression with non-nuclear arms, is basically weak since it rests on the implicit assumption that leaders will behave rationally and will not embark on ventures that may turn out to be suicidal. There is enough historical evidence that irrational people do come to power, even if not frequently.

Nuclear weapons cannot be disinvented, but this does not mean that they have to be deployed, or kept in storage, and that research must continue to invent "better" weapons. The same applies of course to chemical and biological weapons.

Has nuclear deterrence provided stability? The evidence from the history of the nuclear arms race points to the opposite.[7] At no time since the arms race began in 1949 has either of the superpowers been satisfied that what it had in its nuclear arsenals was sufficient to give it security. Each side felt compelled to keep on increasing and modernizing its arsenals, so that they have grown to the present monstrous sizes. Two main reasons for this are: technological advances and changing strategic concepts. Scientific and technological progress of research in military establishments keeps eroding the value of the deterrent, making it vulnerable and raising the specter of a first disabling strike; this creates the need for further research and for modernizing the weapons; a continuous arms race. Moreover, in the name of making the deterrent more credible, strategic concepts are changed, for example, from counter-city to counter-force, and this necessitates the introduction of new categories of weapons. But the strategy of flexible response does not make the nuclear deterrent any more credible. Even if only military installations were targeted, their proximity to population areas would result in enormous civilian casualties, particularly in Europe. A recent study has shown that even a very limited nuclear exchange in Europe, with less than 100 megatons on military targets, could result in more than 100 million casualties, mostly fatalities.[8]

The result of the unending arms race, in the quest for a reliable deterrent, was an increased probability of a nuclear war starting accidentally, by miscalculation or misperception. This is due to the ever increasing reliance on computers and other sophisticated technology, which may go wrong, and the greatly reduced time interval in which a decision has to be made about response to a perceived attack. Several events from the recent past have added to the serious worry about such responses in time of crisis.

The best evidence of the lack of reliance of nuclear deterrence to ensure security was President Reagan's SDI project, originally designed to protect populations by intercepting incoming missiles.[9] Even if it were technologically feasible--an assumption completely unwarranted according to the majority of independent expert opinion--it would destabilize the situation even further by encouraging the other side to augment its offensive arsenals, quite apart from the inherent high degree of instability of space weapons. The recent proposals from U.S. defence analysts of a new strategy, called "discriminate deterrence", is further evidence of the failure of the current deterrent policy.[10]

The Minimum Deterrent

The dangers inherent in the current strategic policies have been generally recognized, and even ardent advocates of nuclear deterrence accepted the need to halt and reverse the arms race. Hence the efforts to reach agreements in international negotiations on the reduction of military arsenals of all kinds, nuclear, chemical, conventional, as well as on confidence-building measures. The first outcome of these efforts is the INF Treaty signed in 1987.[11] Negotiations have been going on since on a treaty to reduce the strategic nuclear arms by 50%, in the first instance (the actual reduction is likely to be about 30%).

These developments are of great importance and were justly acclaimed by all who desire genuine nuclear disarmament. But the enthusiasm is tempered by concern that the gains may be illusive. There is a real danger of circumventing the INF Treaty, under the pretext of modernizing other categories of weapons; in effect this might mean a return to the status quo ante even in the range of weapons to be eliminated. In addition, new weapons coming into deployment as a result of modernization programmes of recent years will more than make up for the agreed reductions. In this connection it should also be recalled that the INF Treaty does not include the actual destruction of the warheads, and either sides permitted to transfer them to other missiles.

Nevertheless, a start has been made on nuclear disarmament. The important questions now are: how far should it go? what other types of weapon should be reduced, and by how much? what should be the ultimate aim of these efforts?

The advocates of the concept of extended deterrence would agree to a reduction of nuclear weapons to a value which, while posing a smaller risk of a first strike, would still retain the potential of adequate retaliation to an attack with nuclear or other types of weapons. This minimum deterrent would, therefore, have to contain enough weapons of different categories to satisfy the given strategic policy, e.g. flexible response. But whatever the contents, a certain number of nuclear weapons will have to stay in the arsenals as long as there exists a risk of military confrontation; in the opinion of some politicians this means in perpetuity.

For the proponents of simple deterrence, i.e. threat of retaliation against the use of nuclear weapons, a certain number of these weapons would have to be retained as an insurance against cheating. Such an insurance might be provided by one class of weapon, the most invulnerable one. The actual value of the minimum deterrent would be determined by the effectiveness of the verification system designed to prevent cheating and able to detect early enough any attempt to violate agreements. With improvements in performance of the verification system, the minimum deterrent could be gradually decreased.

In the early stages of the disarmament process, this approach would not differ in practice from that called for by the exponents of a nuclear-weapon-free world. They too would like to ensure compliance with agreements to eliminate nuclear weapons. But the difference in the basic philosophy about nuclear deterrence makes them seek the achievement of their objective by bolder measures.

A quantitative evaluation of the minimum deterrent policy has to include types, numbers and time of implementation. Concrete proposals about these were made by Richard Garwin.[12] His main concern is the increasing instability of the current system associated with the counter-force strategy, and he sees de-MIRVing as the key to deep cuts. By the single stroke of removing all but one warhead from present MIRVed launchers, the number of strategic warheads held by each side could be reduced from about 10,000 to 2,000; this could be accomplished in two years. Garwin recommends a minimum deterrent of 1,000 warheads each for NATO and WTO, the number to consist of 400 ICBMs with single warheads (the Midgetman an the USA), 400 SLBMs, carried on 50 submarines, and 200 air-launched cruise missiles carried on 100 aircraft. The whole process of disarmament to these levels could be achieved over a period of ten years in the following order of dismantling: all non-strategic missiles; reduction of MIRVs to one warhead per silo; elimination of half of remaining launchers.

A lower minimum deterrent, about 600 warheads for each side, was suggested by the Committee of Soviet Scientists for Peace against the Nuclear Threat, which carried out a detailed study of the problem.[13] They want to see the whole deterrent based on ICBMs, some of them mobile, with single warheads.

At a Pugwash Workshop in June 1988, a still lower value for the minimum deterrent, to be achieved by the year 2000, was discussed, namely, 500-invulnerably based weapons by each side. For the NATO side the distribution of the warheads was envisaged as follows: 200 in the United States, 100 each in France and UK, and 100 non-strategic weapons to be held in Europe.[14] This last item implies retention of nuclear weapons for the purpose of extended deterrence.

If the above value of the minimum deterrent, a total of 1000 warheads, were achieved, it would represent a reduction to less than 2% of the present nuclear arsenals, a truly remarkable accomplishment. However, the remaining arsenals would still contain about 200 megatons of explosives, 25 times more than has been used in all previous wars. Even this very low "minimum" would have been considered unacceptably high 30 years ago when the notion of minimum deterrence was first discussed. It is certainly not acceptable as a permanent solution by those opposed to the whole concept of deterrence, and who are convinced that a finite--even if very low--nuclear deterrent is no more likely to be stable than the current nuclear arsenals.

One of the doubts about the stability of the minimum deterrent is whether we can really conceive that the deterrent will be maintained constantly at the agreed minimum value. We are contemplating going back to a situation, in terms of numbers, that existed many years ago, but is there reason to believe that this time the arsenals will not start growing as they did then? As long as either side has nuclear weapons, however small in number, there will be the need to maintain them. A core of scientists and engineers will be necessary for this purpose. And as is their habit, they will think of ways of making their own weapons more effective, and those of the other side more vulnerable. A nuclear arms race is most likely to start all over again. It is very doubtful whether the minimum deterrent will stay at the minimum for long, unless there is an even more radical change in the political climate than has occurred recently.

Another question is, who will be entitled to possess the minimum deterrent? The schemes described above envisage the deterrent being retained by NATO and WTO, which effectively means the two superpowers. Some schemes allow the retention of some nuclear weapons by China, France and UK. But what about the other countries, like Israel and South Africa, which may already have in their nuclear arsenals more than allocated to China, France and UK, although undeclared? Will they be given tacit approval to retain these weapons, or will they be forced, by military, political or economic means, to give them up? Neither of these solutions seems likely.

This raises a more general question. If the permanent retention of nuclear weapons is allowed for some countries, in order to make them immune from attack with any type of weapon, then how can one deny the same means of immunity to other countries? Such a denial would contain an inherent element of division, and therefore of mistrust and tension in the world: in our hands nuclear weapons are guarantors of peace, but their possession by other countries would increase the danger of war. According to article VI of the Non-Proliferation Treaty, the nuclear weapon states undertook to pursue the aim of nuclear disarmament, as part of the ultimate objective of general and complete disarmament; there is no provision in the NPT for a permanent retention--even if at a very low level--of nuclear armaments. Horizontal proliferation of nuclear weapons has been kept under control so far, but this cannot go on for ever. What is likely to happen is that the NPT Treaty will be scrapped, all restraints it contains will be removed, and a number of countries will acquire the "minimum" nuclear deterrent. Some of these countries are sufficiently unstable to make us view this prospect with much anxiety.

It has been suggested that if the disarmament measures included a comprehensive test ban, this would prevent a build-up of nuclear arsenals by other countries. However, the testing of weapons is no longer a necessary element in the attainment of a nuclear arsenal. The technology of manufacturing bombs is now so well known, that they can be put in the arsenals as reliable weapons, without testing them.[15] Witness the case of Israel: everybody accepts that it has a credible nuclear arsenal even though Israeli tests have never been reported.

The retention of nuclear weapons - at a minimal level - is being justified on the basis of the premise that the existence of these weapons has secured peace in Europe and will reduce the risk of war in the future. Even though this premise is unproven, its plausibility is sufficiently high to make many peace-loving people accept nuclear deterrence as the lesser evil. But in this interdependent world, we must be concerned not only with avoidance of war in Europe but everywhere else. The extension of that premise to other parts of the world, where wars have been raging all the time, would justify the acquisition of nuclear arsenals by other states--unless the superpowers, plus perhaps the other three nuclear-weapon states, take upon themselves the role of a world police, intervening in every military conflict, a role far exceeding that of the Security Council. This is likely to create even more tension and generate violent reaction, and would in any case not be acceptable even to the citizens of the nuclear-weapon states. When balancing the possible risks of military confrontation resulting: (a) from such tension, (b) from the removal of the nuclear deterrent, the former seems to present the greater risk.

The Elimination of Nuclear Weapons

Having arrived at the conclusion that the retention of nuclear weapons in perpetuity will not guarantee peace in the world--and may in fact undermine it-- one needs to discuss the feasibility of the alternative policy, the elimination of nuclear weapons.

There are two dimensions to this problem: (a) technological, i.e. insurance against a violation of treaties involving complete nuclear disarmament; (b) political, i.e. build-up of the necessary climate of trust. Both are essential, and, as will be shown, interact and reinforce each other.

Verification of reductions to very low values

A frequent argument against complete nuclear disarmament is that even if all existing weapons were dismantled, it would not take long to reintroduce them, should this be required by a military or political contingency. However, even if the incentive to use nuclear weapons did arise in a nuclear-weapon-free world, the situation would still be much safer than if nuclear weapons were ready in the arsenals. If military establishments had stopped research on nuclear weapons (an essential element of nuclear disarmament), it would take some months for either side to manufacture and deploy the weapon, particularly if no weapon-grade plutonium or uranium were kept in storage, and this would provide time for negotiations to end the conflict by peaceful means.

The main difficulty about complete nuclear disarmament is the worry about cheating. The destructive potential of nuclear weapons is so enormous, that the concealment of even a small number of such weapons could give the side that has done this an overwhelming advantage. Therefore, we have to address the problem of verification of compliance with undertakings during the process of nuclear disarmament.

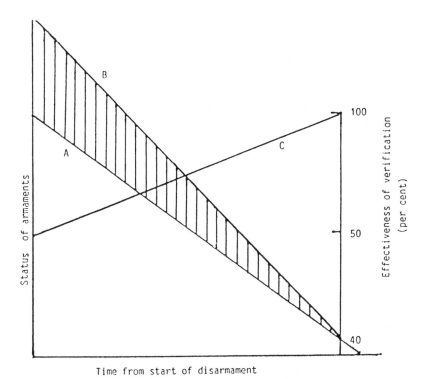

Figure 1.

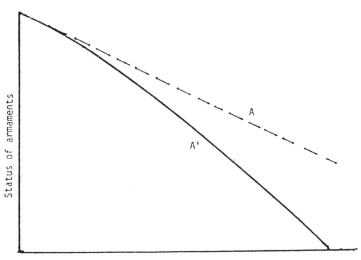

Figure 2.

Obviously, getting rid of nuclear weapons will have to be a lengthy and gradual process, strictly correlated with verification effectiveness. The connection between reduction of nuclear arms and verification is usually described by the so-called Wiesner graph, first put forward at a Pugwash Conference.[16] A modified form of the Wiesner graph is shown in Fig. 1.

The vertical axis on the left is a measure of the status of armaments, for example, the number of nuclear weapons held by one side, or some other quantity characterizing the potential of these weapons. The horizontal scale gives the time from the start of the disarmament process. Both these scales are arbitrary. Let line A indicate the number of weapons held at a given time by our adversary, as declared by him. Natural caution will make us assume that he is cheating, that he managed to conceal some weapons. Let line B be the real number held by him. Note that at the beginning, when the arsenals are still large, even a considerable concealment would not matter, but the situation changes as the arsenals become smaller. Even a small amount of cheating could then be decisive. Therefore, the necessary condition to proceed to low levels of armaments is effective verification of compliance. The state of necessary verification is indicated by line C, with its percentage scale on the vertical axis on the right. The shaded area between A and B represents the degree of uncertainty at a given stage of disarmament; it is inversely related to the effectiveness of the verification procedures achieved at that time.

It should be noted that Fig. 1 is an idealized presentation. In reality, neither the process of nuclear disarmament nor the increase in the effectiveness of the verification system, would be linear functions of time, but it is the general trend that matters.

The main difficulty arises when the level of declared armaments approaches zero. Either side will agree to take the last step of complete disarmament only after the effectiveness of verification has reached 100%. But since this can never be assured, a different approach will have to be adopted when that stage is reached. This is discussed below.

Elimination of missiles

There are several ways to achieve arms reduction. One of them is reduction across the board, i.e. all types of weapons are reduced by agreed amounts in any stage of the disarmament programme. This type of approach is being attempted, in relation to strategic weapons, in the "50%" cut negotiations in START, and has encountered many difficulties. A more efficient way would be the complete elimination of weapons in a given category, one at a time, as was shown by the relatively quick agreement on the INF Treaty, which is characterized by thoroughness and precision. Obviously, it is easier to verify the complete removal of a given class of missiles than to reduce them gradually by agreed numbers or proportions.

Bearing in mind the probable requirement to maintain an invulnerable deterrent during the process of disarmament, and the anxiety not to lower the nuclear threshold in the meantime, the following sequence of eliminating weapons seems indicated. First, the short range missiles, in their great variety an numbers of theatre or tactical nuclear weapons, should be destroyed. In the completely changed political map of Europe their deployment has become an anachronism. Indeed, during the transition period, with its inherent instability, the possession of such weapons by troops is potentially highly dangerous. A reduction and restructuring of conventional forces, preceding or simultaneous with that step, would of course be of great value in this respect.

The next weapons to be eliminated would be land-based ICBMs, followed by missiles and bombs carried by aircraft, and lastly submarine-launched missiles.

The specific techniques required to verify that the missiles and warheads have been destroyed, such as sealing, tagging and "fingerprinting", are described in Chapter 5 of this book.

Disposal of nuclear-weapon materials

Unlike the INF Treaty, the programme of complete nuclear disarmament calls for the elimination of warheads, as well as missiles. In a nuclear-weapon-free world there is no need for nuclear warheads. The main problem is the disposal of the special materials needed to make nuclear weapons, i.e. highly enriched uranium, plutonium and tritium.

A prerequisite for a programme of nuclear disarmament is a halt to the production of these materials. The requirements for verifying a production cut-off of such materials are presented in Chapter 6.

The amounts already in existence are estimated to be 1000 tonnes of 90% uranium-235, 200 tonnes of plutonium and 200 Kg of tritium, these quantities being about equally shared between the USA and USSR.[17] The relatively short half-life of tritium (12.3 years) ensures its natural elimination within a few decades (down to one-fifth in 30 years). With regard to the other two materials, there is the legitimate desire to make use of their very high energy content while being rendered unsuitable for military purposes.[18]

The problem of uranium is simple. Its dilution with uranium-238, so as to reduce the U-235 content to about 4%, ensures that it is no longer a weapon material, but highly suitable as fuel in thermal reactors. The disposal of plutonium is more difficult, because there is no practical way of rendering it militarily useless by isotopic dilution. The suggested method of getting rid of the plutonium without wasting its energy content is to fabricate fuel consisting of mixed oxides of uranium and plutonium for existing thermal reactors.

The burning of plutonium in such reactors is accompanied by the production of new plutonium from uranium-238; the overall rate of eliminating plutonium stores would therefore be rather slow. Since the use of mixed fuels would in any case require a change in design of reactors--due to problems of reactivity control (see chapter 5 of this book)--it may be sensible to go a step further and build reactors which use plutonium as the only fuel, i.e. without uranium. This will be more costly, but the expense is justified in view of the very large stockpile of plutonium. The advantageous feature of such reactors is that they would be the only generators of nuclear energy (until thermonuclear reactors come into being) without producing at the same time new plutonium. The plutonium remaining in the spent fuel elements would be intrinsically mixed with the fission products and thus inaccessible for a very long time. The fabrication of the plutonium fuel for such reactors would have to be carried out under very exacting safeguards, and the control of material flow would have to be very strict, to prevent loss of plutonium by theft or by terrorist acts.

Another way of disposing of the plutonium in the arsenals is to recycle it in molten-salt reactors, in which the fuel (in liquid state) would consist of a mixture of thorium and plutonium fluorides.[19]

Apart from the plutonium in nuclear warheads, there are huge quantities of plutonium produced in electricity-generating stations, based on thermal reactors. Although the Pu-240 content of such plutonium is too high to classify it as weapon-grade material, it could still be used in nuclear weapons.[20] For this reasons it would be desirable that the existing stores of plutonium from civil reactors, separated in reprocessing plants, should also be burned in the special reactors mentioned above.

As an independent measure, to prevent further availability of plutonium, the practice of reprocessing spent fuel elements from reactors should be abandoned in favor of the "once-through" cycle, i.e. storage without processing. The highly radioactive fission products in the spent fuel constitute an effective barrier to access to the plutonium.

The measures proposed here would not affect adversely the economy of nuclear energy production, since the era of the fast breeder reactor--for which separation of plutonium is needed--is receding further into the future, mainly due to the glut of uranium in the world. The extra uranium becoming available from the military stockpiles would add to this glut.

Dual purpose weapons

If the materials for nuclear weapons were eliminated, the existence of missiles that could be converted to carry nuclear warheads would be much less of a problem. Nevertheless, methods of verifying that dual-purpose missiles are not equipped with nuclear warheads would have to be included in a programme of nuclear disarmament. Again, the simplest solution is to eliminate such weapons altogether, in a complementary programme of conventional disarmament.

Difficulties with the Complete Elimination of Nuclear Weapons

The main concern about establishing a nuclear-weapon-free world is how to ensure that one side will not be cheating in the last stages of nuclear disarmament, and conceal a small number of such weapons with which it could gain political power, if not world domination. The verification techniques, discussed in this book, could ensure compliance with agreements to reduce weapons to very low levels, but cannot be 100% effective. Although full effectiveness is generally not required, the enormous destructive power of nuclear weapons makes this a necessary requirement when complete nuclear disarmament is reached.

One of the major causes of uncertainty is the amount of plutonium that might be concealed. Despite the stringent accountability of materials in nuclear facilities under IAEA safeguards, a certain amount of plutonium is lost in the various stage of the nuclear fuel cycle; this comes in the category of MUF (material unaccounted for). It would be difficult to reduce MUF to much below a few percent, and this may add up to a few tonnes of plutonium. Only a fraction of this might possibly be concealed by any one state but this would be sufficient to make a number of bombs, theoretically enough to blackmail another state into submission.

The most radical way to deal with this is to remove the incentive for such an act, by creating a climate of relations between nations such that nobody will want to threaten others. But such a climate, described by one scientist as "nuclear weapons: who cares?",[21] will never be reached as long as states possess nuclear weapons. As argued earlier , if nuclear weapons were retained by the present five states, or even by the two superpowers only, this would be a constant irritant, a perpetual cause of tension that would preclude the establishment of the necessary political climate. If many states were allowed to have nuclear weapons, the situation would be even more precarious, because there can be no guarantee that an irrational person will never become the leader of a state. Another possibility is the acquisition of nuclear weapons by anarchic groups in a civil war which might follow, for example, the collapse of Perestroika in the Soviet Union.[22] The notion that we could live with nuclear weapons and nobody be concerned about them is absurd; the risk involved is far too great to be ever acceptable. For this reason we may have to turn to a different measure to ensure that no state will resort to threaten the use of nuclear weapons acquired or made clandestinely.

Such a measure would be the setting up of an international authority endowed with a small nuclear weapons capability. In a way, this resembles the Baruch Plan to create an International Atomic Development Authority.[23] But the world has changed since 1946, when anything even remotely resembling a World Government was rejected out of hand. We are still not ready for World Government--although there is much less adversion to it--but there is now much more respect and trust in joint international undertakings. The United Nations has proved itself in a variety of policing duties and peace negotiations, and has acquired enough status to be entrusted with an even mightier task, to be the custodian of an instrument designated to prevent a threat to world security.

Specifically, the proposal is to create a new organ of the United Nations, to be the keeper of a small number of nuclear weapons and means of delivery, with an international police force to make the cache invulnerable. The purpose of this UN nuclear arsenal would be to prevent a state, which suddenly disclosed the possession of a nuclear armory, from threatening its use as a political instrument of submission of another state. To be effective, the decision of the UN organ to initiate retaliation must not be allowed to be overridden by the veto of one state, which might itself be the offender or its sponsor. A decision by n-x of its n members, where x might be 1,2 or even higher, depending on the value of n, would be sufficient.

An intermediate step, suggested by Garwin, would be a formal agreement by nuclear-weapon states that weapons possessed by them would be used in retaliation only *through* the United Nations.[24]

Inasmuch as the scheme outlined above relies on deterrence, it is abhorrent to those who object to the very concept of deterrence on moral grounds; it could not therefore be accepted as a permanent solution. As a transitional measure it has the appeal that it would reduce the number of nuclear arsenals from five to only one. It should also be noted that the only purpose of the single arsenal would be to prevent a nuclear threat, and that it would come into being at a time when nations have pledged themselves to get rid of their nuclear weapons. The need for the international depository of nuclear weapons will diminish as time goes on, because of better technological means of verification being developed and a conducive political climate.

The Political Climate

The discussion of the ways towards a nuclear-weapon-free world has so far been based on the technological aspect of the problem. But the political aspects are as important. Indeed, in the opinion of many, the whole problem is a political one; the decision to use, or to threaten to use, nuclear weapons is said to be entirely political, and that therefore the solution must be sought in political terms.

While it is true that the decision whether to employ a weapon is political, such decision would be meaningless unless the state had the technical wherewithal to implement it. Similarly, the political decision to eliminate certain weapons by a treaty would lack credibility unless there were the technical means to verify compliance with the treaty.[28] Both aspects, the technological and the political one, are necessary elements. Moreover, not only do they both play a vital role, but they reinforce each other.

The pursuit of an arms race, and the existence of large military arsenals, go hand in hand with a climate of mistrust, antagonism and fear. One is the father and the child of the other. In order to justify the enormous military spending, it is necessary to create the image of an enemy, who is depicted as evil and aggressive, waiting for any sign of slackness in our defence posture to pounce and overwhelm us.

Conversely, the mutual reduction of arsenals alleviates anxiety and creates trust and good will, which is conducive to further measures in the same direction. It is a process of positive feedback. Disarmament measures reduce fears and bolster confidence, which in turn makes it easier to implement further reductions, which create a better climate, and so it goes on.

In terms of the Wiesner graph (Fig. 1), which was based only on the technological aspect, the inclusion of the effect of an improved political climate would accelerate the process of disarmament, by changing the idealized straight line A (Fig. 2) into a downward bending curve A'. Again, these graphs are meant to show trends and do not imply meaningful mathematical relations.

The above considerations apply not only to nuclear weapons but to all types of military arms. Indeed, it would be folly to aim at nuclear disarmament in a world increasingly armed with other weapons. Nuclear weapons have been singled out because of their enormous destructive potential; should these weapons be used they would threaten the whole fabric of our civilization and the lives of most of the world population. The removal of this menace must therefore have top priority. But the process of nuclear disarmament must be accompanied by steps towards the reduction and eventual elimination of stockpiles of chemical and conventional weapons. Recent moves in this direction, for example the unilateral decisions by the Soviet government to reduce significantly the numerical strength of its army and the numbers of its conventional armaments,[26] as well as its stock of chemical weapons,[27] and the statement by President Bush in the same direction,[28] are highly encouraging. Here again the positive feedback between technical measures and better international relations, would greatly help in the overall eradication of the threat of military confrontation, eventually leading to the ultimate objective, general and complete disarmament.[29]

The Role of Scientists

The scientific community has an important role to play in helping to devise and improve the ways to nuclear disarmament, as well as encouraging the creation of the necessary political climate.

It is appropriate to recall Einstein's statement of 1946 soon after the birth of the nuclear age: "The unleashed power of the atom has changed everything save our modes of thinking, and thus we drift toward unparalleled catastrophe. We scientists who unleashed this immense power have an overwhelming responsibility in this world life-and-death struggle to harness the atom for the benefit of mankind and not for humanity's destruction".[30] With the recent evidence of a change in the mode of thinking on these issues by political leaders, it is even more incumbent on scientists to fulfil actively their social responsibility.

In the first instance, scientists working in military research establishment can help directly. If nuclear and other arms are to be eliminated, the existing establishments will have the cease work, to prevent a renewal of the arms race. But they could be kept going if they were converted entirely for peace research, specifically to enhance verification techniques. Some research of this kind is already going on there--in parallel with work on new weapons--but it would have to be considerably expanded. The scientists and engineers should be asked to use their talents to discover new methods of surveillance, new techniques to identify missiles and warheads, new ways to reduce the likelihood of undetected cheating.

Other scientists can also help in these tasks. The contributors to this book-- nearly all independent scientists not connected with military establishments-- have already shown their ingenuity in advancing verification techniques. Much more could be achieved if a larger number of scientists put their minds to this problem.[31]

Another role of the scientific community is to act as a watch-dog of compliance with treaties. Through their contacts with other scientists in universities and research institutes, and through careful reading of the literature, they can discover whether clandestine work is being carried out, or sensitive material is being diverted, in this way lessening the possibility of cheating. A network of information about suspicious events, including a register of scientists and technologists, will strengthen societal means of verification. And the very knowledge that scientists are on the alert would help in reducing anxiety among the public about non-adherence or circumvention of treaties.

In this context, there is also a significant role for scientists in educating the public about the importance of verification of treaties, and preventing their violation, as part of common security. Several specific measures towards this objective have been proposed.[32] There is a need to foster a general feeling of loyalty to the world community as an extension of the loyalties to one's country and family. Due to the universality of science, which cuts across geographic and ideological boundaries, scientists have developed this sense of belonging to the world community, of being citizens of the world, more than any other group of society, and therefore they are in a good position to nurture such ideas.

Another way for scientists to contribute to the formation of a suitable political climate is by promoting and taking part in global projects of scientific collaboration. Such projects, involving scientists from many countries, not only serve to improve the image of science, but the result of such collaboration can be of great benefit to the peoples of the world, raise standards of living, create more good will on earth, thus lessening the need to resort to military solutions.

Conclusions

Two questions were posed in the title of this paper: is the elimination of nuclear arsenals desirable; and, if so, is it feasible?

The answer to the first question is an emphatic yes. Quite apart from the moral objections to reliance on retaliation with weapons of mass destruction, nuclear deterrence is not a reliable means to ensure security, if based on current arsenals and the inherent danger of an accidental war. Nuclear disarmament down to a "minimum deterrence" will still not bring stability; in the long run a new arms race is bound to occur, and more nations are likely to acquire nuclear weapons for their security, thus increasing the risk of nuclear war.

The answer to the second question is a qualified yes. The known means of verification can ensure compliance with undertakings to reduce nuclear arsenals down to a very low level. With the present state of technology, they cannot be made 100% effective, a necessary condition for the complete elimination of nuclear weapons. Further research is needed to elaborate the approach to that state. As an interim measure, the treaty abolishing national nuclear arsenals would need to be accompanied by the setting up, under the aegis of the United Nations, of an international depository of nuclear weapons and means of delivery, sufficient to deter a potential violator of the treaty.

Apart from continuing efforts to perfect the technological means of verification, the attainment of the objective of a nuclear-weapon-free world would be accelerated by the creation of a climate of good will and trust, itself a result of arms reduction. Scientists have a vital role in these tasks as well.

Notes

1. UN General Assembly, Resolution 1(I), 24 January 1946.

2. Statement by Mikhail Gorbachev, General Secretary of the CPSU Central Committee, 15 January 1986, Novosti Press Agency.

3. "Action plan for ushering in a nuclear-weapon-free and non-violent world order". Tabled by India at the Third Special Session on Disarmament, June 1988.

4. Lord Zuckerman, "The World Without INF". *The New York Review of Books*, 2 June 1988, p. 37.

5. British Prime Minister Margaret Thatcher, in a B.B.C. interview, 7 December 1987.

6. William Waldegrave, British Foreign Office Minister, *The Times*, 6 January 1989.

7. J. Rotblat, "Technology, the Arms Race and Disarmament" in C. Schaerf, B. H. Reid & David Carlton, eds., *New Technologies and the Arms Race*, (London: Macmillan, 1989), pp. 332-344.

8. Andrea Ottolenghi, "Limited Nuclear War in Europe" in *Effects of Nuclear War on Health and Health Services*. (Geneva: World Health Organization, 1987), pp. 121-125.

9. Address to the Nation by President Ronald Reagan, "Peace and National Security",

23 March 1983.

10. F.C. Iklé & A. Wohltsetter,"Discriminate Deterrence". Report of the Commission on Integrated Long-Term Strategy". January 1988.

11. "Treaty between the United States of America and the Union of Soviet Socialist Republics on the elimination of their intermediate-range and shorter-range missiles", December 1987.

12. R. Garwin, "A blueprint for radical weapons cuts," *Bulletin of the Atomic Scientists,* March 1988. See also *Proceedings of the 37th Pugwash Conference,* Gmunden, September 1987, pp. 267-280.

13. A.A. Kokoshin, "A Soviet view on radical weapons cuts," *Bulletin of the Atomic Scientists,* March 1988.

14. Report on 16th Pugwash Workshop on Nuclear Forces. *Pugwash Newsletter,* vol 26, July 1988, p. 14.

15. V.I. Goldanskii in *Nuclear Tests: Prohibition or Limitation?,* (V. Goldblat and D. Cox, eds), Oxford University Press, 1988, p. 332-334.

16. *Proceedings of the 6th Pugwash Conference,* Moscow, 1960, p. 298.

17. F. von Hippel, D.H. Albright, B.G. Levi, "Quantities of Fissile Materials in U.S. and Soviet Nuclear Weapons Arsenals". *PU/CEES Report* No. 168, Princeton University, July 1986.

18. E. Amaldi, U. Farinelli, C. Silvi, "The Utilization for Civilian Purposes of the weapon-grade nuclear materials that may become available as a consequence of nuclear disarmament". Workshop on International Security and Disarmament, the Role of Scientific Academies, Rome, 23-25 June 1988.

19. A. Lecocq, "Disposal of Fissile Materials and Verification" in J. Hassard, T. Kibble, P. Lewis, eds., *Ways Out of the Arms Race* (Singapore: World Scientific Publishing Co., 1989), pp. 77-83.

20. T.B. Taylor, private communication.

21. V. Weisskopf, "A change of Emphasis". *Proceedings of the 37th Pugwash conference,* Gmunden, 1987, pp. 85-88.

22. V.I. Goldanskii, *Physics Today,* March 1990, pp. 53-55.

23. "International Control of Atomic Energy: Growth of a Policy". U.S. Department of State, June 1946.

24. R.L. Garwin, private communication.

25. V.I. Goldanskii and M. Intrilligator, "US-Soviet Relations: from Confrontation to Cooperation through Verificational Deterrence" in *Proceedings of the 38th Pugwash Conference,* Dagomys, 1988, pp. 196-202.

26. Mikhail S. Gorbachev: United Nations Address, 7 December 1988.

27. Eduard A. Shevardnadze: Speech at Paris Conference on Chemical Weapons, 8 January 1989.

28. George Bush, speech at NATO meeting, 30 May 1989.

29. J. Rotblat, "Time to Think Again about General and Complete Disarmament" in *Ways Out of Arms Race,* op. cit., pp. 195-200.

30. O. Nathan & H. Nordon, *Einstein on Peace,* (New York: Simon & Schuster, 1980), p. 376.

31. J. Rotblat, "Dilemmas for Scientists with a Social Conscience" in *Proceedings of the 38th Pugwash Conference,* Dagomys, 1988, pp. 105-112.

32. T.B. Taylor, "Global Abolition of Nuclear Weapons - Verification of Compliance

and Deterrents to Violation," paper prepared for the 40th Pugwash Conference, Egham, September 1990.

12

Arms-Control Verification in a Changing World

John P. Holdren (USA) & Andrei A. Kokoshin (USSR)

Most of this book was written before the remarkable events of late 1989 and early 1990 initiated what is obviously an entirely new phase in East-West political and military relations. Although the full ramifications of these developments still cannot be discerned as this concluding chapter is being written in early 1990, we two authors who come last cannot escape the task of speculating on how the changes of the last few months will affect the issues treated by our colleagues in the chapters preceding this one. Which of the themes and recommendations elaborated there will remain germane in the world of 1990 and beyond? Which might need to be modified? What new challenges and opportunities in arms-control verification are likely to accompany today's and tomorrow's rapidly changing international-security agenda?

The changes that already have occurred in the security landscape are indisputably fundamental. The sweeping reforms and political restructuring that are transforming the political face of Europe have essentially eradicated, in the space of a few months, the core of the ideological and political basis for the Cold War. Withdrawals of Soviet troops from one Eastern European country after another amount to a unilateral dismantling--at a pace unimaginable half a year earlier--of the most visible and to many minds the most threatening part of the Cold War military confrontation. No less a pillar of the Western threat-assessment establishment than the Director of the US Central Intelligence Agency declared in March 1990 that a drastic diminution in Soviet military potential for use in central or western Europe was already irreversible.

Yet as much as has changed, there is much that remains the same. The bloated military forces of the East-West confrontation--nuclear and chemical as well as conventional--have on the whole barely begun to be trimmed. There is still no START agreement, no Chemical Weapons Convention, no treaty on Conventional

Forces in Europe.

Meanwhile, other threats to international security and stability that had been suppressed or had lain dormant during the long winter of the Cold War--threats arising from ethnic and racial tensions, from economic discontent, from diverse forms of nationalism, from long-standing territorial disputes--are popping up in and around Europe like weeds after the spring thaw.

In the South, while the amelioration of superpower competition may bring some reduction in the security threats that have been associated with interventions from the North in pursuit of geopolitical advantage, the indigenous roots of instability--extreme poverty and inequity, religious and ethnic hatreds, competing claims on territory, the inevitable frictions of self-determination and emerging statehood, the struggle for regional hegemony--are probably becoming more rather than less dangerous over time. The sources of increasing danger include: (a) worsening economic and environmental conditions in many parts of the South--compounded by continuing rapid population growth and by regional droughts that may be the leading edge of global climate change--leading to increased misery, threats to the stability of governments, and expanded flows of environmental refugees; (b) the effect of partial withdrawal of the superpowers in lifting some of the restraints previously imposed by their presence on independent local aggressive action; and (c) the growing size and sophistication of the arsenals in the South, fed not only by continuing transfers of sophisticated weaponry from the North but also by the rapid growth of indigenous arms industries in the South.

Against this evolving backdrop of international security concerns, it seems reasonable to us to conceive the arms-control agenda for the 1990s--and, accordingly, the verification agenda--in terms of three sets of interrelated challenges.

- First, it is essential to proceed with all possible speed to complete, while conditions remain highly favorable, the basically bilateral framework needed to address such primary elements of the US-Soviet military competition as strategic nuclear forces, ballistic missile defenses and space weaponry, deployments of US and Soviet shorter-range nuclear forces and conventional forces in and near Europe, and navies. This framework must aim at force levels much lower than today's, and it must limit qualitative characteristics as well as numbers. Unless such a framework can be completed and solidified quickly, there will be a danger that the deeply embedded competitive tendences of the militaries and weapons industries on the two sides will promote a continuing series of arms races, notwithstanding the virtual disappearance of the political rationale for such an adversarial relationship. And if the United States and the Soviet Union fail to move decisively to rule out these forms of bilateral military competition between them, there will be no hope of persuading other countries to relinquish the pursuit of military power as a critical currency of international relations.
- The second set of challenges is, naturally, that of developing the multilateral

as opposed to bilateral dimensions of an expanded arms-control framework, with special attention to classes of armaments whose importance tends to be magnified by the diminishing dominance of superpower postures in international security affairs. These challenges include limiting the offensive potential of conventional forces in all countries, restraining the spread of nuclear and chemical weapons and sophisticated technologies for their delivery, and constraining the global trade in weapons more generally.

• The third set of challenges involves broadening and deepening the concepts of arms control and arms-control verification, so that they become integrated with a more comprehensive approach to the definition and limitation of threats to international security. Issues in this category include the development and implementation of restraints on third-party intervention in regional conflicts, the management of research and development to minimize both the emergence of destabilizing weapons technologies and fears about such emergence, the redirection into more productive channels, worldwide, of the excessive flows of technological and economic resources now devoted to weaponry ("conversion"), and the monitoring and management of regional and global environmental problems with the potential to aggravate international tensions.

In what follows, we consider the relevance of the contributions of the preceding chapters to these three sets of challenges, as well as identifying some issues on which further work is clearly warranted.

The US-USSR Arms-Control Agenda

The recent political transformations have not yet affected the size of the strategic nuclear arsenals held by the United States and the Soviet Union, nor have these transformations even altered in a significant way the terms of the discussion about the prescriptions by which these forces are to be reduced. This situation will surely change, as policy makers and publics come to recognize that the main rationales under which these forces were built up over the past decades have now been pulled from beneath them. The primary official rationale for the design of U.S. nuclear forces was the idea that deterring the Soviet Union from a potentially successful conventional attack against Western Europe could only be accomplished by an explicit threat that the United States would be prepared to respond to such an attack by initiating the use of nuclear weapons and by escalating if necessary to global nuclear war. The U.S. attempt to deploy nuclear forces that would give this threat credibility through the capacity to inflict more harm on the Soviet Union with nuclear weapons than the Soviet Union could inflict in return--and the Soviet attempt to deploy nuclear forces that could deny the United States any such potential advantage--shaped the nuclear arms competition for forty-five years and led to the accumulation of the 55,000 nuclear warheads still residing in the two arsenals as this is written.

We do not think there was ever really a good case for the sorts of nuclear arsenals that the United States and the Soviet Union built up; but now that everyone can see that there is no chance at all of a successful conventional-forces attack by the Soviet Union across Europe, it must be completely clear that nuclear arsenals of these kinds are useless anachronisms. Whether or not one agrees with the arguments in the chapter by Rotblat and Goldanskii, that nuclear weapons can and should be eliminated entirely from the armaments of nations, it is now obvious at least that much smaller nuclear arsenals than those deployed by the United States and the Soviet Union today would be adequate for any imaginable deterrent need. It therefore seems very likely that a phase-one START agreement, which would reduce these two arsenals by at least 25 to 35 percent, will have been signed by the time this book is in print, that pressure will build rather rapidly to design and agree upon much deeper subsequent cuts in strategic nuclear forces, and that pressure to remove from the territory of Europe all of the shorter-range nuclear weapons deployed by the United States and the Soviet Union (mainly missiles, nuclear artillery shells, and aircraft-delivered bombs) will also intensify rapidly.

In the context both of an initial START agreement and of subsequent steps toward deeper cuts in strategic forces, the points made by Fetter and Rodionov in their chapter on verifying numerical limits on strategic delivery systems will remain highly germane. Two of these points seem to us to be of particular importance.

- First, it is possible to verify, with high reliability, reductions in deployed numbers of long-range ballistic missiles *regardless of their type* (that is, whether silo-based or road-mobile or rail-mobile or submarine-launched) by using combinations of data exchange, on-site inspections, perimeter-portal monitoring, enhanced "national technical means", and tags and seals; thus verification considerations need not govern the choice of each side about what basing mode may be used for its allotment of ballistic missiles under a treaty, and this should make it easier to reach agreement.
- Second, the problems posed for strategic arms verification by air-launched and sea-launched cruise missiles--particularly because of the problem of distinguishing strategic nuclear versions from tactical conventional ones--are likely to remain severe. It seems to us that in today's world and tomorrow's it should be possible just to do without the military benefits of cruise missiles, by banning them altogether, in   order to avoid the serious complications they will otherwise pose for nuclear arms control. At the very least it should be possible to ban *nuclear* cruise missiles entirely--which would simplify the verification problem considerably--given that the idea of selective uses of nuclear weapons in warfare is being rapidly discredited and given that other types of strategic weapons are more than

adequate for any residual deterrent role that might be deemed necessary.

As for verifying the complete removal of U.S. and Soviet shorter-range nuclear forces from the territory of Europe, the numbers and actual or potential dispersal of these systems implies challenges in some ways even more demanding than those already faced in the INF Treaty and in the proposals for verifying START limits. (A separate chapter on this topic in our book would surely have been deemed warranted, had the political transformations been foreseen that have made the denuclearization of Europe so much more salient an issue.) Certainly a combination of verification ideas from the strategic and intermediate-range nuclear-forces regimes, as well as from the conventional-forces regime as treated in this book by Altmann, Deak, Kelleher, and Makarevsky, will prove to be germane to the shorter-range nuclear forces question. It can also be noted that some of the potential verification difficulties posed by this category will surely be considerably alleviated by a situation in which the individual countries within Europe see it as strongly in their own interests that their territories be free of nuclear weapons.

As cuts in strategic and nonstrategic nuclear forces go deeper, it will become increasingly important that not only delivery systems but also the nuclear warheads themselves be destroyed (as opposed merely to being returned to a nondeployed reserve, or being "recycled" onto delivery sytems that have not yet been restricted) in the case of tactical and operational-tactical weapons it will be even more important. In this connection the ideas developed in the paper by Taylor and Feoktistov on destruction of nuclear warheads and the sequestering of their nuclear-explosive materials will deserve careful attention in the future. We endorse their proposal for the formation of an official joint US-Soviet working group to design and assess specific procedures and corresponding facilities for verified elimination of nuclear warheads, and urge that this step be undertaken promptly.

Attempts to constrain the size and qualitative capabilities of offensive nuclear forces cannot succeed in the long run unless strategic defensive weapons also remain constrained. This was the fundamental insight that led to the Anti-Ballistic Missile Treaty of 1972, and the insight remains as true and as important in the 1990s as it was in the 1970s. The ideas about space-based missile defenses that gained so much attention in the 1980s not only failed to discredit the concept that offensive and defensive limits are prerequisites for one another but rather, by underlining the ambiguity betweeen offensive and defensive uses of anti-missile weapons, strengthened the point. Nor have the political and military changes that started in late 1989 altered in any way the need to preserve and strengthen the limitations in the ABM Treaty. Indeed, ballistic missile defenses and space weapons more generally provide perhaps the best example of an area in which technological change, if not scrupulously constrained, could prove capable of stimulating a dangerous and expensive military competition despite the absence of any political rationale for it.

The recommendations in the article on space weapons by Garwin and Sagdeev, therefore, remain completely valid. The United States and the Soviet Union should move expeditiously to negotiate effective and verifiable bans on testing and deployment of space weapons and on testing of anti-satellite weapons, in order to close off fruitless competitions in these categories of weapons and above all to avoid undermining the ABM Treaty and thus unraveling the whole fabric of strategic arms control. It is worth emphasizing, especially, that banning all weapons from space, as well as tests of weapons in space and from Earth to space, would be far simpler to verify than an array of detailed numerical limits on particular space-weapon capabilities and activities, as well as much more reliable as a means of averting the dangers of competition in space weapons. Given such comprehensive bans, the effectiveness of an inspection regime centered around pre-announcement of nearly all launches and space activities, with at least limited on-site monitoring of payloads at the launch sites, should be very high.

In contrast to the attention that has been devoted to the problems of limiting the use of space as an arena for military competition between the United States and the Soviet Union, the focus on the more traditional arena of the oceans--that is, on naval arms control--has been neither very vigorous nor very successful. (This is partly because the navies, and particularly the U.S. Navy, have wanted it that way.) Nonetheless, and notwithstanding the absence of a chapter devoted to verifying naval arms control in this volume, we think that limitations on navies would be desirable and will inevitably be seriously considered in the years ahead. The U.S. and Soviet navies today contain about 30 percent of the strategic and tactical nuclear warheads in the combined arsenals of the two countries, and the combination of the mission of many of these weapons and the command-and-control arrangements governing them means that they represent in some respects an even bigger menace than nuclear weapons based on land.

Verifiability of reductions in numbers and restrictions in categories of naval nuclear weapons is likely to pose many difficulties, but these become much easier the moment one contemplates a ban rather than numerical limits. We believe the most sensible proposal from the standpoint of efficacy as well as verifiability, in fact, is one of the most radical ones: ban all nuclear weapons on all surface vessels, and ban all but strategic ballistic missiles on submarines. It is increasingly difficult to justify any real military need for nonstrategic nuclear weapons on naval vessels, and retaining them on U.S. and Soviet ships patrolling the world's trouble spots is likely to become more and more troublesome in the future as an irritant to allies, a provocation to adversaries, and another embarrassing bit of hypocrisy in a world in which our two countries are trying to persuade others to forego acquiring nuclear weapons.

With respect to *all* of the issues on the bilateral US-Soviet arms-control agenda, the arguments made by Duffy and Loukiantzev in their chapter on compliance will remain germane well into the future. They are surely correct that the recently initiated period of reduced tensions and cooperative inclinations in US-Soviet relations will not mean the end of disputes about compliance with agreements in the future, and they provide a useful categorization of the ways in which such disputes can arise--with examples of issues in US-Soviet arms-control agreements that could easily become problematical in the years to come. We strongly agree with them that the present period of good relations should be exploited to institutionalize, insofar as possible, more systematic and more cooperative approaches for minimizing disagreements about compliance and for dealing with those that do arise. The needed prescriptions include the strengthening of existing compliance institutions, such as the Standing Consultative Commission connected with the SALT and ABM agreements and the counterpart organization associated with the INF Treaty; incorporating such institutions in new agreements as they are formulated; and developing mechanisms of recourse for use when these dispute-resolution bodies fail.

The Multilateral Arms-Control Agenda

Besides the United States and the Soviet Union, which between them possess more than 95 percent of the world's 55,000 nuclear warheads, national nuclear arsenals of some hundreds of nuclear warheads each are possessed by France, the United Kingdom, and China. In addition, Israel is widely supposed to possess a nuclear arsenal that may also be larger than 100 weapons; India tested a nuclear weapon in 1974 and may have since acquired a modest stockpile; and Pakistan and South Africa are suspected of having at least a few weapons or the capacity to assemble them quickly. Although the spread of nuclear weapons capabilities to an ever larger number of nations has so far taken place more slowly than many people feared at the dawn of the nuclear age, there is nonetheless much reason to worry that each addition to the "club" of nations possessing nuclear weapons makes the world a less predictable and more dangerous place.

It is far from clear that the recent drastic improvement in East-West relations will reduce the dangers of nuclear proliferation. Quite the contrary, it could even aggravate them, both by reducing the dominance of the United States and the Soviet Union in defining the security postures of countries within what have been the Western and Eastern blocs and by reducing the restraining influences of U.S. and Soviet military presences and commitments in the South. The problem of proliferation is in any case, by its nature, a multilateral and not a bilateral one. It cannot be solved by U.S. and Soviet actions alone, although very clearly what the United States and the Soviet Union do (or do not do) can exert a considerable influence. What the two countries have mainly done in support of non-proliferation up until now is to serve as principal architects and promoters of the Non-Proliferation Treaty (NPT) of 1968, which today has more than 130 parties, and of the associated International Atomic Energy Agency safeguards against diversion of nuclear materials from civilian into military applications. What they have mainly *failed* to do is make significant progress toward reducing their own nuclear arsenals (as called for in Article VI of the NPT) or agree on the cessation of nuclear testing (as endorsed in the NPT's Preamble and in that of the Limited Test Ban Treaty of 1963). Both failures represent significant obstacles, in our view, to achieving a climate that minimizes the incentives for additional countries to acquire their own nuclear weapons.

While it is widely agreed that the two most useful steps the nuclear-weapons powers could take in support of nonproliferation would be agreement on significant reductions in nuclear stockpiles and agreement on a Comprehensive Test Ban (CTB) covering nuclear explosions in all media (space, the atmosphere, the oceans, underground), policy makers and the arms-control community more generally have tended to give much higher priority to the first goal than to the second. One reason for this is that arms reductions have been thought to have greater direct bearing on the cessation of the nuclear arms race than a CTB would have, thus being more valuable in their own right as well as being more influential as a reducer of proliferation incentives. Another reason is the idea that a CTB would be extremely difficult to verify. We have no quarrel with the usefulness of reducing nuclear arsenals, but we think both the importance and the verifiability of a CTB have been under-rated.

Concerning importance, we think continued nuclear testing manifests a conviction that nuclear weapons have military functions which can benefit from continued refinements in weapon design. This conviction is itself a major driver of the nuclear arms race, which has always been as dangerous for its qualitative innovations as for the growth in numbers of weapons alone. (It was only through nuclear testing, of course, that nuclear weapons small enough to be put in artillery shells--or small enough to bring about extensive MIRVing of ballistic missiles-- could be developed, and it would only be through nuclear testing that nuclear directed-energy weapons for "Star Wars" and other applications could be developed, as well.) As long as nuclear-weapons states insist, moreover, not only that their security requires retaining nuclear arsenals but that these need continuing refinement through nuclear testing, the advice of these countries that other countries should forego acquiring such weapons cannot be expected to carry much weight. Only when nuclear testing stops will it become believable that the commitment of the nuclear-weapons states to the military and political value of nuclear weapons is coming to an end.

Up until the Reagan Administration came to power in the United States in 1980, the ostensible reason for the failure of the original parties of the Limited Test Ban Treaty--the United States, the Soviet Union, and the United Kingdom--to agree on extending it into a Comprehensive Test Ban was the difficulty of agreeing on what would constitute adequate verification. As verification capabilities, particularly by seismic means improved, and as these improvements became widely known, the idea that verification was an insurmountable obstacle to a CTB steadily lost credibility. As a result, the Reagan Administration was forced to admit that verification was not the only issue: it announced, notwithstanding commitments to the contrary by six previous Administrations, that the United States did not favor agreement on a CTB in the foreseeable future because it regarded modernization of its nuclear forces through nuclear testing as essential to U.S. national security in view of "the Soviet threat". The Reagan Administration stuck to this position despite the pressures generated by General Secretary Gorbachev's 18-month unilateral moratorium on Soviet nuclear testing in 1985-87, and until now the Bush Administration has not reversed it.

It seems certain, however, that the recent revolution in East-West relations--accompanied, as it has been, by the rapid evaporation of any sense that there is a plausible "Soviet threat" to the West--will undermine support for the proposition that continuously modernizing nuclear forces is necessary or desirable, and thus will undermine support for continued nuclear testing. This situation is likely to return the emphasis in the CTB debate to the question of verifiability, making more relevant than ever this book's chapter by Archambeau, Gokhberg, Kedrov and Leggett on seismic and other means of test-ban verification. The essence of their conclusion is that present capabilities, given moderate numbers of in-country seismic monitoring stations, should be adequate to verify that no program of underground nuclear tests with explosive yields above a threshold in the range of 2 to 5 kilotons could escape detection. (This is of course far below the 150-kiloton threshold currently being observed under the terms of the Threshold Test Ban Treaty of 1974.) With the larger set of monitoring stations that would seem to be achievable in the current atmosphere of cooperation, the threshold of confidence in detection might well be pushed to 1 kiloton or below.

The question that probably will come to dominate the test-ban debate in the months and years immediately ahead is whether to seek a treaty establishing a threshold in the range of 1 to 5 kilotons or whether to seek a true comprehensive test ban barring nuclear explosive tests at any yield. Proponents of the first alternative argue that it is unwise, or at least politically impractical, to agree to any ban tighter than what can be reliably verified. Proponents of a comprehensive ban--and here we include ourselves--argue that no arms control agreement of any sort is *absolutely* verifiable, in the sense that no conceivable violation could ever escape detection, but that this should not be an obstacle to agreement. The key question governing whether to agree on a treaty is whether the risks associated with the possibility of cheating below the threshold of detectability are greater or smaller than the risks associated with having no treaty at all. In the specific case of a Comprehensive Test Ban versus a low-threshold treaty, settling for the latter fails to secure the main benefits that a test ban should be seeking: by not stopping testing altogether, it does not force the nuclear-weapons states to renounce the *concept* that continuing improvement of nuclear weapons is necessary and desirable, and thus it loses both the main anti-arms-race benefit and the main anti-proliferation benefit that a Comprehensive Test Ban would secure. We do not find it credible that, in the era of the 1990s and beyond, there are either gains from testing below (say) 1 kiloton, or risks from potential adversaries doing so undetected, large enough to stand in the way of agreeing to a CTB and gaining the anti-arms-race and anti-proliferation benefits it offers.

The links between the behavior of the current declared nuclear-weapons states and the prospects for containing the spread of nuclear weapons to additional countries include not only the influence of progress in nuclear arms reductions and the potential role of a Comprehensive Test Ban, but also the rules applied to the production of fissile materials in all countries. Currently there is a striking asymmetry in this last connection, in that weapons states openly produce fissile materials for addition to their nuclear-weapon stockpiles, while all non-weapons-state parties to the Non-Proliferation Treaty are expected to adhere to rules and safeguards intended to prevent either the construction of dedicated facilities for acquisition of weapons materials or the diversion of materials from civilian facilities to weapons purposes. Any anti-proliferation prescription that is to have much chance of success will need to counter the pernicious influence of this asymmetry, and the only obvious solution is to eliminate it by imposing a universal cutoff on production of fissile material for weapons purposes.

This idea, which is considered in the chapter by Scheinman and Gverdziteli, seems considerably closer to attainability now than it did a few months ago. For it is even harder now than before to see what justification can possibly be offered for nuclear arsenals as large as those that already exist, and therefore it becomes extremely difficult to argue that a continuing flow of new fissile material into the stockpiles is required. If the United States, the Soviet Union, and the other nuclear-weapons states were to agree to such a cutoff (and given their much larger arsenals it would not be unreasonable to expect the United States and the Soviet Union to do so in advance of the other weapons states), most if not all of the required verification machinery could be put in place--as Scheinman and Gverdziteli point out--simply by generalizing the safeguards system and authority already extant in the International Atomic Energy Agency and applied to nonweapons states under the NPT. With such a rationalization of the international regime regulating production and use of fissile materials, say Scheinman and Gverdziteli, it might become possible to insist that all new nuclear fuel-cycle activities with potential weapons applications be structured and operated on an international basis. We strongly agree that this would be highly desirable; indeed, it is hard to see how expanded use of nuclear fission for energy supply worldwide can be countenanced *without* the combination of a universal cutoff of fissile-material production for weapons purposes, submission of all existing fuel-cycle facilities to international inspection, and the placing of new enrichment and fuel-reprocessing facilities under international management.

Chemical weapons represent another arena in which the largest stockpiles are held by the United States and the Soviet Union but the issue has long since become a multilateral much more than a bilateral one. Nothing less than a comprehensive, worldwide prohibition on the production, stockpiling, and use of these indiscriminate weapons of mass destruction can offer adequate protection against them. A Chemical Weapons Convention with these aims has been under formal negotiation since 1984 in what is now the 40-nation Conference on Disarmament (CD) in Geneva, but the problem of verification has proven to be an intractable obstacle to concluding an agreement. One of the most difficult features of the problem is the interchangeability of chemical manufacturing capabilities having legitimate commercial applications with those associated with the manufacture of chemical weapons. There is a parallel here with the usability of civilian nuclear-energy facilities for producing nuclear-weapons material; but the chemical problem is more difficult in that the relevant kinds of chemical-manufacturing facilities are much more diverse, more numerous, and more thoroughly integrated with the industrial sectors of modern societies. That means that a convincing scheme for verifying non-production of chemical weapons probably needs to be much more pervasive and intrusive than those in place or envisioned for the nuclear sector.

In parallel with the official CD negotiations, a series of fifteen Pugwash workshops on chemical weaponry, emphasizing verification issues, has been conducted in Geneva, with members of the negotiating teams and many other leading experts on chemical-weapons problems taking part. The very thorough treatment of chemical-weapons verification presented in the chapter by Lohs, Perry-Robinson, and Smidovich in this book owes much to that workshop series, in which all of the authors have been regular participants. We believe that their arguments--both about the ingredients of the satisfactory verification solutions for chemical weapons that are now within reach, and about the general lessons derivable from the CD negotiations process with relevance to other arms-control arenas--are sound and certainly not less relevant after the recent transformations in Europe than before. Indeed, the new openness and more vigorous scientific and industrial interactions linking Western and Eastern Europe should strengthen the authors' conclusion that inspection procedures of the needed pervasiveness and intrusiveness can be agreed--at least as concerns the countries in that part of the world. (Even as they wrote, the authors noted that obstacles to agreement were looming larger on the North-South axis than on the East-West one, and that is surely even more true now.) It must be hoped, in any case, that the relaxation of tensions in Europe does not produce any reduction in the sense of urgency attached to concluding the Chemical Weapons Convention, for the dangers of chemical weapons use in the South are growing even faster than they are shrinking in Europe.

In the case of biological and toxin weapons, a comprehensive ban already exists in the form of the Biological Weapons Convention of 1972, to which more than 100 states are parties. As Meselson, Kaplan, and Mokulsky point out in their chapter on this topic, the verification provisions originally embodied in this convention have been considerably augmented since through agreements entered into by its parties in review conferences and through actions taken at the United

Nations. Nonetheless, there is more that could and should be done. The authors recommend, among other measures, some steps relating to openness of biological research activities--that there should be *no* secret military facilities, programs, or research in biology or medicine, and that there should be an expansion of long-term exchanges of working scientists, as well as exchanges of scientific administrators, among the biological and medical research facilities of different nations--which we think may have much wider relevance in maintaining confidence that research and development activities in other fields are not being turned to threatening ends.

Limitations on conventional forces are, in general, the most complex of arms control agreements to negotiate and the most difficult to verify, for reasons developed at length in the chapter on this subject by Altmann, Deak, Kelleher, and Makarevsky: the problem is as multilateral as can be, since virtually all countries have such forces; the numbers of sites and weapons are greater than in other arms-control contexts; almost always one is dealing with non-zero ceilings, which are harder to verify than the total bans sometimes possible with other weapon types; and problems of definition are often more complicated (e.g., answering the question "What is a tank?" offers more opportunity for ambiguity and disagreement than answering the question "What is a nuclear warhead?").

At the same time, some of the most difficult problems of formulating and verifying limitations on conventional forces may have become, through the recent changes in the European political landscape, no longer very relevant--at least in that part of the world. For example, the complicated zonal prescriptions which a few months ago were the heart of every prescription for conventional-forces arms control in Europe, and to which the chapter by Altmann et al. naturally devotes considerable attention, are almost certain to be made practically irrelevant within a year or so by the removal of Soviet forces from Hungary, Poland, Czechoslovakia, and probably East Germany. It would be an understatement to say that there does not now seem to be much danger that these removals could be reversed surreptitiously--and that this assurance does not depend on any details of negotiated verification capabilities.

There will almost certainly, nonetheless, be a treaty emerging from the Vienna negotiations on Conventional Forces in Europe (CFE), and a strong interest on all sides in verifying that its provisions are being obeyed. For this purpose, both the general principles and the specific prescriptions for conventional-forces verification enunciated in the Altmann et al. chapter will certainly remain applicable; it is only that the magnitudes and dispositions of the forces, and perhaps the foci of some of the main concerns, are likely to be rather different than those the authors were reasonably hypothesizing a few months ago. In the way of concerns, for example, a number of countries will now be interested in the capabilities of a CFE agreement and associated verification measures to provide assurances that a reunited Germany cannot become a threat to any of its neighbors--an issue on no one's agenda a year ago. (The array of verification measures treated by the authors should certainly be adequate for this purpose, and might be made politically palatable if applied equally to all countries in Europe with a multilateral organization responsible for the monitoring.)

Both for the European context and elsewhere, we welcome the authors' stress on the complementary roles of diverse approaches and means for verification: permanent and temporary observation posts; scheduled, random, and challenge inspections; overlapping sensor systems that are mutually reinforcing and differentially vulnerable to failure; tags and seals; overflights by reconnaissance aircraft; space-based monitoring; and more. Reading this chapter could be recommended as an antidote to the somewhat excessive preoccupation with overflights alone that has been engendered by the recent revival of the "Open Skies" approach first proposed by Eisenhower in 1955; it is a useful concept, but far from the whole solution or even most of the solution to conventional-forces verification problems. As noted earlier, there is also much of value in this chapter for application to the task of verifying the removal of nuclear weapons from the territory of Europe.

As in a number of other arms-control problems already discussed here, the locus of greatest dangers and greatest arms-control difficulties in respect to conventional military forces is in the process of shifting from Europe and the associated US-Soviet dimension to the South and the associated North-South issues. The potential causes of military conflict are more diverse and more intractable in the South than in the North; the arrangements for arms control, confidence building, crisis avoidance, and crisis control are far less well developed in the South than in the North; and the arsenals in the South have been growing dramatically in firepower, range, and sophistication, drawing both on extensive arms transfers from the North and on increasingly capable indigenous arms industries.

Of particular concern in the last few years has been the drastic upsurge of testing and deployment of ballistic missiles in the South: the U.S. Arms Control and Disarmament Agency (ACDA) publication *World Military Expenditures and Arms Transfers 1988* lists 16 Third World countries (9 in the Middle East, 5 in Asia, 2 in South America) that possess such missiles or are in the process of developing them. These capabilities of course relate not only to the capacity to deliver conventional warheads over large distances, but also to the delivery of the chemical and nuclear weapons whose proliferation among these same countries we mentioned above. The need for negotiated restraints (and means for verifying them) on the transfer and development of such delivery systems is desperate and obvious.

Although some of the verification concepts for conventional forces as discussed in the chapter by Altmann et al. could, in theory, find application in the conventional-forces confrontations that exist in the South, there seems little real prospect at the moment of agreements that would establish the arms-control context into which these verification concepts would fit. A chapter on the transferability of conventional-forces arms-control and verification concepts into the South would have been an appropriate addition to this book, but we have the sense that this difficult topic might easily have expanded toward book length on its own.

We do want to give special mention here to an aspect of the issue of conventional weaponry in the South that deserves particularly urgent attention in view of its connection with recent rapid changes in Europe: this is the problem of North-South arms transfers, and most particularly the danger that large quantities of conventional weaponry being eliminated from Europe will simply be transferred to the burgeoning regional military confrontations in the South. According to ACDA, arms transfers to the developing countries in the 11 years from 1977 through 1987 totalled 356 billion current dollars, 50 percent of it from the Soviet Union and other Warsaw Pact countries and 38 percent of it from the United States and other NATO countries. These rates are likely to increase sharply as the United States, the Soviet Union, and European countries attempt to convert into foreign exchange earnings and political credits the military aircraft, missiles, tanks, armored personnel carriers, artillery, machine guns, and ammunition made surplus by arms reductions in Europe. A number of very large sales of this kind have been admitted recently by U.S. officials to be pending, and neither the U.S. or the Soviet government--nor presumably many European ones--are thought to be interested in foregoing the revenues and political influence they expect such arms transfers to bring them.

Expanding Conceptions of Arms Control and Verification

Nearly all of the chapters in this book have been devoted to those issues of arms-control verification that seemed, toward the end of the 1980s, to be most likely to be germane for the negotiation and implementation of arms control in the closing years of the century--and with some considerable emphasis on the arms problems that have been most prominent in East-West as opposed to North-South relations.

The main exception to the relatively "near term" focus is the chapter by Rotblat and Goldanskii on the elimination of nuclear weapons, in which they tackle some of the issues that must be faced if ways are to be found to get nuclear weapons out of the hands of nations altogether: the disposal of the weapons-grade fissile material from the existing arsenals (they propose burn-up in thermal reactors); the insurance against one country's withholding a small stockpile and using it to devastating effect (their solution is a UN nuclear weapons authority with a well-guarded stockpile it could use to retaliate against such an offender); and the potential for re-invention of nuclear weapons some time after they had been eliminated (they would depend on an international network of socially responsible scientists to blow the whistle on any attempt to do this). The Rotblat-Goldanskii assault on these questions is instructive and admirable. The topic needs and deserves a lot more work.

So also do a wider array of questions that fall under a broad interpretation of the arms-control-and-verification heading but were not treated here in detail because they were seen as less pressing than the topics treated, or less well developed (or simply because the book would otherwise have been too long). The drastic changes of the last year, however, have made it seem likely that the traditional arms-control agenda may move more quickly than had been expected, upgrading the salience of many of the issues that were neglected here. It seems all the more important, therefore, at least to mention in this closing chapter what some of these issues are, and to identify some of the key questions concerning them.

Research, development, and testing. How to constrain the processes by which new and potentially destabilizing weapons technologies are invented and developed to the point of deployment has long been a thorny topic in arms control. The basic dilemma is that, on the one hand, to constrain research--the "mere" acquisition of knowledge--is philosophically problematical as well as extremely difficult to enforce, while, on the other hand, once new insights relevant to weaponry emerge from research activities, the natural tendencies pushing toward embodiment of the new ideas into actual weapons and the deployment of these with military forces are very difficult to stop. The usual practice in arms control has been to settle for prohibitions on particular kinds of testing, as the only practical and verifiable way to draw a boundary between permitted research and forbidden development. Some kinds of investigations are so potentially pernicious, however--such as research on new kinds of nerve gases or biological toxins, or research on nuclear-weapons design in a future world in which nuclear weapons had been banned altogether--that it seems desirable to seek ways to define and enforce proscriptions against them. In any prohibition of research short of large-scale testing, verification will inevitably be a significant problem. Relevant ideas from chapters in this book include the elimination of secret research facilities (Meselson et al.), large-scale international exchanges of scientists and research administrators so that prohibited activities would be difficult to conceal (Meselson et al., Lohs et al.), and commitments by scientists to certify regularly to a responsible national body that their work is consistent with treaty obligations (Garwin and Sagdeev) or to report suspicious activities by others (Rotblat and Goldanskii). This is a subject that deserves further systematic attention.

Conversion, military budgets. The normalization and substantial demilitarization of East-West relations can be expected to entail significant reductions in military budgets and the "conversion" of military equipment and personnel to civilian applications. It is possible that eventual agreements on conversion will go considerably beyond the force reductions now being contemplated in the CFE negotiations and discussed in the chapter by Altmann et al. on conventional forces, and new issues of verification would then emerge. One of the more obvious kinds of potential agreements in this context would be direct limitations on military budgets; how such an agreement would be verified raises many interesting questions (exchanges of permanent observers in parliamentary committees and defense-industry managements seem intrusive in the extreme, but perhaps should not be ruled out). It is not too early, in any case, to begin to study some of these possibilities now. Even where conversion is not required by agreement, there is clearly confidence-building value in being able to verify that it has taken place, and that it is not reversible on a short time scale. There may of course be considerable benefit in working on conversion collaboratively, not only from the standpoint of sharing of insights but also for the benefits in mutual verification that conversion is actually taking place.

Non-intervention. Building international security is clearly not just a matter of placing quantitative and qualitative limits on arsenals and providing assurance that these limits are being observed; it is also a matter of avoiding situations in which the interests of potential adversaries may collide with enough force to generate armed conflict--or to widen an existing conflict. The growing likelihood that this problem is now practically solved as concerns the potential for US-Soviet conflict relating to Europe calls attention to the desirability of seeking similar reductions in the potential for clashes of major-power interests elsewhere in the world. It seems to us not too much to hope that the present period of cooperative relations between the United States and the Soviet Union could be used to achieve a pact in which the two countries agree to refrain from attempting to exploit political instabilities in the South for unilateral gain. The precise parameters of such a "non-intervention" pact and the means of verifying it and enforcing compliance would need careful attention; but certainly there is some basis for optimism in the growing stature and potential effectiveness of international bodies, most notably the United Nations, for regional peacekeeping.

Nonmilitary aspects of security. There has been increasing attention in recent years to broadening conceptions of security to encompass the roots as well as the more immediate mechanisms and means of international conflict. The economic and environmental dimensions of international security have been particular focuses of discussion and debate. It is possible that some of the international agreements that emerge to deal with these issues will have elements that raise questions of verification not entirely unlike those associated with arms-control agreements. For, example, it is conceivable that international agreements restricting national emissions of carbon dioxide, in order to prevent intolerable global climatic change, would be seen as so critically influencing both economic and environmental well-being that some formal provision for verification would be required. Verification issues of this sort have scarcely begun to be examined, but when they are the discussion will surely profit from application of the sorts of insights about more traditional verification issues to be found in this book.

An Annotated Bibliography

Itshak Lederman (Israel)

Introduction

The literature on arms control verification has received considerable attention throughout the 1980's. The main reasons are the following:

1. The persistent demand by the Reagan Administration to have "efficient verification" for any arms control agreement, has brought the subject to the center of national and international debate.
2. There have been pathbreaking changes in the Soviet Union's approach to verification since Gorbachev came to power. After decades of resistance to Western demands to establish intrusive verification regimes, the Soviets have agreed to include such measures both in the Stockholm Agreement (September 1986) on the monitoring of exercises and out-of-garrison activities in Europe and in the INF Treaty (December 1987).
3. The precedent-setting provisions in the INF Treaty, now will set the standard for future verification regimes including START, CFE, and the Chemical Weapons Convention.
4. The revolutionary changes in Eastern Europe and in the Soviet Union during 1989/90 have raised new questions on the future utility of both arms control in general and verification in particular. These questions have to be addressed in light of the evolving new world order.

There are several approaches to classifying the literature on verification in arms control agreements. First, one can examine the topic as a part of the material dealing with the agreements themselves. A second approach sees verification as an independent area and divides the literature into six categories: descriptive, prescriptive, structural, multinational, technical, and game-theoretic. Finally, there is the differentiation between verification regimes according to weapon systems criteria--nuclear, conventional, or chemical.

The following annotated bibliography addresses the many facets of verification. It includes sources dealing specifically with verification, covering political and technological aspects; but it also contains sources dealing with the contexts of verification: arms control, defense policies, and security agendas. To provide a comprehensive perspective, older materials as well as the most recent publications are included.

Annotated Bibliographies on Verification

Cheon, Seong and Fraser, Niall, "Arms Control Verification: An Introduction and Literature Survey," *Journal of Arms Control and Disarmament*, Vol. 9, No.1, May 1985, pp. 30-58.
An introduction to arms control verification; a comprehensive survey of the literature on verification, and a short history are included. The literature is categorized into six groups: descriptive, prescriptive, structural, multilateral, technical, and mathematical (game-theoretic).

Scott, Robert and Scribner, Richard, *Strategic Nuclear Arms Control Verification: Terms and Concepts*, Washington, D.C., American Association for the Advancement of Science, January 1985, 40 pages.
A glossary of terms and concepts relating to the specifics of arms control verification.

Scribner, Richard and Scott, Robert Travis, *Strategic Nuclear Arms Control Verification: An Annotated Bibliography, 1977- 1984*, Washington, D.C., American Association for the Advancement of Science and the Arms Control Association, August 1985, 90 pages.
The focus is on verification of strategic and theater nuclear arms control agreements, during 1977-1984. The work includes contrasting viewpoints on the strengths and weaknesses of verification, and covers both the technological and political aspects of verification. The book also includes extensive cross-references, and a summary of earlier bibliographic coverage of verification.

Disarmament and Security Yearbooks 1986, 1987, 1988-89, USSR, Academy of Science, Institute of World Economy and International Relations (IMEMO). The Soviet yearbook provides a comprehensive survey and analysis of the developments in arms control and Disarmament (see section 5, Yearbooks, for more details). Summaries of recent publications on disarmament and security are included in the appendices of every Yearbook.

Books

Berkowitz, Bruce D., *Calculated Risks*, New York, Simon and Schuster, 1987, 221 pages.
Describes the limitations of current approaches to arms control and proposes new conceptual and organizational ways to promote it in the US context.

Brams, Steven J., *Superpower Games*, New Haven and London, Yale University Press, 1985, 176 pages.
Deterrence, the arms race, and verification are examined through the lens of game theory.

Borawski, John, *From the Atlantic to the Urals: Negotiating Arms Control at the Stockholm Conference*, Washington, D.C., Pergamon Brassey's, 1988, 260 pages.
Provides a detailed description of the road to Stockholm 1986 and a full account of the negotiations that led to agreement. The book details Confidence Building Measures (CBM) proposals from 1954 to date.

Byers, R.B., Larrabee, F. Stephen, and Lynch, Allen (eds.), *Confidence Building Measures and International Security,* New York, Institute for East-West Security Studies, 1987, East-West Monograph Series No. 4, 156 pages.
The conceptual framework of CBM and their regional implementation in Europe, the Middle East and Latin America, are in the center of this collection. CBM as a verification aspect is given special place.

Carter, April, *Success and Failure in Arms Control Negotiations,* New York, Oxford University Press, 1988, 308 pages.
Analyzes the reasons for success and failure in arms control negotiations. Several case studies (Test Ban talks, SALT I, SALT II, INF, MBFR, START) illustrate the analytical framework.

Clarke, Duncan L., *The Politics of Arms Control*, London, The Free Press, 1979, 277 pages.
Tells the story of how US arms control policy is made in the Executive Branch and in Congress; focusing on ACDA's roles.

Duffy, Gloria, *Compliance and the Future of Arms Control*, Report of a project sponsored by the Center for International Security and Arms Control, Stanford University and Global Outlook. Cambridge, MA, Ballinger Publishing Co., 1988, 258 pages.
A review of compliance and non-compliance in the context of overall US-Soviet relations. Focus is on the dispute resolution process and the role of the Standing

Consultative Commission.

Dupuy, Trevor N. and Hammerma, Gay M, *A Documentary History of Arms Control and Disarmament*, New York and London, T.N. Dupuy Associates, 1973, 629 pages.
Provides the texts of arms control proposals and agreements, from ancient and medieval times to the SALT I Agreement.

Freedman, Lawrence, *Arms Control: Management or Reform,* London, Routledge and Kegan Paul, Chatham House Papers, No. 31, 1986, 102 pages.
Verification is put into the context of arms control and security from the 1960's through the 1980's. An important feature is the negotiation history of SALT, START, INF, MBFR and CSCE process.

Garfinkle, Adam M. (ed.) *Global Perspectives on Arms Control,* New York, Praeger, 1984, 172 pages.
The relationship among arms control, stability, and international security are in the center of this collection. European security and global stability are examined through arms control concepts and prospects.

Jasami, Bhupendra and Barnaby, Frank, *Verification Technologies: The Case for Surveillance by Consent,* London, Berg Publishers, The Center for International Peacemaking, 1984, 130 pages.
Covers technologies for verification, particularly satellites. The focus is on the suggestion to create an International Verification Agency. Also useful are the appendices listing multilateral arms control agreements.

Jasami, Bhupendra and Toshibomi, Sakata, (eds.), *Satellites for Arms Control and Crisis Monitoring,* SIPRI, Oxford, Oxford University Press, 1987, 176 pages.
Presents the technical capabilities of satellites and remote sensing technologies for arms control and crisis management. Also, various organizational schemes are reviewed, such as international and regional satellite monitoring agencies.

Keliher, John G, *The Negotiations on Mutual and Balanced Force Reductions,* New York, Pergamon Press, 1974, 204 pages.
Describes the background and analyzes the development of the MBFR talks in their initial phase.

Kolkowicz, Roman and Joeck, Neil (eds.), *Arms Control and International Security,* Boulder and London, Westview Press, 1984, 157 pages.
Summarizes the discussions and results of a conference on international security and arms control, proposed by York University and hosted by UCLA. Questions on the impact of technology on arms control, proposals for future arms control

measures, and regional dimensions of arms control are discussed in the collected papers.

Krass, Allan, *Verification, How Much Is Enough?*, SIPRI, London, Taylor & Francis, 1985, 271 pages.
Analyzes in detail the technologies of verification and its politics as well as the interrelations between them. Twelve propositions are proposed to outline the field of verification.

Krepon, Michael, *Strategic Stalemate: Nuclear Weapons and Arms Control in American Politics*, New York, St. Martin's Press, 1984, 191 pages.
Analyzes the conflicting impulses within the US governing elite and body politic, relating to the nuclear armament and to arms. Different approaches of various US administrations to verification and compliance are presented.

Krepon, Michael and Umberger, Mary, (eds.), *Verification and Compliance: A Problem-Solving Approach*, Cambridge, MA, Ballinger Publishing Co., 1988, 308 pages.
A collection of fourteen essays that examine the technical and political aspects of arms control verification and compliance. Intrusive verification, NTM, and cooperative measures are thoroughly reviewed.

Lehman, John F. and Weiss, Seymour, *Beyond the SALT II Failure*, New York, Praeger, 1981, 195 pages.
Concentrates on the process that lead to SALT II failure and includes discussion of the policies of the Soviets, and the allies, and of the verification debate.

Luck, Edward C., *Arms Control, the Multilateral Alternative*, New York, New York University Press, 1983, 258 pages.
Addresses the problem of global and regional arms control. The book deals with the major international forces affecting arms control and verification. A chronology of multilateral arms control in the postwar era as well as selected bibliography 1976-1982 are included.

Melman, Seymour (ed.), *Inspection for Disarmament,* New York, Columbia University Press, 1958, 291 pages.
Political and technical characteristics of inspecting and verifying compliance with different types of arms control curbs and limitations are discussed.

Newhouse, John, *Cold Dawn: The Story of SALT,* Washington, D.C., Pergamon Brassey's, 1989, 302 pages.
Portrays the negotiation and conclusion of the SALT I Agreement.

Payne, Samuel B., *The Soviet Union and SALT*, Cambridge MA. and London, The MIT Press, 1980, 155 pages.
The two SALT Agreements (1972, 1979) are at center of this analysis of Soviet arms control policy. The book reveals the domestic interplay within the Soviet Union related to foreign policy in general and to arms control in particular.

Potter, William C., *Verification and Arms Control*, Lexington, MA, Lexington Books, 1985, 266 pages.
A collection of twelve essays examining the major issues of verification, both technical and political. Soviet and American approaches are reviewed.

Potter, William C., *Verification and SALT: The Challenge of Strategic Deception*, Boulder, CO, Westview Press, 1980, 256 pages.
Through the prism of the debate over SALT II, the political and technical problems of arms control verification are reviewed. Major issues of the verification process, such as US capabilities to verify Soviet compliance with SALT II; Soviet views on verification; the relationship between US verification and intelligence communities are included. An appendix contains the report of the Senate Select Committee on Intelligence, evaluating US capabilities to monitor SALT II.

Rowell, William F., *Arms Control Verification: A Guide to Policy Issues for the 1980's*, Cambridge, MA, Ballinger Books, 1986, 167 pages.
Touches the main areas of verification: its concept, its relationship to intelligence, the impact of technology, the role of cooperative measures, on-site inspection, negotiations, standards and strategies, and the handling of the public and Congress. The challenge of verification is presented as one of simplicity versus complexity.

Scribner, R., Metz, W., and Ralston, T., *The Verification Challenge: Problems and Promise of Strategic Nuclear Arms Control Verification*, Boston, Birkhauser, The American Association for the Advancement of Science, 1985, 249 pages.
Politics and technologies of verification, verification measures, compliance issues, and future prospects are in the center.

Sheare, Col. Richard L. Jr. (USAF), *On-Site Inspection for Arms Control: Breaking the Verification Barrier*, Washington, DC., National Defense University, 1984, 65 pages.
A monograph examining the problems of verification, the need to improve verification techniques, and the role of verification in on-site inspections.

Sherr, Alan, *The Other Side of Arms Control: Soviet Objectives in the Gorbachev Era*, Boston, Unvin Hyman, 1988, 325 pages.
Examines arms control and verification within the framework of new Soviet reality under Gorbachev. A chapter on Soviet approach to verification is included.

Smith, Gerard, *Doubletalk*, New York, Doubleday,1980, 556 pages.
The US Chief negotiator tells the story of the negotiation and conclusion of SALT I.

Seaborg, Glenn T., *Kennedy, Khrushchev and the Test Ban*, Los Angeles, University of California Press, 1981, 320 pages.
Analyzes in detail the process of negotiating and concluding the Partial Test Ban Treaty of 1963.

Talbott, Strobe, *Endgame: The Inside Story of SALT II*, New York, Harper and Row, 1979, 319 pages.
The inside story of SALT II as researched and analyzed mainly from the American perspective. The process and the actors at the negotiation end are portrayed against the deliberations and bureaucratic play in Washington and Moscow.

Tsipis, Kosta, Hafemeister, David W., and Janeway, Penny (eds.), *Arms Control Verification: The Technologies That Make it Possible*, Washington,D.C., Pergamon-Brassey's, 1986, 419 pages.
The technologies that can be applied to arms control verification in the future are the focus of this collection of twenty-three articles.

Wainhouse, David W., *Arms Control Agreements: Designs for Verification and Organization*, Baltimore, Johns Hopkins University Press, 1968, 179 pages.
Focuses on the organization of an international arms control organization.

Nuclear Arms Control, Background and Issues, Washington, D.C., National Academy of Science, 1985, 378 pages.
Describes and analyzes nuclear arms control agreements. Provides both process of negotiation and texts of agreement for SALT, INF, Nuclear Test Ban, Nuclear Non-Proliferation Treaty, anti-satellite arms control, and nuclear freeze.

Strategic Disarmament, Verification and National Security, SIPRI, London, Taylor and Francis, 1977, 174 pages.
The relative role of verification in disarmament versus other factors such as deterrence, international law, and public opinion is discussed in this SIPRI volume.

Articles

Adam, A. John, "Ways to Verify the U.S.-Soviet Arms Pact," *IEEE Spectrum*, February 1988, pp. 30-34.
Reviews in detail the verification regime of the INF Treaty, and points out several

weaknesses.

Alexander, Michael, "MBFR - Verification is the Key," *NATO Review*, Vol. 34, June 1986, pp. 6-11.
Verification problems in the MBFR talks.

Arbatov, Alexei G., "START: Good, Bad or Neutral," *Survival*, July/August 1989, pp. 291-300.
Describes the current principles and problems of START.

Bertram, Christoph, "The Future of Arms Control: Part II," *Adelphi Paper* No. 146, London, IISS, Summer 1978, 42 pages.
Points out the limits of the existing arms control philosophy and practice, dealing with quantitative aspects. Bertram argues that a new approach should be adopted, limiting new units of accounts: missions instead of weapons. The verification system of implementing the new approach is based on NTM and "justification by challenge" in the procurement of new weapons systems.

Borawski, John, "U.S.-Soviet Move Towards Risk Reduction," *Bulletin of the Atomic Scientists*, Vol. 43, No. 6, July-August 1987, pp. 16-18.
The history, concept and roles of the Risk Reduction Centers are described.

Cohen, Samuel and Douglas, Joseph, "Arms Control, Verification, and Deception," *National Security Record*, December 1985.
Reviews the inadequacies of NTM to gather verification data, and clarifies the role of OSI.

Davis, Paul K., "Towards a Conceptual Framework for Operational Arms Control in Europe's Central Region," *Rand Report*, R-3704-45DP, November 1988, 81 pages.
Sketches a military framework for conceiving and evaluating measures for operational arms control in Europe's Central Region, i.e., arms control affecting operations and readiness of forces.

Davis, Lynn, "Lessons of the INF Treaty," *Foreign Affairs*, Vol. 66, No. 4, Spring 1988, pp. 720-734.
An initial assessment of the INF Treaty, focused on the US and its European partners.

Dean, Jonathan, "CFE Talks - Overtaken by Events," *Arms Control Today*, Vol. 19, No. 10, January 1990, pp. 12-16.
Urges an updating of Western objectives vis-à-vis the momentous changes in Eastern Europe and the Soviet Union.

Dean, Jonathan, "Verifying Conventional Force Reductions and Limitations," in Robert Blackwill and F. Steven Larrabee (eds.) *Conventional Arms Control and East-West Stability,* Durham, NC, and London, Duke University Press, 1989.
Examines in detail the problems of verifying conventional forces reductions in Europe (CFE talks) and proposes the principles of a suitable verification regime.

Duffy, Gloria, "Study Finds Treaty Compliance," *Bulletin of Atomic Scientists,* Vol. 43, No. 8, October 1987, pp. 30-31.
Summarizing the findings of a Stanford report on Soviet and U.S. compliance with existing arms control agreements. The role of the Standing Consultative Commission (SCC) as a cooperative verification tool is accentuated.

Einhorn, Robert, "Treaty Compliance," *Foreign Policy,* No. 45, Winter 1981-82, pp. 29-47.
Stresses the need for cooperative verification measures, in addition to NTM, in future arms control.

Farley, Philip, "How to Negotiate a Treaty," *Bulletin of Atomic Scientists,* Vol. 43, No. 8, October 1987, pp. 33-36.
A summary of a Stanford working group on compliance with arms control agreements. The role of the SCC is accented as a tool for a "healthy arms control process," and the author predicts Soviet flexibility on intrusive inspection.

Fetter, Steve and Garwin, Thomas, "Using Tags to Help Verify Compliance with CFE Limits," in Richard Kokoski and Sergey Koulik, (eds.), *Verification of Conventional Arms Control in Europe: Technological Constraints and Opportunities* (in press).
CFE and Tags, in this SIPRI forthcoming book.

Fetter, Steve and Garwin, Thomas, "Using Tags to Monitor Numerical Limits in Arms Control Agreements," in Barry M. Blechman (ed.), *Technology and the Limitation of International Conflict,* Washington, D.C., The Johns Hopkins Foreign Policy Institute, 1989, pp. 33-54.
An evaluation of how tagging could be applied to five arms reduction scenarios, based on the type of weapon systems to be monitored and the deployment of the system. The authors also address the benefits and problems associated with negotiating and implementing a tagging system for verification.

Graybeal, Sidney, and Krepon, Michael, "The Limitations of On-Site Inspection," *Bulletin of Atomic Scientists,* Vol. 43, No. 10, December 1987, pp. 22-26.
A review of the risks and benefits associated with on-site inspection. Clear distinctions are made between routine and challenge inspection.

Hansen, Lynn, "Verifying Conventional Force Reductions," Occasional Paper 1, Washington, D.C., The Henry L. Stimson Center, February 1990, 37 pages. Emphasizes the increasing role that Europeans are playing in negotiating and concluding arms control agreements in Europe and their verification regimes.

Hirschfeld Thomas J., "The Toughest Verification Challenge: Conventional Forces in Europe", *Arms Control Today*, March 1989, pp. 16-21. Analyzes the prospects of CFE verification.

Iklé, Fred Charles, "After Detection - What?", *Foreign Affairs*, January 1961, pp. 208-220. One of the few detailed treatments of the issue of invoking sanctions or penalties against violators of arms control agreements.

Kelleher, Catherine M. and Lederman, Itshak, "Verification: Overview of Issues", in Philip Rogers (ed.), *European Conventional Arms Control: New Hope and Old Dilemmas,* New York, St. Martin's Press, 1990. Presents the difficulties of constructing a robust verification regime for a CFE agreement and provides several principles on how to cope with this role.

Krepon, Michael, "Verification of Conventional Arms Reduction," *Survival*, Vol. 30.No. 6, November/December 1988, pp. 544-555. A review of the available verification measures that can be used to monitor conventional arms reductions and provide indications and warning of offensive military preparations. The measures reviewed are: NTM, ground observers, data exchanges, on-site inspections, unmanned sensors, tagging, aerial reconnaissance, and commercial or multilateral observation satellites.

Krepon, Michael and Graybeal, Sidney, "How to Streamline the Arms Control Bureaucracy," *Arms Control Today*, November 1988, pp. 11-14. A review of US bureaucracy behavior in the INF era and a consideration of basic management objectives for successful treaty implementation.

Krepon, Michael, "High Stakes in INF Verification," *Bulletin of Atomic Scientists*, Vol. 43, No. 5, June 1987, pp. 14-16. The author argues that "reasonable verification... could pave the way for INF agreement, but overly intrusive verification measures may compromise national and industrial security and generate endless controversies."

Kunzendorff, Volker, "Verification in Conventional Arms Control," *Adelphi Paper* 245, London, IISS, Winter 1989, 80 pages. Focuses on the various components of a robust verification regime of a CFE agreement in Europe, such as OSI, NTM, exchange of information and permanent observation. Management and cost considerations of such a regime are also included as well as lessons of past experience of verifying conventional arms agreements.

Lederman, Itshak, "Arms Control and Verification: Past Development, German approaches to CFE Verification, and Possible Models of Verification in the Future," Hamburg, Institute for Peace Research and Security Policy at the University of Hamburg, 1990.
German approaches to verification of a CFE agreement are at the center of this monograph. Also, possible models of verification of the next phases of CFE are examined. Based on a research project completed in Germany, during November-December 1989.

Lederman, Itshak, "The Arab-Israeli Experience in Verification and its Relevance to Conventional Arms Control in Europe," Occasional Paper 2, Center for International Security Studies at Maryland (CISSM), College Park, 1989, 23 pages.
Describes verification regimes of four Arab-Israeli agreements and examines their lessons and relevance to the European scene.

Maxfield, Russell and Meerburg Arend, "Two Techniques for Verifying Conventional Reductions," *Arms Control Today*, Vol. 19, No. 6, August 1989, pp.18-21.
Examines the use of sampling techniques to decide on OSI and the use of tags, in verification of conventional arms control agreements in Europe.

Meyer, Stephen, "Verification and Risk in Arms Control," *International Security*, Vol. 8, No. 4, Spring 1984, pp. 111-126.
A consideration of the verifiability of arms control agreements, the risks inherent in a less than 100 percent verifiable agreement, and the implications for US national security. An innovative distinction between monitoring and verification is presented.

Nolan, Janne E., "The Politics of On-Site Inspection," *The Brookings Review*, Fall 1988, 15-22 pages.
Reviews the implication of and political problems associated with arms control and on-site inspection in the wake of the INF Treaty.

Oelrich, Ivan and Utgoff, Victor, "Confidence Building with Unmanned Sensors in Central Europe", in Barry M. Blechman (ed.), *Technology and the Limitation of International Conflict*, Washington, D.C., The Johns Hopkins Foreign Policy Institute, 1989, pp. 13-31.
Analyzing the capabilities of unmanned sensors in verifying arms control agreements

in Europe and concludes that a monitoring system that could give reliable warning of surprise attack preparations is feasible and affordable.

Siovall, Don. D., "A Participant's view of OSI", *Parameters*, Vol. 19, No. 2, June 1989, pp. 2-17.
Portrays author's experience as inspector of the Stockholm Agreement. Concludes that so far the inspections were smoothly accomplished.

Tsipis, Kosta, "Arms Control Can Be Verified," *Discover*, April 1987.
A review of U.S. verification capabilities (both NTM and OSI) and their application to arms control agreements.

Yazov, Dmitri, "The Soviet Proposal for European Security", *Bulletin of the Atomic Scientists,* Vol. 44, No. 7, September 1988, pp. 8-11.
Describes Soviet current approach to European security.

"Verifying a CFE Agreement", *Issue paper*, Program on Science, Arms Control and National Security, American Association for the Advancement of Science, Publication No. 90-105, January 1990, 12 pages.
Follows the CFE negotiation process, focusing on verification and comparing positions of East and West.

Reports

Crawford, A., Cleminson, F.R., Grant, D.A., and Gilman, E.A., *Compendium of Arms Control Verification Proposals,* 2nd Edition, Operational Research & Analysis Establishment, ORAE Report No. ORAE-1282, Ottawa, Ontario, March 1982, 517 pages.
A reference catalogue of 296 arms control verification proposals. Each proposal has been abstracted and catalogued according to two main criteria: arms control objective and the type of verification method.

Government of Canada, Ottawa, Ontario, *Verification in All Its Aspects: A Comprehensive Study on Arms Control and Disarmament Pursuant to UNGA Resolution 40/152,* Report PB87-13758, April 1986, 78 pages.
A Canadian study of the history, problems, and prospects of the arms control verification process.

Proceedings of the Thirty-Eight Pugwash Conference on Science and World Affairs, Dagomys, USSR, 29 August - 3 September 1988, 576 pages.
A Report on the 38th Pugwash Conference; the report covers statements and reports from the conference, and includes papers submitted to the conference on:

strategic nuclear disarmament, prevention of proliferation of nuclear weapons, nuclear and conventional forces, prevention of chemical warfare, European security, military research and development, global environmental problems, and alleviating underdevelopment.

U.S. Arms Control and Disarmament Agency, *Verification: The Critical Element of Arms Control*, Publication 85, Washington DC, Government Printing Office, March 1976, 32 pages.
An overview of verification--its history, its mission, the available methods, misconceptions, and possible violations.

U.S. Senate Committee on Foreign Relations, Committee Report, The INF Treaty, 100th Congress, 2nd Session, Executive Report, 100-15, April 14, 1988, Volume I.
Provides a full description and analysis of the INF Treaty, its history, text, impact on NATO, verification and compliance, and other related issues. Testimony on the treaty, a comparison to SALT and the additional views of Senator Helms, objecting to the agreement, are presented in detail.

Western European Union, *Requirements of a Tag for Conventional Arms Control*, WEU Publication AG I (88) D/10, July 15 1988, 24 pages.
An unclassified version of a WEU confidential report on the methods and techniques that could be applied in the verification of potential conventional arms control agreements. The report examines the tagging concept and its applicability to conventional arms control agreements as a verification measure.

Western European Union, *Past Experiences of Verifying Restrictions on Conventional Forces and Armaments*, WEU Publication AG I (88) D/8, March 1988, 34 pages.
This report provides a useful review of past experiences in verifying restrictions on conventional forces and weapons systems. The experiences examined include the inter-allied control commissions (1920-26), the German and Italian armistice commissions, the Agency for the Control of Armaments (1954-85), and the Peacekeeping Force in the Sinai (1974-1988).

Occasional Reports

Basic Reports from Vienna, British-American Security Information Council, Washington, D.C. and London, 1989.
A regular update on the CFE and CSBM negotiations by the British-American Security Information Council. Director, Daniel T. Plesch.

Trust And Verify, The Bulletin of the Verification Technology Information Center (VERTIC), London, VERTIC Research Organization, 1989.
VERTIC is an independent research organization aiming to research and provide information of the role of verification technology and methods in present and future arms control agreements. Director, Dr. Patricia Lewis.

Vienna Fax, Institute for Defense and Disarmament Studies, Brookline MA., 1989.
News and analysis from the Vienna talks on CFE and CSBM. Bi-monthly reports are issued. Director: Randall Forsberg.

Yearbooks

Disarmament and Security Yearbook, 1988-1989, USSR, Academy of Sciences, Institute of World Economy and International Relations (IMEMO).
This is the third volume published by IMEMO; the first two were published in 1986 and 1987. The yearbook concentrates mainly on analyzing the approaches of different states, primarily the Soviet Union, the US, their allies neutral and nonaligned countries, to problems of arms control and disarmament, the lowering of military conflicts in various regions of the world and strengthening of international security. This year issue emphasizes the military balance in Europe and the CFE talks. The whole array of arms control negotiations and agreements is covered (START, INF, the Chemical Weapons Convention, Comprehensive Test Ban and space based weapons) as well as problems of verification. A chronology of events (January 88 - May 1989) and summaries of interesting publications on disarmament and security are included in the appendices.

SIPRI Yearbook 1989: World Armaments and Disarmament, Stockholm International Peace Research Institute, Sweden.
SIPRI's yearbooks offer four parts: weapons and technology; arms trade, military expenditures and armed conflicts; developments in arms control, and special features. Arms control agreements and negotiations are closely followed.

Index

259

verification, 21-22
Nuclear weapons
  China 5, 211
  France 5, 210
  Gorbachev speech on elimination of, 205
  Gorbachev-Reagan joint declaration on nuclear war, 206
  Great Britain, 5, 210
  India, 7, 231
  Israel, 211
  Pakistan, 231
  Pugwash workshop on, 210
  role in NATO, 97, 206
  South Africa, 211, 231
  Soviet Union 5, 103-119, 229, 231
  United Nations, 218
  United States 5, 103-119, 210, 229, 233
  use on Japan, 205
  see also Air-Launched Cruise Missiles, Intercontinental Ballistic Missiles, Intermediate Range Ballistic Missiles, Intermediate-range Nuclear Forces Treaty, Non Proliferation Treaty, Nuclear deterrence, Sea-Launched Cruise Missiles, Strategic Arms Limitation Talks, Strategic Arms Reduction Talks, Strategic Defense Initiative, Submarine-Launched Ballistic Missiles
Outer Space Treaty
  prohibition of orbiting nuclear weapons, 32
  provisions for compliance disputes, 15
Pakistan
  as a potential nuclear power, 231
  IAEA safeguards, 79
  Non-Proliferation Treaty and, 8
Peaceful Nuclear Explosion Treaty
  on-site inspection provisions, 98
Pechora (Soviet radar site), 24, 26
Pike, John, 39
Perry-Robinson, Julian P., 235
Poland
  removal of Soviet forces, 236
  within "Jaruzelski zone", 168
  within NATO and WTO CFE zonal

schemes, 170-172
Portugal
  within NATO and WTO CFE zonal schemes, 170-172
Pugwash Conferences on Science and World Affairs
  CW workshops, 143, 234
  June 1988 workshop on nuclear weapons, 210
Reagan Administration
  policy on CTB, 232-233
  policy on SALT 7
  signing of the INF Treaty 8-9
  stance on ABM, 24
Reagan, Ronald
  joint declaration (with M. S. Gorbachev) on nuclear war, 206
Reykjavik
  November 1986 U.S.-Soviet summit, 95, 205
Rodionov, Stanislav V., 228
Rotblat, Joseph, 228, 238, 239
Rumania
  within NATO and WTO CFE zonal schemes, 170-172
Safeguard (ABM system), 27
Sagdeev, Roald Z., 230, 239
Saudi Arabia
  party to BWC, 159
Seabed Treaty
  provisions for compliance disputes, 15
Sea-Launched Cruise Missiles (SLCM)
  SS-N-21, 114, 116
  SS-NX-24, 114, 116
  Tomahawk, 114, 116
  verification under START, 114-119
Schear, James A., 16
Shevardnadze, Eduard A.
  comment on Bush CFE proposal, 169
  March 1989 CFE proposal, 168-169
  speech on Krasnoyarsk radar, 24
Smidovich, Nikita P., 235
Soviet Union
  Academy of Science, 24
  bilateral (with United States) arms control agenda, 227-231
  CFE proposal on manpower cut, 170
  compliance with ABM Treaty and with limits on space weapons, 23-42

Pugwash Conferences on Science and World Affairs

The purpose of the Pugwash Conferences is to bring together, from around the world, influential scholars and public figures concerned with reducing the danger of armed conflict and seeking cooperative solutions for global problems. Meeting in private as individuals, rather than as representives of governments or institutions, Pugwash participants exchange views and explore   alternative approaches to arms control and tension reduction with a combination of candour, continuity, and flexibility seldom attained in official East-West and North-South discussions and negotiations. Yet, because of the stature of many of the Pugwash participants in their own countries (as, for example, science and arms-control advisers to governments, key figures in academies of science and universities, and former and future holders of high government office), insights from Pugwash discussions tend to penetrate quickly to the appropriate levels of official policy-making.

The Pugwash Conferences take their name from the location of the first meeting, which was held in 1957 in the village of Pugwash, Nova Scotia. The stimulus for that gathering was a "Manifesto" issued in 1955 by Bertrand Russell and Albert Einstein--and signed also by Max Born, Percy Bridgman, Leopold Infeld, Frederic Joliot-Curie, Herman Müller, Linus Pauling, Cecil Powell, Joseph Rotblat, and Hideki Yukawa--which called upon scientists of all political persuasions to assemble to discuss the threat posed to civilization by the advent of thermonuclear weapons. The 1957 meeting was attended by 22 eminent scientists (seven from the United States, three each from the Soviet Union and Japan, two each from the United Kingdom and Canada, and one each from Australia, Austria, China, France, and Poland).

From that beginning evolved both a continuing series of meetings at locations all over the world--with a growing number and diversity of participant--and a rather decentralized organizational structure to coordinate and finance this activity. By the end of 1989 there had been 167 Pugwash Conferences, Symposia, and Workshops, with a total attendance of some 8400 (there are now in the world some 2500 "Pugwashites", namely individuals who have attended a Pugwash meeting and are hence considered associated with Pugwash, and therefore eligible to receive our quarterly Newsletter). The Conferences, which are held annually, are attended by 125 to 250 people; the more frequent topical Workshops and Symposia typically involve 30 to 50 participants. A basic rule is that participation is always by individuals in their private capacity (not as representatives of governments or organizations). International arrangements and communications are coordinated through small permanent offices in Geneva, London and Rome, while National Pugwash Groups--usually sponsored and/or administered by academies of science--nominate participants from their countries and rotate the work of hosting meetings. Formal governance of the organization is by a 27-member Council elected at the "Quinquennial" Conferences held every five years since 1962; the President of Pugwash is the titular head of the organization; the Secretary-General has the overall executive responsibility.

The first half of Pugwash's three-decade history coincided with some of the most frigid years of the Cold War, marked by the Berlin Crisis, the Cuban Missile Crisis, the invasion of Czechoslovakia, and the Vietnam War. In this period of strained official relations and few unofficial channels, the forums and lines of communication provided by Pugwash played useful background roles in helping lay the groundwork for the Partial Test Ban Treaty of 1963, the Non-Proliferation Treaty of 1968, the Anti-Ballistic Missile Treaty of 1972, and the Biological Weapons Convention of 1972. Subsequent trends of generally improving East-West relations and the emergence of a much wider array of unofficial channels of communication have somewhat reduced Pugwash's visibility while providing alternate pathways to similar ends, but Pugwash meetings have continued through the seventies and eighties to play an important role in bringing together key analysts and policy advisers for sustained, in-depth discussions of the crucial arms-control issues of the day: nuclear forces, chemical weaponry, space weapons, conventional force reductions and restructuring, and crisis control in the Third World, among others.

Starting in January 1980, for example, the Pugwash series of Workshops on nuclear forces provided an off-the-record forum where not only military and civilian analysts but also some members of the official negotiating teams compared notes and sought solutions to obstacles in the official negotiations (18 Workshops of this series have been held to the end of 1989, most of them in Geneva, Switzerland). The Pugwash chemical warfare Workshops--15 of them since 1974 to 1989--have similarly engaged technical experts from the official negotiating teams, as well as academic and industry experts; this series led in early 1987 to the first visit of Western chemical weapons specialists to an Eastern European chemical-production complex, and Pugwash contacts were also instrumental in setting up the first access by a U.S. expert to the medical records associated with the disputed 1979 anthrax outbreak in Sverdlovsk. The Pugwash study group on conventional forces, which originated in the European Security Working Group of the 1982 Pugwash Conference in Warsaw, has played a pioneering role in developing concepts for restructuring conventional forces and doctrines into modes less suited for attack, and in gaining credibility for these concepts with Eastern as well as Western military planners and policy makers.

While Pugwash findings reach the policy community most directly through the participation of members of that community in Pugwash meetings and through the personal contacts of other participants with policy makers, additional means of airing Pugwash ideas are also used. A quarterly *Pugwash Newsletter-* -distributed worldwide to policy makers, past Pugwash participants, and libraries- -contains communiqués issued by the Pugwash Council, summaries of issues addressed in Pugwash meetings, and, with the authors' permission, excerpts from commissioned and proffered papers presented at the meetings. (The summaries are prepared by participant/rapporteurs and do not quote or commit other participants.) The *Annals of Pugwash*, which have been published as a book series (now by Springer Verlag), contain the most significant communiqués, summaries, and papers from each year's activity. Participants are often interviewed by the press during and after the meetings, but in these instances they speak only for themselves and do not attribute statements made by others in the meetings (which are generally closed to the press, to foster uninhibited discussions).

Recently, Pugwash has undertaken some research projects requiring a more sustained organisational effort than a single meeting or even a series of meetings. One such instance has been the production of this book. Another instance (jointly with SIPRI) is a detailed technical study of the production and marketing of one chemical substance, thiodiglycol, from the point of view of the verifiability of a convention banning chemical weapons.

Costs of operating the Pugwash offices in Geneva, London and Rome are met by a combination of donated services, contributions from individuals, from foundations, and from the National Pugwash groups (in proportion to their participation and ability to pay: for instance, the U.S. and Soviet annual contributions are equal at about US$ 25,000 per year). Costs of participants' food and lodging during meetings are generally covered by the host Pugwash group; participants find their own support for travel costs, either individually or through their home Pugwash groups. No honoraria or other fees are paid to participants in Pugwash meetings, nor to the officers of Pugwash (who serve on a voluntary--unremunerated- -basis).

National Pugwash groups raise the funds they need from foundations and individuals, and in some instances from their governments, often through national academies of science or analogous institutions.

PUGWASH CONFERENCES ON SCIENCE AND WORLD AFFAIRS

| President | : | Professor Joseph **Rotblat** |
| Secretary-General | : | Professor Francesco **Calogero** |

Pugwash Council

Chairman	:	Academician Maciej **Nałecz**	(Poland)
Members	:	Academician Angel T. **Balevski**	(Bulgaria)
		Academician Dénes **Berényi**	(Hungary)
		Professor Francesco **Calogero**	(Italy)
		Professor Ubiratan **D'Ambrosio**	(Brazil)
		Professor Hans Peter **Dürr**	(FRG)
		Professor Bernard T. **Feld**	(USA)
		Mr. Shalheveth **Freier**	(Israel)
		Professor Essam E. **Galal**	(Egypt)
		Professor Virginia **Gamba**	(Argentina)
		Academician Vitalii I. **Goldanskii**	(USSR)
		Professor Lameck K.H. **Goma**	(Zambia)
		Professor Anatoly A. **Gromyko**	(USSR)
		Professor Andrew **Haines**	(UK)
		Professor John P. **Holdren**	(USA)
		Professor Serguei P. **Kapitza**	(USSR)
		Dr. Martin M. **Kaplan**	(Switzerland)
		Professor Catherine M. **Kelleher**	(USA)
		Academician Karlheinz **Lohs**	(GDR)
		Dr. Peter **Markl**	(Austria)
		Professor Samuel E. **Okoye**	(Nigeria)
		Professor Joseph **Rotblat**	(UK)
		Professor Jack **Ruina**	(USA)
		Professor Philip B. **Smith**	(Netherlands)
		Professor Bhalchandra M. **Udgaonkar**	(India)
		Professor **Zhou** Peiyuan	(China)

Pugwash Executive Committee

Chairman	:	Professor John P. **Holdren**
Members	:	Professor Francesco **Calogero**
		Professor Bernard T. **Feld**
		Professor Essam E. **Galal**
		Academician Vitalii I. **Goldanskii**
		Dr. Martin M. **Kaplan**
		Academician Maciej **Nałecz**
		Professor Joseph **Rotblat**
		Professor Bhalchandra M. **Udgaonkar**

Geneva office	*London office*	*Rome office*
11A, Avenue de la Paix	Flat A Museum Mansions	Palazzina dell'Uditorio
1202 GENEVA	63A Great Russell Street	Accad. Nazionale dei Lincei
(Switzerland)	LONDON WC1B 3BJ	Via della Lungara 229
Phone **41-22-7331180	(Great Britain)	00165 ROMA (Italy)
Fax **41-22-7337313	Phone **44-71-4056661	Phone **39-6-6872606
Telex 412 151 pax ch	Fax **44-71-8315651	Fax **39-6-6878376